Democratic Vistas

JEDEDIAH PURDY, *Editor*
ANTHONY T. KRONMAN &
CYNTHIA FARRAR, *Advisory Editors*

Democratic Vistas

REFLECTIONS ON THE
LIFE OF AMERICAN
DEMOCRACY

Yale University Press
New Haven &
London

Set in Sabon type by Keystone Typesetting, Inc.
Printed in the United States of America.

Library of Congress Cataloging-in-Publication Data

Democratic vistas : reflections on the life of American democracy / Jedediah Purdy, editor ; Anthony T. Kronman and Cynthia Farrar, advisory editors.
p. cm.
"The essays in this volume began as the Tercentennial DeVane Lectures at Yale University" — Introduction.
Includes bibliographical references and index.
ISBN 0-300-10256-9 (alk. paper)
1. Democracy — United States. I. Purdy, Jedediah, 1974– II. Kronman, Anthony T. III. Farrar, Cynthia.
JK1726.D498 2004
320.973 — dc22   2003020521

A catalogue record for this book is available from the British Library.

The paper in this book meets the guidelines for permanence and durability, of the Committee on Production Guidelines for Book Longevity of the Council on Library Resources.

10 9 8 7 6 5 4 3 2 1

Contents

Introduction

JEDEDIAH PURDY

The essays in this volume began as the Tercentennial DeVane Lectures at Yale University. These were public lectures, attended by students and other residents of New Haven. Their purpose was to consider the nature and prospects of American democracy. They took their title, *Democratic Vistas,* from a prose work by Walt Whitman, perhaps America's greatest celebrator, and also a critic who wrote with the passion of one saddened by the failings of what he most loves.

These essays explore democracy *in America,* because democracy, although it is today's universal creed, is by its nature a particular thing. Self-rule has no abstract existence; it always belongs to one specific people, and a fair part of its business turns out to be expressing, or deciding, who *we* are. Even if the goal is to talk about democracy in general, it is usually best to start with someone's democracy in particular.

The authors gathered here do not assume that everything American is also democratic, from hip-hop and gun ownership to private medicine and a written constitution. Instead, most of these essays are attempts to sort out democracy from other aspects of American experience — free markets, religion, family life, the Cold War, higher education. Democracy gives its shape to each of these, and sometimes it threatens to overrun them all, turning schooling or faith or childrearing into mere handmaidens of political values. At the same time, these other realms can threaten democratic values: the inequalities of capitalism and the putative certainties of some religious belief are only the most notorious examples of nonpolitical practices that can endanger democratic values.

What, though, are democratic values? Precisely because almost everyone nowadays claims to be a democrat, and democracy is presented often as necessary and sometimes as sufficient to cure all social ills, the meaning of democracy can be hard to pin down. One place to begin, as Anthony Kronman does in the opening essay of this volume, is at the origin of the critique of democracy: Plato's account of democratic character, exemplified by the undisciplined Athenian citizen who follows his impulses from a feast to the gym and back again, dabbles now in music and now in philosophy, and cannot decide whether he most admires merchants or wishes to become a soldier. Plato considered democracy the second-worst regime, better only than tyranny, and Kronman reminds us that Plato understood democracy to be not just a political system but a disposition of character, a shape of the soul.

Since Plato, democracy's many critics have sounded the same themes. They identify democracy with a leveling spirit that obliterates rank and authority, producing equality among persons, among opinions, and among appetites. This equality may be said to be a presupposition of democratic government: if a people believed some individuals or opinions to be superior, should it not wish to be ruled by them? The equality of opinion and appetite may also be, as Alexis de Tocqueville suggested, a product of democratic rule: a social life without distinctions of rank teaches people to trust their own spontaneous attitudes and shifting impulses. Whichever way the diagnosis runs, the democratic soul is said to lack any compass more definite than whim, to be a shapeless thing blown about by thoughtless passion and blind appetite. It answers to no standard of refinement or excellence that might lend it discipline or form. The democrat is insensible to reverence, except perhaps for crude awe or animal self-regard. Because he does not honor anything or anyone as his superior, his world is flattened into banality, unleavened by higher, purer, or nobler impulses. In contemporary imagery, democracy is strip malls and designer outlets, earning money to spend it, too much beer at night followed by the gym in the morning, many choices and no particular reason to prefer one over another, and à la carte spirituality to salve any prick of discontent.

Kronman's purpose in beginning from this account of democracy is to make a pair of points: first, it does describe us, however unsettlingly; and, second, we would not give it up if we had the chance. Our modern idea of democracy, in America above all, includes a deep commitment to the idea of individuality:

that our lives are worthwhile because they are self-created and unique. Because we believe that, we must dispense with every old hierarchy of value: contemplation over action, sober piety over ecstatic enthusiasm, discipline over pleasure, or Latin over the vulgate. Any such hierarchy would rob us of our total and final ownership of our own lives, and since that is the basis of our dignity, the hierarchies must go. Democracy involves tearing down distinctions — an act of barbarism, perhaps, but one performed in the service of a new ruling value. If we do not recognize this, then we fail to see ourselves clearly.

Kronman's essay exemplifies the aim of this volume: to bring large and perennial questions into fresh focus. The point is to ask how we think of ourselves, and what our ideas imply for how we live together — not because the answers are likely to be altogether new, but because there is no final answer, and the questions are always inescapable. Kronman's essay also sets out the challenge that animates many of the volume's discussions: What is the basis of dignity in a democratic society? How does a democracy do what any social order must: elevate people's lives in their own eyes, and give form to the inchoate feeling that one's existence has significance?

The essay that most directly takes up this challenge is David Bromwich's treatment of Abraham Lincoln and Walt Whitman as "representative Americans." Bromwich means that term in the way that Ralph Waldo Emerson wrote of "representative men" — individuals who embody some aspect of human character to perfection, and who, by their conduct, teach us about that part of our own potential. For Bromwich, the poet and the politician, both self-made men who became American archetypes, wrestled with questions that are universal for democrats: How can a democrat, a member of a creed of equality, prove him- or herself *worthy* of respect without betraying the principle of equality? What is the relationship between the democratic insistence on equality and the need to insist on one's own uniqueness? Both men's answers lay in an irresolvable tension between devotion to the equal worth of all — no slaves and no masters, no lords or servants — and a vast capacity for solitude, for looking inward, for remaining fully and even mysteriously themselves for all the democratic hurly-burly they moved in and honored.

Bromwich's essay reflects his intimate acquaintance with a long tradition of anxiety that democracy might be the ruin of human dignity. Whitman and Lincoln would have known that tradition as well — indeed, Whitman acknowledged it in *Democratic Vistas*. Skeptical observers of democracy, such as Alexis de Tocqueville and Edmund Burke, stressed that no one is born human, or worthy of dignity. We learn to be ourselves by participating in our cultures, our polities, and our families. There we develop the habits and refinements that make a person a member of a civilization, the loyalty and affection that form membership in political and other communities, and the higher aspirations that make us more than vehicles for our appetites. None of these qualities can be justified by the exercise of pure reason or generated by sheer will. They become a part of us, and we learn to love them — indeed, learn to love through them — first of all because they are ours, binding on us as part of an inheritance. Burke believed that only such a system of manners could elevate people above pettiness, rampant appetite, and the impulses to cruelty and domination — which Lincoln and Whitman also abhorred above all else. He praised "all the pleasing illusions, which made power gentle, and obedience liberal, which harmonized the different shades of life, and which, by a bland assimilation, incorporated into politics the sentiments which beautify and soften private society, [which] are to be dissolved by this new empire of light and reason. . . . All the super-added ideas, furnished from the wardrobe of a moral imagination which the heart owns, and the understanding ratifies, as necessary to cover the defects of our own naked shivering nature, and to raise it to dignity in our own estimation."

What did democracy do to these "pleasing illusions"? Its principles of equality destroyed the authority of the aristocracy, the churches, the whole social order in which the "super-added ideas" of tradition were preserved and reproduced. By wrecking the home in which humane customs lived, democracy turned loose individuals to be merely human, untutored by tradition, without awe for their inherited institutions, left with only their "own naked shivering nature." Naked human nature was not merely undignified but often violent. People loved to rule arbitrarily over others. Those who took power in a democracy would not be schooled in the practices "which made power gentle," nor would their subjects know the habits that made "obedience liberal." They were likely to end at each other's throats. By pulling down the edifices on which the soul models itself, democracy, in Burke's most anxious imaginings, created a personality as isolated and untutored as Plato's democrat. A life of elevation, dignity, and mutual restraint seemed to him possible only with support from practices and beliefs that democracy undid.

Because Tocqueville had less fear than Burke of democratic violence, he was better able to see democracy's less apocalyptic dangers. Tocqueville's democratic man, like Plato's, was not so much brutish as fatuous. The French lawyer and aristocrat looked at democracy with an air of mourning for what it destroyed. "Equality of conditions," the definition Tocqueville gave to democracy, meant the same dismantling of old hierarchies that alarmed Burke. In equal conditions, each person's worth was judged not by the position she had inherited but by what she made of herself in the all-embracing scramble for wealth and status. The general pursuit of success created a restless, pervasive energy, but also ubiquitous anxiety among democrats who could never be secure in their place, and whose achievements might disintegrate as suddenly as they had arisen. Despite the fact that every person was running off in his own direction, democratic individuals were much alike, because distinctiveness, refinement, and high ideals were produced only within traditions that remained stable from generation to generation. A people made up of equally insecure, equally ambitious individuals, all chasing the same prizes, would not preserve such traditions.

The old aristocratic virtues would not survive, Tocqueville concluded, because a democratic society could not "raise mankind to an elevated and generous view of the things of this world . . . inspire men with a certain scorn of material goods . . . engender deep convictions and prepare the way for acts of profound devotion." It was unsuited to "refining mores, elevating manners, and causing the arts to blossom." Democratic culture was self-concerned and philistine, flat because all its appetites, ambitions, and loyalties were directed at this world, in the present time, with no sense of history or the transcendent. "I see," Tocqueville wrote of the democratic character, "an innumerable multitude of men, alike and equal, constantly circling around in pursuit of the petty and banal pleasures with which they glut themselves. Each one of them, withdrawn into himself, is almost unaware of the fate of the rest. Mankind, for him, consists in his children and his personal friends. As for the rest of his fellow citizens, they are near enough, but he does not notice them. He touches them but feels nothing."

There is no mistaking the echo of Plato here. Nor, more pertinently, is there any mistaking these anxieties in Whitman's denunciations of the present-minded, self-interested "realism" that he saw flattening and sapping the American character. To the claim that democracy could not make the arts blossom, Whitman answered with a democratic poetry that celebrated the American collective but was premised on the power of one unique individual to stand apart and describe it all, without claiming to be better than any part of it. Both Whitman and Lincoln, as Bromwich presents them, wrestled constantly with the question of how to "feel" one's fellow citizens without being either absorbed or repulsed by them. And Lincoln, perhaps, had the last word on democrats' capacity for "acts of profound devotion" when at Gettysburg he spoke, as plainly and precisely as ever, of "the last full measure of devotion."

Most Americans, though, do not take the balance of their satisfactions from democratic politics, nor do they find most of their dignity there. Instead, a great deal of our devotion is lodged in two areas that Americans have learned to think of as the very opposite of political: the family and religious faith. Nancy Cott's historical treatment of the family's place in American politics explores a persistent paradox. On the one hand, political rhetoric and constitutional law have both enshrined the family as a perfectly private realm, home to intimate connections that politics must not disturb. In early America this meant that a man's home was his castle, sometimes to the point of tyrannizing over his subjects — his wife and children. More recently this idea has expressed itself in the Supreme Court's protection of sexual and reproductive freedom, especially in the question of abortion. On the other hand, from the time of the American Revolution the family has been seen as a political institution. Good families were thought necessary to breed good citizens, as much in John Adams's time as in today's debates over family values and welfare policy. At the same time, activists have always been eager to extend democratic principles of freedom and equality to the family. The fruits of this effort include liberal divorce law and the prohibition on domestic violence, to name two important examples.

Cott points to another paradox, one that might not have surprised Tocqueville. Although political values often press into family life, in the twentieth century the private values of comfort and security have been the ultimate bases of American political identity. In World War II, efforts to rally soldiers did not concentrate on the public principles of liberty and democracy; instead, American propaganda focused on the home front, the family life and prosperity that soldiers were fighting to defend, and to which they hoped to return. The enemy was not a competing political theory, whether communism or fascism, but fear itself: anything that threatened to disrupt the peaceful private existence that Americans treasured. Cott's theme is recognizable in the tenor of today's public discussions of terrorism. It was already present in Tocqueville's qualified endorsement of democracy:

> If you think it profitable to turn man's intellectual and moral activity toward the necessities of physical life and use them to produce well-being, if you think that reason is more use to men than genius, if your object is not to create heroic virtues but rather tranquil habits, if you would rather contemplate vices than crimes and prefer fewer transgressions at the cost of fewer splendid deeds, if in place of a brilliant society you are content to live in one that is prosperous, and finally if in your view the main object of government is not to achieve the greatest strength or glory for the nation but to provide for every individual therein the utmost well-being, protecting him as far as possible from all afflictions, then it is good to make conditions equal and to establish a democratic government.

The American democrats whom Cott describes would surely agree.

Stephen Carter takes aim at another platitude of political rhetoric: the separation of church and state. Contemporary Americans are accustomed to think of this as a constitutionally enshrined principle, one of the axioms of a liberal and democratic way of life. Carter invites us instead to view it as a historically particular compromise, deeply shaped by the American experience and the cast of Protestant Christianity — not an eternal law that precedes our politics but part of the fractious political community we have made together. Many of us are also in the habit of viewing the separation of church and state as a one-sided battle, in which self-certain zealots teem outside the walls of the state, trying to break in and impose their creeds on the rest of us. Carter proposes a different view: from the beginning of American history, religious and political leaders have been duly wary of each other's realms, and the wall they built between them was understood to preserve the integrity of each side. Even today — just one moment in a long history — most of the evangelical Christians who press for a larger religious presence in public life are not expansionist theocrats; instead, they see their "garden" of religious life as under assault by secular politics, and they understand their activism as a defense of the properly modest relationship between the church and the state.

This description may seem to put Carter on the side of the evangelicals (and indeed he describes himself as an evangelical Christian). So may his prescription: that religiously inspired arguments deserve equal status in public life with other moral positions, so long as they are not made in a spirit of bad faith, violence, or other violations of the standard of civility. Carter's real target, though, is any view that would assimilate all human values under one flag, whether the banner belongs to democratic politics, the Christian religion, or any other creed. People legitimately value, even revere, many kinds of things, and some of those things are irreconcilably different. The wall between church and state, however shifting and contingent it may be, exists in acknowledgment of a division within the soul. To try to break down that division, as fanatics of one stripe or another are sometimes inclined to do, would be a disaster. In Carter's view, democracy may not need religion, nor religion democracy; but here they are, consigned to live together, with many people committed comfortably or awkwardly to both.

The public schools have been less successful than either religion or the family in preserving any claim to be more than the handmaidens of politics. They were a political creation from the beginning, and, as Richard Brodhead points out in his essay, there are few problems that have not been blamed on bad schools, and fewer that schools have not been called on to solve. Since Thomas Jefferson envisioned a public school system as a way of cultivating civic virtue and meritocracy, and Horace Mann proposed common schools as a way to impart civic unity in an age of immigration and factory labor, reformers have imagined the schools as the forge of democratic life.

That would be a lot to ask of one institution under the best of circumstances. The schools, as Brodhead points out, do not operate under the best of circumstances. Besides the persistent problems of insufficient funding and profound inequality in the social and economic backgrounds of their students, the schools are asked to serve two democratic masters: the democratic value of meritocracy and individual opportunity, on the one hand, and the democratic value of equality, on the other. We sometimes suppose that because these are "democratic" ideals, they must be compatible. In fact, to advance one is often to compromise the other. Brodhead uses the example of the Scholastic Aptitude Test (SAT) to drive home the point. The SAT was introduced, in good part, to break down the old, class-based and racist barriers that reserved elite education for those born to the elite. It succeeded magnificently, turning old colleges such as Harvard and Yale into the flagships of American meritocracy, and shaping the huge and sometimes great state schools that expanded mightily after World War II. At the same time, it created a new elite, and drew fresh attack from the proponents of equality, who believe it has once more made schools into bastions of inequity, now moving under the name of merit. As long as we take "democracy" to mean many things, some of them mutually contradictory, we are likely to create paradoxes like this one. The lesson Brodhead draws from this difficulty is not at all despairing; rather, his essay is a modestly phrased and entirely unpompous plea for recognizing our competing values and, in consequence, being a bit less self-righteous about any one of them.

A more contentious account of democratic paradox comes from James Scott, who also takes the SAT as one of his examples. For Scott, democracy creates problems for social decisions: how to spend public money, whom to admit to elite schools, and other choices that affect the prospects of individuals and communities. The democratic premise of equality—that anyone's judgment should count as much as anyone else's—produces a demand to take these decisions away from traditional elites, whether old boys' networks or powerful political families. What makes *their* judgment any better than yours or mine? Because the democratic answer is "Nothing," a political imperative arises: to create ways of making these decisions that replace subjective judgment with impersonal, objective, and scientific standards. These enable us to give out elite education on the basis of SAT scores, public-works money on the basis of cost-benefit analysis, jobs on the basis of aptitude tests, and so forth.

The problem, Scott argues, is that these "objective" decision-making techniques contain their own, concealed politics. Inherent in any test or cost-benefit analysis are judgments about what counts as valuable, what is a cost and what a benefit, what counts as aptitude or intelligence or merit, and how numerical value should be assigned to all of this. By measuring "verbal" and "mathematical" intelligence but not attempting to capture any other "merit," such as compassion or patience or broad experience, the SAT represents a huge decision about who will make up our elite. So do the other techniques Scott examines. Yet because they are presented as scientific and nonpolitical, their politics is invisible. Thus, they have the profoundly undemocratic effect of enforcing large and contestable value judgments without ever putting them up for democratic debate. What began as an expression of democratic ambition has become a shackle on democracy. Scott has a good deal more than this to say about the bewitching quality of "scientific" or quantitative substitutes for qualitative judgments, but this democratic paradox is at the core of his argument. He takes the side of a rather radical conception of democracy, preferring to bring these hidden value judgments into the open even at potential risk to the ramshackle compromises that Cott, Carter, and Brodhead explore. To address the paradoxes of democracy, he is inclined to prescribe more democracy.

To many observers, the most basic paradox of American life is the relationship between democracy and capitalism. Depending on what one means by democracy, the pairing can indeed seem disastrous. Free markets in labor, capital, land, and commodities produce enormous inequality in wealth, social status, and, by extension, political power. Thus they undermine the democratic premise of equal political and social standing. They can also erode the democratic value of self-determination, by throwing women and men into a labor market where they barter their best years and hours for sustenance, with evenings and weekends added into the bargain. Markets unseat the solidarity that Whitman and David Bromwich put near the center of democratic virtue, replacing it with the age-old contest between bosses and workers.

This is the view Michael Denning advances in his essay. For Denning, the American conceit that "we are all democrats" conceals a struggle between nominal democracy — limited to elections — and real democracy, which would include much greater popular control over the workplace and private institutions such as universities and foundations. Denning offers a revisionist view of history: most democratic gains, from the universal franchise to the forty-hour week, arose from the struggle of the masses against the elites, carried out in a spirit of solidarity and in response to concrete abuse and exploitation. Only once the battle had receded, and the masses had won the day, did elites accommodate themselves to the new dispensation and eventually embrace the changes as part of "our" shared democratic values. In today's conflicts, Denning puts himself on the side of labor unions, anti-globalization activists, and anyone else who stands in the way of free-market economics' ascent to dominance in all areas of life. I suspect that a thinker such as Stephen Carter would judge that Denning is himself an absolutist, who would order all areas of life by a single set of — political — principles. Denning would respond that those are the right — democratic — principles and that others must give way. The reader will, perhaps, be provoked to consider both positions carefully.

Richard Levin, president of Yale University, offers nearly the opposite view of the relationship between markets and democracy. In his essay, he contrasts

America's democratic capitalism not to an ideal democracy but to the authoritarian regimes that were its main competitors in the twentieth century. Following Adam Smith, he points out that markets both presuppose and help to create "natural liberty" — to move from place to place, to leave bad jobs or hopeless situations, and to enter into agreements with anyone who is willing. Although these may seem banal because they are familiar, they have been the privilege of only a minority of human beings even in recent decades. Without such freedom, political liberty would be meaningless. Moreover, capitalism supports the cultural ferment of democracy by ensuring that wealth builds up in many different centers, creating patrons and spokespersons for a great variety of views — from Ross Perot to Warren Beatty, and many lesser-known supporters of both liberal and conservative causes.

In Levin's view, the excesses of capitalism are ones that democratic politics can do much to address. Although it is true that a market society tends to put everything up for sale, democratic bans on, say, prostitution and baby selling can help to preserve non-market values. Progressive taxation and redistribution can reduce the inequality that markets produce alongside wealth. Well-crafted programs can compensate for the "externalities" that market calculations of profit and loss exclude, such as environmental damage. The essential virtues of a market society, then, reinforce democratic values, while the failings of markets are susceptible to democratic solution. Levin is not entirely sanguine; he worries about growing inequality and admits that politics seldom produces perfect results to correct markets' antidemocratic tendencies. Still, he sees no essential opposition between market realities and democratic values.

The purpose of Ian Shapiro's essay is to ask why democratic politics does not do much more than it does to address economic inequality. Many early observers of democracy, and more recent political theorists, argued that democracy in conditions of economic inequality would produce massive redistribution of wealth from the rich to the poor and lower-middle ranges of society. After all, what reason would voters have not to demand a larger share of social wealth? Yet despite confident and well-argued forecasts of redistribution, history has demurred, and inequality has held steady or grown as the franchise has expanded. Shapiro offers an exhaustive set of reasons for this phenomenon: American government, in particular, is set up to slow democratic will; the political parties are influenced by wealthy campaign contributors; a two-party system prevents the growth of a radical program; and all politicians fear that higher taxes would drive wealth to offshore accounts. Perhaps more interesting are the reasons having to do with social psychology and political beliefs. Most people judge how well they are doing not by reference to the whole social order but in comparison with the people around them — which may be why a huge share of Americans identify themselves as middle class, and 20 percent believe they are in the top 1 percent of personal income, while another 20 percent believe they will end up there. Moreover, Americans, including many of the poor, believe that the market system is fair and that the inequality it produces corresponds to talent and effort; accordingly, they see no good reason to redistribute wealth. They prefer to concentrate on getting their share.

The most provocative part of Shapiro's discussion brings the volume around to its opening theme: the basis of dignity in democratic society. Early theorists, whether worried landowners or hopeful radicals, assumed that the lower orders would use the ballot to get their hands on more material goods. From the American Revolution to post-apartheid South Africa, history suggests that people care more about dignity, the sense of worth and belonging, than about increases in income. They will fight for status before they will fight for bread. Shapiro reports that people do not demand redistribution in the United States because they believe in the American Dream — that democratic capitalism rewards talent and work, that people end up with what they deserve. Part of the reason for believing this, of course, is that it is partly true — and far more than in most of the countries that give the United States its striving immigrant populations. But when belief in the American Dream is so expansive as to create empirical and logical absurdities, such as 20 percent of the population putatively squeezed into the top 1 percent of income, something else is afoot as well. Perhaps it is that people are deeply invested in believing that they live in a fair and decent system, even against some of the evidence, because to believe otherwise would mean being a victim, a loser, a sucker. Our dignity rests on believing in a kind of social membership that is partly imaginary but that elevates us in our own minds. It may be that Burke was wrong: we have our "pleasing illusions," as surely as the subjects of monarchical France did. The empire of light and reason, of which Shapiro is a partisan, has not dissolved them but only changed their form.

John Gaddis's essay, on democracy and American foreign policy, may now seem dated at first glance. It was composed in the spring of 2001, before the attacks on New York and Washington that shifted the tone of America's relations with the rest of the world. Gaddis has since commented elsewhere on the current direction of international relations. We have kept this essay in its original form because it is not so much a comment on the events of the day as it is a reflection on how to think about politics and history — and specifically how Americans are inclined to think of these themes. Gaddis's argument is that, although American-style democracy and markets are triumphant in much of the world, we should not take false reassurance from this fact. The history of the past century might have gone very differently, and that it went our way is not a reason for confidence that the next century will do the same. Human affairs are full of contingency, happenstance, and small incidents with huge consequences.

The implicit target of Gaddis's essay is a strain of triumphalism that has affected the American self-image from the beginning. The first Puritan settlers were building a new Jerusalem in the wilderness; the authors of *The Federalist* presented the Constitution as the test of whether human beings could make their governments by will and reason rather than history and accident; Abraham Lincoln proposed at Gettysburg that the Civil War might decide whether democracy would survive or "vanish from the earth." I mention these figures because they were not, unlike many figures in American history, jingoists or land-grabbers; they were among our most serious and severe ancestors, and still they felt a special providence, a sense of unique historical purpose in the American project. America stood in, somehow, for all the world, and our future was by definition humanity's future. Gaddis proposes a more modest view: history has not chosen us, at least not irrevocably; whatever our virtues, we have flaws as well, which make us imperfect bearers of democracy; and we live in a world of many competing perspectives and values, in which we take a necessarily partial view. The point is not that we are not good, but that we are better when we remember that we are not perfect.

Cynthia Farrar's essay is in some ways a more concrete reflection on the same themes. In the course of the Yale Tercentennial DeVane Lectures that became these essays, she led a weekly discussion group made up of members of the New Haven community, who shared their responses to the lecturers' arguments and observations about American democracy. Her account of these conversations leads her to conclude against conclusion: there can be no theoretical resolution of democratic questions that comes before, or predetermines, the course of actual democratic deliberation. When citizens come together, they bring their existing interests and attitudes, but they also change each other in the course of deliberating together; they obey the rules of civility and argument, but they may also come to new understandings of those rules as they argue together. Democracy is not a vast opinion poll, nor is it a fixed and eternal principle for making decisions: it is an activity, to which people submit themselves, and which sometimes changes them. What David Bromwich judges from the vantage point of literature and history, Farrar concludes by way of political theory and firsthand experience: the life of American democracy has no predetermined shape.

In their essays on science and democracy, Joan Steitz and David Gelernter take opposite and complementary tacks. Steitz asks how American democracy might contribute to this country's status as the world leader in basic scientific research. Gelernter comes closer to James Scott's themes, asking how technology — specifically computers and the Internet — affect democracy.

Steitz's descriptions of the relation of democracy to scientific research have something in common with Richard Levin's treatment of democracy and the market. She is interested less in political democracy than in cultural features we associate with democratic values, such as individuality, entrepreneurialism, and meritocracy. Her basic contrast is between the United States and the Pacific and European countries, where she portrays national bureaucracies and autocratic laboratory directors setting top-down research agendas. In the United States, by contrast, competitive research funding, allocated by multiple public and private sources according to highly meritocratic criteria, makes bottom-up initiative the core of the research process. In Steitz's picture, the institutional advantages of the United States do not mean that the government stays out of research; instead, by fostering a competitive and merit-based system of funding, federal policy makes research *less* rather than more top-down. All this chimes with American cultural habits: self-confident dissent and the compulsion to distinguish oneself from the crowd. Nonetheless, Steitz's argument is not really a cultural one. It has to do with the effects of large-scale institutional decisions, which can either inhibit or foster a culture of small-scale initiative in ideas and research. If we have the research culture we deserve, it is not because our political culture guaranteed it to us but because our political decisions created it.

In reading Steitz's essay, one is reminded of an additional factor in American scientific success: our as-yet unique power to draw the finest scientific talent from around the world, an ability that is a function both of political and cultural openness and of the meritocratic openness of our research institutions. James Wilson, the constitutional framer, remarked that America might become the Rome of the modern age because, like its imperial predecessor, it need not impose itself on the world; instead, the world would pour itself on America. As Steitz points out in passing, it is impossible to imagine the American scientific triumphs of the past sixty years without waves of immigration from Europe in the 1930s and 1940s, and from south and east Asia in recent decades.

David Gelernter asks a somewhat different question: How will computers and the Internet reshape democracy? His answer is a democratic one: we can't know yet because we have not decided. That is, it's up to us. He suggests two basic alternatives, a pairing that echoes Thoreau's remark that when we go to ride upon the railroad, we must beware lest it ride upon us. On the one hand, Gelernter suggests, we can use new sources of information to do what we already do, only better and more efficiently. He imagines online voting with an icon next to each candidate's ballot line linked to a short statement of the candidate's positions. Another click would lead to a longer statement, or to position papers on particular issues, perhaps even a handful of selected campaign speeches. Rather than diffidently absorbing the flotsam of a long campaign, then staring blankly at a ballot and trying to remember who said that thing we liked about health care, we would gather information on candidates exactly when we needed it and use it to vote more intelligently.

In Gelernter's second alternative, we would use nimble technology to distract ourselves more profligately than ever, snapping up entertainment, unvetted and fragmentary facts, and anything else that caught the eye, at the expense of deep reading, careful thinking, and distinguishing between sense and nonsense. This warning has become more poignant in the years since Gelernter delivered his DeVane lecture. We are now much more sharply aware than we were then that all forms of fanaticism, including the nationalism and fundamentalism that fuel terrorism, thrive on the Internet. Small communities of the discontented reinforce one another's resentments and delusions, building up alternative versions of history and their own dark interpretations of the latest events. Whoever wants to be inducted into Hindu nationalism, militant Islam, or white supremacism should start online, where such ideas flourish in noxious hothouses of the like-minded.

Gelernter stipulates at the start of his essay that any programs for computer-based voting must be tamper proof, and proposes that any company providing such programs be required to explain how they work, in less than five minutes, in a way an ordinary person can understand. The second is a credible goal, and the first is positively indispensable. Considered together, however, they suggest an even more pessimistic possibility for the relation of democracy to technology. At the time of writing, freelance computer scientists are contending that the programs now used in computerized voting systems in several states, and being hurried into place elsewhere, are susceptible to tampering — that vote totals could be changed by hackers without leaving a trace. The software companies have responded by suing the whistleblowers for revealing the contents of internal memoranda discussing the programs' vulnerabilities.

C. S. Lewis once wrote that, human character being what it is, any new form of power over nature — that is, any new technology — will tend to become a form of power over other human beings. Gelernter adds to this that the more sophisticated our technology becomes, the more obscure our lives may grow, the more of what we inhabit we may be unable to understand. Stuffing ballot boxes is nothing new; but what would it mean if a losing candidate alleged that an election had been stolen by a means that 95 percent of Americans could not understand, and that left no trace? If the workings of democracy became unintelligible to us, would the system be the less able to withstand crises? Reading Gelernter's sorting-out of reasons for optimism and pessimism, one can hardly help concluding that the answer is, Maybe. *Maybe* is enough to cost a democrat some sleep.

All of these essays, then, are contributions to a national project — the project of the nation itself — that cannot be completed unless by an unhappy ending. Because they are calls to historical and philosophical reflection, though, they cut against the American current, which is always rushing forward in a spirit of eager forgetfulness. Our national life is founded on movement: migration and immigration, the constant churn of commercial culture, and the amnesia of a present-minded and forward-looking people. These qualities are related to our virtues: the openness to cultural and demographic change that makes us a model for an increasingly plural world; the capacity to forgive historical injuries that stands in contrast to the embittered ethnic and national politics of so many places; the capacity to leave behind our own bigotry, as we have begun to do in matters of race, sex, and sexuality. Because we do not dwell on the past, we are not trapped or pursued by it.

The habit of amnesia, though, makes a people vulnerable to certain dangers. Forgetting our history and neglecting abstract questions of principle can leave us untutored at times when we need guidance. When we have to balance liberty against security, to weigh fear or threat in the moment against a compromise of constitutional principles — as we have increasingly had to do in recent years — it is important to remember why those principles were enacted to begin with, and why we might want to preserve them even if they are inconvenient to us just now. As Richard Brodhead points out, Jefferson wanted even citizens with just a few years of education to know classical history, so that they would recognize the signs of encroaching tyranny and be able to defend their liberty. Even if we do not take Rome as our model of liberty and tyranny, we might do well to hold ourselves to a similar standard. Constitutional and other shared principles ensure that a people remains itself even in times of crisis, and a forgetful people is most at risk of losing itself.

These essays are public exercises in reflection, meant to remind us of ourselves in all our paradox and imperfection. At their best, they are the living stuff of a tradition: plural, open to change, but united by a body of principles and concerns that tracks the present back to its past. They are not programmatic or didactic, but they are for our democracy what Robert Frost once called on poetry to be: a momentary stay against confusion.

The Democratic Soul

ANTHONY T. KRONMAN

The first great work of political philosophy in the long tradition of Western thought has come down to us in its original Greek, almost perfectly preserved through twenty-five centuries of transmission. This by itself is a miracle of sorts, given the library of works, composed by authors writing in periods much closer to our own, that have disappeared completely or been corrupted beyond repair. And the feeling that there is something miraculous about the preservation of this text must deepen when one considers that it not only contains the first organized examination of many of the most basic questions of political life, but treats them with a depth of understanding that has never been surpassed, and a stylistic genius that remains the standard by which all philosophical compositions are judged. I am speaking, of course, of Plato's *Republic*, the miraculously wise and beautiful book with which the tradition of Western political philosophy starts.

The *Republic* is still the book that a student of political philosophy is most likely to encounter at the beginning of his or her study of the field, and its central arguments and images — the myth of the cave, the image of the sun, the proposal to abolish family life, the argument for philosopher-kings — remain required knowledge for anyone who wants to grasp, even in a basic way, the main lines of Western political thought. Even today, a young person reading Plato's *Republic* for the first time, at such vast distance from the time and circumstances of its creation, is bound to be impressed by its arguments, perhaps even persuaded by them, and to be moved by its unforgettable images.

But there is one feature of the *Republic* that no modern student can accept, and that must cause the thoughtful reader to reconsider, and in the end, I believe, to reject, the central premise on which its entire argument is based. I have in mind the harsh assessment that Socrates and his companions offer of democratic government and of the way of life associated with it.

Most of the *Republic* is devoted to an examination of the conditions under which the very best kind of political regime might emerge and to a description of its features. Having completed this part of their inquiry, Socrates and his friends turn, toward the end of the *Republic,* to an exploration of four less good regimes, concluding with the rule of the tyrant, the worst regime of all. In this descent from the best regime to the worst one, democracy comes next to last, after timocracy (which distributes authority on the basis of honor) and oligarchy (rule by the rich). In Socrates' view, only tyranny is less attractive than democracy and farther from the best political scheme.

With rare exceptions, modern readers of the *Republic* start with a view of democracy sharply different from Socrates' own. For them—for us— democracy is not the next-to-worst system of government but the very best, the one we most respect and to which we owe our deepest allegiance. To be sure, we often disagree about the exact meaning of democracy and the sound-est methods for achieving its ends. We do not all share the same conception of democracy or the same idea of how best to secure it. But our disagreements are family quarrels among those who embrace the basic principles of liberty, equality, and tolerance on which every form of democratic rule is based. In this broad sense, we are all democrats today, and Socrates' ironic skewering of these principles, and of the democratic way of life that rests on them, cannot help but offend the modern reader who admires the very things that Socrates mocks.

It is possible, of course, to put brackets around the passage in question, to treat Socrates' antidemocratic views as an aristocratic prejudice that has little or nothing to do with the main arguments of the *Republic,* and in this way to contain the damage the passage does to the credibility of the work as a whole. But this is not an adequate response, nor can it achieve its goal of containment. For if one asks, with any seriousness at all, where we and Socrates differ in our views of democracy, the answer is bound to call into question not just this one passage but the most fundamental assumption on which the entire argument of the *Republic* is based.

What we value about democracy, above all else, is its commitment to the individual. This is a commitment that Socrates does not—and I believe cannot — share. And those who endorse the value of individuality, as we modern democrats all do, must also reject the methodological premise on which Plato's *Republic* is founded: the claim that political order is the analogue and product of psychological order, that order at the level of the city both reflects and derives from order at the level of the soul. The truly individual soul cannot be an orderly soul, in the sense in which Socrates understood this idea. For democrats, who affirm the value of the individual, the greatest challenge of political philosophy is therefore to explain how political order can be derived from psychological disorder, from souls whose individuality makes them disorderly in a deep and defining way — an explanation that cannot be found within the framework of Plato's *Republic*. The history of post-Platonic political thought, inspired and shaped by the tradition of religious belief from which our democratic commitment to individuality derives, is the history of the search for such an explanation.

This is all, of course, much too compressed, and in need of further elaboration. Let me start by describing more carefully the assumed connection between political and psychological order on which the argument of the *Republic* is based.

Plato's *Republic* is an extended conversation among Socrates and a small group of friends regarding two questions: First, what does it mean for a person to be just? And, second, is it better to be just or merely to appear so? Early in the conversation, Socrates proposes that he and his companions shift their inquiry to a larger stage and consider the meaning and value of justice not in the soul of a single person but in the constitution of a whole city instead. Socrates observes that their investigation of justice in the soul is a difficult one, even for those, as he puts it, "who see sharply." He then makes the following famous remark. "If someone had ordered men who don't see very sharply to read little letters from afar and then someone had the thought that the same letters are somewhere else also, but bigger and in a bigger place, I suppose it would look like a godsend to be able to consider the little ones after having read these first, if, of course, they do happen to be the same." The bigger place that Socrates has in mind is the city, a political association composed of many individuals. Socrates proposes that he and his friends first examine the nature of justice in cities, where this quality is displayed on a larger scale and is easier to see, and then, using the justice of cities as a model, return to their original inquiry into the justice of souls, where the essential character of justice, though appearing in smaller letters, is presumed to be the same.

This presumption itself is never tested, even though Socrates introduces it in an explicitly conditional form. In a conversation that subjects so many other hypotheses to rigorous examination, this one is never exposed to critical review. No one ever asks whether justice in cities really is the same thing, writ large, as justice in individual souls. The structural identity of political and psychological justice, of justice at the level of cities and souls, is simply taken for granted, and from the point in book 2 where it is first introduced, until the end of the *Republic,* the assumption of this identity remains the unchallenged premise on which the entire argument of Plato's masterwork is based. Indeed, when Socrates and his friends return to the subject of individual justice midway through book 4, Socrates asks the others whether "it isn't quite necessary" for them "to agree that the very same forms and dispositions that are in the city" are in the souls of each of us as well, and then answers his own question by asserting that it would be "ridiculous" to think otherwise. In that uncontested judgment we may discern the foundation of Plato's *Republic* and the limits of its author's intellectual world, indeed, as I shall suggest, the limits of Greek thought generally.

As the argument of the *Republic* unfolds, the relationship between political and psychological justice proves to be even closer than first appears. Not only does the justice of souls look like that of cities. Not only do these two species of justice conform to the same pattern or idea — to use one of the most potent words in the lexicon of Greek philosophy. In the end, Socrates insists, a city can be just only if there is justice in the souls of its individual members, and vice versa. Political justice and psychological justice are not merely alike in form. Each is also, he argues, a condition of the other's existence, a cause of its coming into being.

At the beginning of his description of the four defective regimes, the ones that are less good than the truly just city whose origin and character are the subject of the central books of the *Republic,* Socrates observes that to each of these four regimes there corresponds a particular type of character or soul, and in the discussion that follows he moves methodically from an analysis of each regime's political constitution to an examination of the character type associated with it. As the reader quickly discovers, however, the relationship between city and soul in these four defective regimes is not a static one. It is not a relation of mere resemblance. It is a doubly dynamic, causal relation as well, each system of rule originating in the emergence of a new character type that demands political recognition, the attainment of which in turn establishes that character type as a norm, as the model to which souls in the new regime are expected to conform.

This same doubly dynamic relation of city to soul, so vividly displayed in the genesis and transformation of the four inferior regimes that Socrates dissects in books 8 and 9 of the *Republic,* also exists in the best city, where true justice prevails at both the political and psychological levels.

For a city to be truly just, Socrates says, its members must accept their proper places in the civic order, each one practicing the single function for which, in Socrates' words, "his nature [makes] him naturally most fit." A regime is just, on Socrates' view, only when the individuals who compose it "mind their own business" and refrain from meddling in the exercise of functions properly assigned to others, and when, as a result, the supervision and direction of those performing lower functions in the city remain in the control of those who by nature are equipped to guide and direct them.

But for the members of a political association to acknowledge their proper places within it and to accept the hierarchy of supervision this implies, their own individual souls must be in order. The parts of their souls must themselves be in their proper places, each performing its function in a hierarchy of command and without interfering in the business of the others — a condition we are told, at the end of book 4, that constitutes the true meaning of psychological justice. Only if a person's soul is internally so ordered, only if he does not let the different parts of his soul "meddle with each other" but seeks instead to keep them in their proper relation of subordination, only if he is in this sense inwardly just, will he be disposed to mind what Socrates calls "his external business," and to accept his place in the city to which he belongs, thereby contributing to the establishment of a regime of political justice, which on Socrates' view not only looks like its psychological counterpart but is produced by it as well. And the reverse is equally true. For in order to establish that internal order within the souls of its citizens that constitutes their justice as individuals, a city must deliberately cultivate, through myths and other devices, the belief in a natural hierarchy of command and the acceptance of one's proper place within it that for Socrates is the essence of justice in cities and souls alike. So in the best city too, as well as in the four defective ones, the kind of order that exists at the level of the individual not only resembles the order that characterizes the political community itself but is also a cause of its coming into being and vice versa, the order of cities and souls conforming to the same idea and dynamically producing each other.

With this as background, let us return to the passage in book 8 in which Socrates portrays democracy as the next-to-worst regime and examine his reasons for doing so.

The democratic city that Socrates describes is marked by two features, by the freedom of its citizens and by their attachment to the principle of equality, which they interpret to mean that the many different pursuits of those living in the city cannot be ranked according to their natural dignity or value. The democratic city, Socrates says, is "full of freedom and free speech." Its citizens have license to do as they wish, choosing those activities that happen, for whatever reason, to please them at the moment. All different ways of life, from the sordid to the sublime, flourish in the democratic city, which from the point of view of its citizens looks, in Socrates' words, like "a general store" that contains every imaginable pattern for living. Some choose one pattern, others another, and for a time at least adopt it as a guide, though most move restlessly from activity to activity, pursuing different pleasures with impatient curiosity. Socrates describes the life of the democratic citizen in the following way. "He lives along day by day," Socrates says, "gratifying the desires that occur to him, at one time drinking and listening to the flute, at another downing water and reducing; now practicing gymnastic, and again idling and neglecting everything; and sometimes spending his time as though he were occupied with philosophy. Often he engages in politics and, jumping up, says and does whatever chances to come to him; and if he ever admires any soldiers, he turns in that direction; and if it's money-makers, in that one."

In the mind of the democratic citizen, of the "all-various" man as Socrates calls him, "full of the greatest number of dispositions," no distinctions of inherent worth exist among these different pursuits. He does not divide the desires that motivate them into the "necessary" and the "unnecessary," the beneficial and destructive. He considers them all equally legitimate and worthy of pursuit, and he rejects the idea that they can be ranked in some definitive order of value. Above all, he believes in freedom and equality. These are the principles that guide his life, that define the soul of the democratic citizen, and they are reflected in the constitution of his city, where slaves and masters, men and women, children and adults, teachers and students all behave as equals, and the rulers are chosen by lot — the only method, we are led to conclude, that does not entail the acknowledgment of a rank order among those selected. How much this portrait looks like us! Do we not believe, passionately, in the very things that define the democratic way of life, in freedom and equality? Are we not devoted to the idea that each of us must be free to choose the life that seems to him or her the best? Are we not profoundly sympathetic to the claim that there can be no fixed and authoritative ranking of these choices according to the degree to which they approach the one true conception of how human beings should live? Are the lives we live not strikingly like the one that Socrates caricatures as the democratic norm: full of restless energy and insatiable curiosity, devoted to a multitude of heterogeneous pursuits — to music and drinking and dieting and exercise and politics and study — that form no overall pattern?

In his account of democracy, Socrates shows us how we live today. He holds a mirror up to our lives. His contempt for democracy is a contempt for us, and if we are honest with ourselves we must admit the truth of what he says. Our democratic culture is shallow, inconstant and vulgar, driven by fashion and fad, shameless in its refusal to acknowledge the distinction of better and worse and the authority that flows from it. But all of this we accept for the sake of an ideal that Socrates does not recognize, and could not have recognized, given the metaphysical assumptions on which his political philosophy rests. We accept the pathologies of democracy as the necessary if sometimes unappealing consequence of our commitment to the ideal of individuality — the ideal of being or becoming an individual. For us, this goal is supremely important, and we love our democracy, with all its flaws, because it honors this goal and makes it its central value.

The idea of individuality, to which we assign such importance, has two distinct but related components. The first is the notion of singularity, and the second that of invention or, more exactly, of self-invention. To be an individual means, first, to be a unique presence in the world, a person whose biography constitutes an original and distinct story, unprecedented and unrepeatable in all of time, a singular trajectory between the common points of birth and death. For us, individuality implies a distinctiveness in living that sets one apart from others — from all others — and that stamps one's mortal career as something perfectly particular and uniquely one's own. The opposite condition we call conformity, the condition of being indistinguishable from others, and to it we assign a strongly negative value.

The second component of our concept of individuality is the idea of self-invention. To be an individual one must lead a singular life. But this by itself is not enough. It is merely a necessary, not a sufficient, condition of individuality. In addition, one must be the author of that life, the source of invention from which its distinctiveness flows. One must lead a life that is unique, and that uniqueness itself must be the consequence not of some accidental combination of forces working from without — in the way that the uniqueness of every wave on the beach is produced by a singular combination of wind and water — but the upshot of a series of choices and actions for which the person living the life is him- or herself responsible. The uniqueness of my life must have its source in me, and only if it does will it possess an individuality of the sort we judge morally valuable. This kind of self-invention has been called by different names. Some philosophers call it autonomy, and others authenticity, but whatever name we give it, it is an essential feature of the concept of individuality to which we assign such prestige.

We all know, of course, that most lives resemble one another in many ways, that their uniqueness is limited and in certain cases difficult to discern. Our habits, attitudes, and interests are very much alike, and the lives we lead quite similar as well. We all also know that our lives are to a large degree the product of forces and circumstances beyond our control, and that moments of genuine self-invention are rare and their consequences of limited scope. In these respects, our lives typically fall far short of the ideal of individuality, lacking both the uniqueness and the self-invention this ideal implies. But even though we know this, and accept it as a fact of life, the ideal of individuality retains for us its prestige and appeal. Despite the shortfall between its demands and our achievements, this ideal remains the moral benchmark by which we judge our lives and the lives of others, and its tenacity as an ideal is an even more impressive fact than our consistent failure to achieve it.

The moral appeal of democracy as a form of government is, for us, tied to the moral appeal of the ideal of individuality, of the ambition to be, or to become, through acts of self-invention, a person with a biography uniquely one's own. One of the fundamental aims of democratic rule is to provide a framework of laws and institutions and, in the view of many, a system of material support, to enable those living within this framework, and drawing on this support, to pursue the ideal of individuality as fully as they can. Democracy implies a maximum of freedom, which permits each of us to chart our own distinctive course in life in a spirit of self-invention, and it tolerantly abstains from enforcing any hierarchy of public values by which the worth of different lives might be judged — something that would contradict the ideal of self-invention in a fundamental way. In these respects, democracy serves our ideal of individuality by providing the best — indeed, the only — organized form of collective life within which to pursue it. But these characteristics of democratic rule, which we admire and value because of their connection to the ideal of individuality, are the very ones that Socrates finds so ridiculous, and the reason he does is that this ideal itself is one his deepest metaphysical beliefs render not only valueless but unthinkable — incapable of being thought. Let me explain.

Midway through book 5 of the *Republic,* Socrates' most intelligent and devoted student raises a question that Socrates calls "the biggest, and most difficult," question of all. Let us concede, Glaucon says, that the ideal city — the truly just city — is precisely as Socrates depicts it. Let us accept everything he says about it. How, Glaucon asks, can this ideal city ever become a real city? How might it actually come into being? Socrates' famous answer, of course, is that true justice can be realized on earth only if "philosophers rule as kings or those now called kings and chiefs genuinely and adequately philosophize," only if "political power and philosophy coincide." This "paradoxical" reply, as Socrates calls it, immediately raises a further question. How are we to know who the true philosophers are and to distinguish them from those who are not? This is the central question of the *Republic,* and the lengthy discussion that follows, regarding the selection and training of philosopher-kings, depends on Socrates' answer to it. The true philosopher, Socrates tells us, can best be distinguished by contrasting his beliefs and attitudes with those of another sort of person, whom Socrates calls the lover of sights and sounds. The lover of sights and sounds has a passion for the theater and for the drama of public life. He is constantly running around, as Glaucon puts it, from one spectacle to the next. What he loves about the world, above all else, is its dazzling variety, its infinite combinations of noises and colors and shapes, the endless parade of individuals and events that cross the world's stage in such staggering profusion. The attention of the lover of sights and sounds is fixed, as we might say, on the surface of the world, whose ever-changing appearance is to him a source of constant entertainment and delight. By contrast, Socrates says, the attention of the true philosopher, of the person he describes as a lover "of the sight of the truth," is fixed not on the surface of things but on the changeless forms that are reflected or embodied in the world of transient beings. The true philosopher looks through the superficial world of sights and sounds to the eternal forms behind it, and it is with these forms and not their images or reflections that he is in love.

According to Socrates, these enduring forms are the only things that are genuinely real in the ever-changing world of sights and sounds. A beautiful vase, for example, possesses reality on Socrates' view only to the extent that it participates in or exemplifies the form of beauty itself. To that extent, it shares in the reality of the form it reflects. But of course no vase can participate in beauty completely. Every "real" vase, as we normally but wrongheadedly describe it, is marked by imperfections and by a liability to decay that the form of beauty itself — changeless and perfect — can never possess, and to the extent it deviates from the form of beauty, a "real" vase, in our ordinary parlance, becomes unreal in Socrates' opposing conception of what truly has being and what does not.

This conception turns our ordinary view of the world on its head. It reverses the common understanding of reality. Yet it possesses great philosophical appeal, for it helps to make sense of our most basic habits of speech, which depend on the capacity to talk intelligibly about the common properties of different individuals — to say, for example, that two vases are beautiful, or two cities just, or two soldiers courageous. Only the forms of things, on Socrates' view, permit us to make such judgments and to express them in words. And only they, he insists, possess reality because only they last forever. For Socrates, eternity alone is real, and hence only the forms of individual things are real because only they never die. Individual vases and cities and soldiers come and go. They bloom and disappear. Their individuality is transient. It comes into being and passes away again, under the mortal sign of time, and is to that extent unreal. To direct one's attention to the forms of things is therefore to be concerned with what is real in them, but to attend to their individuality, to be excited by the differences among the various things that belong to the same category or class, to love the diversity of beautiful vases or just cities or courageous soldiers rather than the one thing they share in common is, on Socrates' view, to turn away from what is real to what is unreal and possesses no being at all.

With this claim we come to what is perhaps the deepest premise of Plato's philosophy, and of Aristotle's too for that matter: the equation of reality — of being — with form, and the consequent denial of reality to individuals, or more precisely, the denial of reality to all that makes them individuals, and not just exemplars of the timeless and unblemished forms they imperfectly and temporarily embody. From this premise many of the most distinctive features of Plato's philosophy flow: for example, his insistence that our love of individual human beings is a lesser and confused form of our love of the general qualities they represent, and his description of the activity of founding political communities as a kind of craftsmanship, whose success is to be judged solely by the resemblance of the product to the blueprint the craftsman has followed, rather than as a type of artistry whose success is measured, in part at least, by the novelty and singularity of its results.

Plato's equation of form and being is also the source of his negative view of democracy. For us, democracy is made attractive and legitimate by its commitment to the ideal of individuality. We justify democracy on the grounds that it establishes the best framework within which to pursue the goal of becoming an individual, a person with a distinct and self-created career. This goal is, for us, a morally and spiritually compelling one, and the closer we come to achieving it the more fully we feel we have lived. The closer we come to being individuals, the more real our lives become, in contrast to the unreal (or, as we often say, inauthentic) lives of those who follow the herd and take their directions from others. For Plato, this judgment is not merely wrong. It is unintelligible. To pursue individuality is, on a Platonic view, to pursue that element in us that lacks reality. It is to turn away from the only things that possess reality, the forms that lie beyond change and corruption, and to chase after unreality instead. It is to turn our attention from being to nonbeing, and while Plato recognized that most men and women — all the lovers of sights and sounds — are in fact more attached to the world of things that come into being and pass away than they are to the realm of imperishable forms, he would have considered a view that deliberately elevates the pursuit of individuality to a position of supreme moral and political importance metaphysically absurd. He would have thought it a view that turns the relationship of being and nothingness upside down.

But of course Plato does not even entertain the possibility — which seems so obvious to us — that the pursuit of individuality might be defined as something good in itself, and the fact that he does not reveals how deeply his own view of democracy is shaped by the metaphysical equation of form and being. For this equation rules that possibility out. It is a possibility that lies beyond the horizon of Plato's thought, as the nature of his attack on democracy makes clear to a modern reader for whom the value of individuality goes without saying. According to Socrates, democracy is characterized by the dazzling variety of ways of life it encompasses and allows. "It contains," he says, "all species of regimes," both at the political level, in the factions that struggle incessantly for control of the city, and at the psychological level, in the restless souls of its citizens. Democracy is, in Socrates' phrase, a "many-colored" regime, and especially attractive on this account to those living in it, who rush around from one activity to the next, drawn first to this way of life and then to that, just like the lovers of sights and sounds that Socrates describes in book 5 of the *Republic*. Indeed, democracy is, on Socrates' view, the political scheme that best fits the attitudes and desires of the lovers of sights and sounds, the regime that best expresses their own conception of what is valuable and real. For just like their lives, which are filled up with all sorts of different things and which in their unsteadiness reflect the transient splendor of the superficial world on which the attention of the lovers of sights and sounds is fastened, democracy itself is characterized by fluidity and impermanence as it moves from the control of one faction to that of another. Failing to love the forms, the lovers of sights and sounds lead lives that are formless, and in this respect the formlessness of democracy, where the lovers of sights and sounds are most at home, mirrors perfectly their own existence — or perhaps it would be better to say, their nonexistence, for if anything is clear in the long argument of the *Republic,* it is that the lovers of sights and sounds dwell in the realm of nonbeing and live lives as unreal as the changeable and varied things to which they are so attached.

Democracy mirrors the formless lives of its most representative citizens, and, to the extent it does, it lacks reality too. Like the lives of its citizens, the democratic city is characterized by mobility, change, transience, variety, freedom, experimentation, and individuality — and, hence, on Plato's view, by nonbeing. We accept the value of these things and of the democratic institutions that promote them. But for Plato to have done so, he would have had to abandon the equation of form and being so fundamental to his thought. He would have had to have a radically different conception of reality. He would, in a word, have had to be not a Greek but a Jew or a Christian.

I shall return to this last thought in a moment. But before we leave Plato, I must gather up the threads of my argument and explain why, for a modern reader, a proper understanding of the reasons for Socrates' attack on democracy — a form of government whose appeal rests on the acceptance of a proposition that Plato would have found metaphysically absurd — must also lead one to abandon the methodological claim on which the entire argument of the *Republic* is based, the claim that political order and psychological order are analogous and mutually conditional.

This principle is the product of a train of thought whose implicit logic might be expressed roughly as follows. Every political community is a gathering of men and women in accordance with some ruling principle of order, in accordance with what Socrates calls the community's "regime" (the term we use to translate the Greek word *politeia*, which is also sometimes translated as "republic" and is the original title of the dialogue known by that name). A community's regime gives it its shape or form and, with this, its political reality. A group of men and women who happen merely to live in the same place, but whose relations are not governed by any principle of order, who are neighbors in a physical sense but not the citizens of a shared regime, do not constitute a political community, whose very being Socrates equates with the organizing form that gathers its constituent elements — the men and women living in it — into a unified whole. It is the regime, or as we would say today the constitution, of a political community that makes it such, that confers reality on it, and that distinguishes it from those formless collections of human beings that in the strict sense possess no political reality at all. This much follows from the fundamental equation of form and being. But something else follows as well. For political communities must come from somewhere, and this can only be from the men and women who compose them. More precisely, the thing that makes these communities real — the regimes that give them their political reality — can only come from what is real in their individual members; and, so long as we equate reality with form, what is real in the members of a political community can also only be the forms that shape their souls, the internal regimes that provide the organizing structure of their psyches. The individuality of the citizens of a political community can, on this equation, have no reality at all. Their individuality is literally nothing, and if we further assume, as Plato did, that something cannot come from nothing, then what is real in a city can only come from what is real in the souls of its citizens, the reality of both residing in the regimes that give them their respective shapes.

Indeed, a Platonist must go further and say that the kind of reality — the nature of the regime — must also be the same at both levels, at the level of the city and of the soul, for otherwise it would be necessary to assume that one sort of being can arise from another sort that it is not, and again that would be to assume (what Plato thought impossible) that something can come from nothing. Do you suppose, Socrates asks at the beginning of his review of the four imperfect regimes, that they could arise "from an oak or [from] rocks"? It is meant to be a ridiculous question. These regimes can only arise, he reminds his listeners, from the "dispositions" of the people living in them, from the regimes that inform their souls. Something real can only come from something else that is real, and one kind of reality cannot come from another — any more than the form of a human political community can come from that of an oak or of rocks. The same equation of form and being that prevents Socrates and his companions from recognizing in democracy the thing we value most about it — its devotion to the idea of individuality, to the project of living a unique and self-defined life — thus also entails the presumed analogy of political and psychological order on which the whole argument of the *Republic* is based.

A modern reader who believes in the value of individuality, and in the value of democracy as the form of government best suited to promote it, is therefore compelled to ask a question that Socrates' assumption of a structural identity between the order of cities and that of souls makes impossible to answer, one that a modern reader can begin to answer only by rejecting this assumption itself. The question is, how can individual men and women be gathered into a democratic state? Democracy is surely a regime in Plato's sense. It is a principle, or set of principles, for the arrangement of a community's affairs; it is an ordering idea. But if we think of the men and women who belong to a democratic regime as individuals, not just in the sense that they happen to be distinct from one another, but in the deeper and more important sense that they are seized by the ambition to be individuals, living lives whose significance and worth flows from their self-defined uniqueness, then we must abandon the notion, central to Plato's argument, that the order of their political regime is analogous to, or derivable from, the order of their own souls. We must abandon this notion because the soul of the truly democratic man or woman — the one for whom individuality is an ideal — cannot be thought of as possessing a defining order at all, because the democratic soul is defined not by its order, as Plato thought all souls must be, but by its resistance to definition in accordance with any principle of order instead.

Put abstractly, this may sound like an extravagant claim, but it lies at the heart of many of our most familiar modern beliefs. It lies at the heart, for example, of our concept of personal love, which insists that true love can never be captured or explained by a list of the beloved's general qualities, but is always directed toward an inexpressible uniqueness that starts where lists of this sort leave off. It lies at the heart of our concept of the work of art, whose true artistry resides in that indefinable residue of individual achievement that remains when all its general properties have been catalogued. And it lies at the heart of our notion of fulfillment in living, which for us includes, among other things, the achievement of a self-created distinctness that transcends all formal definition. These are all familiar features of our moral civilization, and they all flow, in one way or another, from the positive value we place on individuality, on a condition that for us is paradoxically defined by its transcendence of definitions, by its irreducibility to ordering forms, by its disorderliness in a deep and constitutive sense.

For Plato, this would have seemed a kind of madness. Plato of course understood the nature of conflict in the human soul — he was one of the keenest observers of such conflict the world has ever known — but the notion that the highest achievement of a human soul lies in the attainment of an individuality that transcends any possible combination of forms would have struck him as absurd, given the equation of form and being on which his conception of the world was based. For those of us who accept this idea, the challenge thus arises of explaining how democratic government, which is a species of political order, can be established and sustained by men and women whose moral and spiritual dignity flows from their disorderly individuality, how political order can be derived from disorderly souls. This is not a challenge that Plato had to face. It is not a challenge he would even have recognized. But our commitment to individuality puts it squarely before us, and we can meet it only by rejecting the claim that political order and psychological order are analogous and interdependent, the claim on which the argument of the *Republic* as a whole is founded. Modern readers who reflect on their democratic beliefs will rediscover in these beliefs their commitment to individuality; and if they reflect on this commitment, they will be led to reject not only Socrates' account of democratic rule but also the methodological premise on which Plato's political philosophy is constructed. They will discover a challenge that Plato could not see, and in doing so be compelled to find a new and non-Platonic way to meet it — a new and non-Platonic way of linking soul and city or, as we would say, individual and state.

We modern readers of the *Republic* share a belief in the value of individuality, a belief that to Plato would have been utterly unintelligible. Nothing separates his mental world from ours as fundamentally as this. But where does our belief in the value of the individual come from? I have already hinted at the answer. Our modern, secular commitment to individuality, and to the democratic way of life that honors and promotes it, derives not from the great pagan philosophies of the ancient world, which all accepted Plato's equation of form and being with one degree of self-awareness or another, but from the tradition of religious belief that first challenged this equation in a radical way by insisting on that most un-Greek of all ideas, the idea of creation from nothing. In the creation story of the ancient Jews, God is portrayed as a world-transcending power who brings the universe into being from nothing. Unlike the demiurge of Plato's late dialogue the *Timaeus*, who makes the world by imposing a system of preexisting forms on a shapeless mass of preexisting matter — just as any craftsman makes an artifact by shaping some already given material in accordance with a blueprint or plan — the creator God of Genesis confronts nothing that exists in advance of His own act of creation, neither raw material, whose resistance to His creative efforts God is constrained to accept, nor a preexisting plan that He must follow if His creation is to have an intelligible shape. The difficulties of conceiving such a perfectly unconstrained act of creation are enormous, perhaps insuperable, and many of the most persistent questions with which Jews and Christians and Muslims have grappled over the centuries are the product of these difficulties (for example, the question of whether the laws of nature were fixed in God's mind before He created the world or were brought into being as part of that creation itself). But however great the puzzles to which their belief in God's radically free creation of the world gives rise, the affirmation of this belief has remained for all the descendants of the ancient Israelites a matter of supreme importance, for it is only the idea of such an act, voluntary and unconstrained, that does justice to their conception of God's supreme power, to a divine omnipotence that even Plato's demiurge cannot approach. No idea is more central to the traditions of Jewish and Christian and Muslim belief, and none seemed more absurd to those philosophically cultured Greeks who first encountered it two millennia ago.

Many consequences flow from the idea of creation ex nihilo. Two are of particular importance for our purposes here. The first is that, with this idea, individuals acquire a dignity — a reality — they could never possess within the framework of Greek thought, predicated, as it was, on the equation of form and being. If God has made everything in the world, all its forms and all its matter too, and not merely stamped a set of preexisting shapes on a body of already-given matter, then the individuality of every individual in the world — the absolute uniqueness of every sparrow and elm and human being — must itself be a product of God's creative act, something God brought into being along with the rest of the world, and hence must share in the reality and meaning of His creation as a whole. For Plato, the individuality of things has no reality at all; only their common properties — their forms — have reality, intelligibility, and value. The idea of creation ex nihilo reverses this judgment and compels us also to assign reality and value to individuals, whose uniqueness is as much a part of God's creation as the formal laws of mathematics, and therefore as deserving of our curiosity and respect.

A second consequence of this idea is its revolutionary impact on our understanding of human freedom. Plato's *Republic* is centrally concerned with human freedom. But for Plato freedom means ordering one's life in the right way, and that means in accordance with the proper forms, above all, the form of justice. Freedom, for Plato, is literally a kind of conformity. By contrast, in the creation story of the Jews and Christians and Muslims, God's freedom resides in His absolute independence of any antecedent system of forms; and to the extent that we human beings think of ourselves as having been made in God's image, our freedom must resemble His in this crucial respect. Our freedom, too, must consist in the exercise of an unconstrained power of creation. The name we give this power is "will," a concept that has no real counterpart in Greek philosophy. On this view, to be free is to exercise one's will, to say "yes" to one thing and "no" to another. And even if the standards of conduct to which one says "yes" and "no" are themselves fixed in advance, even if justice and courage and beauty are eternal and unchanging in their meaning, our assent to them — or rejection of them — is always freely given, and it is this freedom, and this alone, that gives our actions their spiritual meaning on a religiously inspired view of the world that starts with God's creation ex nihilo and that defines our spirituality in terms of its resemblance to His. Socrates said, "To know the good is to do the good." St. Paul cried out in anguish, "I do not what I want, but the very thing I hate." Behind these statements lie two fundamentally different conceptions of freedom, and the revolution in thought that separates them is a second consequence of the idea of creation from nothing.

Our modern notion of individuality, and the value we assign it, derives, as I have said, from two connected propositions: first, that it is the uniqueness of a person's life that gives it its meaning and reality; and, second, that this uniqueness must be self-invented to have moral or spiritual worth. To be indistinguishable from others, to be a conformist who follows the crowd, is on our view to be a "nobody" whose life lacks authenticity—and who to that extent we judge not to exist at all, except in a shadowy and unreal way, a judgment that exactly reverses the Platonic equation of individuality with nonbeing. These beliefs, which for us possess such a self-evident plausibility, first become intelligible with the doctrine of creation ex nihilo, from which the reality of every individual's uniqueness follows, and with the invitation to view our human spirituality as the image of God's own, as having its source in a capacity for self-direction, a freedom of the will, which though accompanied in us by limitations that God lacks, is within these limits as unconstrained as the power of divine creation it reenacts on earth. The idea of creation from nothing undermines the metaphysical premise of Plato's philosophy and prepares the way for our modern understanding of individuality, and, with that, our belief in the moral and spiritual value of democracy. The religious tradition from which this idea derives has faded into the background of our democratic civilization, and it has left behind a thoroughly secular morality that no longer betrays its theological inspiration. But the traces of this theology, and of the revolution in thought it produced, may still be glimpsed in the various answers that modern political philosophers have sought to provide to the question of how the relation between a democratic state and its citizens should be conceived, a relation that Plato understood as one of analogy but one that our religiously derived belief in the reality and value of the individual compels us to describe in a fundamentally different way.

Many of the most familiar, and influential, modern answers to the question of how we should conceive the relationship between a political community and the human beings who compose it draw deeply on religious ideas, whether they recognize this or not, and cannot be understood apart from the radical revaluation of individuality that the doctrine of creation from nothing entailed. It would be the work of a lifetime to catalogue and investigate all the ways in which modern political philosophers draw from the armory of religious ideas in their effort to explain the relation of individual to state. Let me therefore mention just one, which may be of particular interest to some here.

Today one hears a great deal of talk, especially in our universities, about the value of diversity. Indeed, in certain quarters, diversity is on its way to becoming not just a value but a supreme value, the yardstick by which all others are measured. From a commitment to the value of diversity there follows a certain conception of what political communities are for: they are for the cultivation of diversity, which some consider the highest and most valuable function that such communities perform. On this view, a state is not merely the guarantor of public order, protecting the rights of its citizens to live in private as they wish. It is also the guardian of an organized space for the display and celebration of diversity, whose aim is to promote the moral pleasure that citizens take in the diverse attitudes and achievements of others as well as in the pursuit of their own plans of life. This is the highest moral ambition of the state, and when that ambition is fulfilled, when the endlessly diverse human beings who are its citizens have been gathered into a community of mutual enjoyment and respect, the state reaches a goal that America's great prophet of diversity, Walt Whitman, describes as nearly divine.

Here we have a political ideal that is exactly the opposite of the one proposed in the *Republic*. Plato's ideal city is marked not by the celebration of diversity, but by its systematic repression, by the ordered arrangement of all citizens in accordance with a single master principle and the functional hierarchy it entails. For Plato, the movement toward diversity is not a movement toward reality. It is a movement in the opposite direction, toward nothingness or nonbeing, and the idea, so appealing to many Americans today, that diversity is a value, something good and worthy of respect, would have struck Plato as completely absurd, given the fundamental equation of reality and form on which his political philosophy was premised.

For Whitman, and for us, the belief that diversity has value and that the highest purpose of the state is to promote its exuberant expression and joyful appreciation — beliefs so commonplace in our contemporary culture that we scarcely even recognize them as such — are the secular by-products of that radical revaluation of individuality entailed by the religious doctrine of creation from nothing, a teaching whose implications could never be absorbed within the limits of Greek thought. For once it is granted that the absolute distinctness of every individual is something real in its own right — a proposition foreign to the whole spirit of Platonic philosophy but required by the doctrine of creation ex nihilo — the way is open to the celebration of diversity as something divine, as the revelation of the Creator in His creatures, and to a view of the state as a union of individuals gathered for the purpose of enjoying their own diversity. Today this view has immense popularity in the United States. In certain circles, one might even say, it is the dominant view of the relation of individual to state. And though it has lost all reference to the religious doctrine that first gave it credence, this view, now so thoroughly secularized and disenchanted, has its true source not in the philosophy of Plato or any other classical thinker, where one will search in vain for a recognition of the value of the individual on which our modern appreciation of diversity, and our modern reverence for democracy, are based, but in the commanding Word of that omnipotent Lord of Creation whose prophets first declared, to the amusement of their Greek critics, that the God to whom they prayed had made the world from nothing.

As I near the end of this discussion, I fear that I may be leaving you in a mood of self-confidence, of self-congratulation even, and that is something I would like to use my last words to try to correct.

We modern men and women believe in the value of individuality, the value of living a life uniquely one's own. And because we believe this, we must reject Socrates' negative assessment of democracy and the organizing assumption on which the *Republic* is based: the assumption that the order of a political community mirrors the order in the souls of its citizens and can be derived from no other source. Socrates' inability to recognize the value of individuality and our inability to deny it leads him to count democracy as the next-to-worst regime and us to rank it as the best. That is the main point I have tried to establish.

But let the point be granted. It does not follow that we must regard everything about democracy — the turmoil and vulgarity and all the rest — as something good. Nor does it follow that Socrates' criticisms of democracy have no bearing on our situation and leave us with no disturbing questions to confront. In fact they do, and even after we have understood the metaphysical divide that separates him from us, and grasped the consequences of this divide for the methods and agenda of political thought, these questions remain to be addressed.

I shall close by mentioning one such question, to my mind the most important of them all. You will recall that Socrates attacks democracy, among other reasons, for its failure to discriminate between two sorts of desires, the necessary and the unnecessary. To grant that desires can be classified in this way is to concede that different lives may be ranked, and judged better or worse, according to the kind of desire those living them seek to fulfill. That is of course a fundamental premise of the *Republic,* indeed of Platonism generally, and it might seem that we cannot grant this premise without compromising our ideal of individuality, an ideal that locates the value of a person's life in something other than its conformity to a standard of right living defined by reference to a hierarchy of more and less worthy desires. Indeed, it might seem that our commitment to individuality requires that we reject the very idea of a standard of right living, as Socrates understood it. But can we in fact do without such a standard altogether? We recognize, and employ, standards for evaluating human achievement in a wide range of specialized activities, from cooking to statecraft. Must we — can we — forsake the use of such standards when it comes to the comprehensive activity of living? Of two lives, each unique and self-directed, can we never say that one comes closer to the goal of human fulfillment, that it has more of worth in it, and is worthier on that account?

We live in a civilization in which the power of reason, in the form of science, is accepted without question on a scale unprecedented in human history. And yet our ideal of individuality, the organizing principle of our moral and political life, seems to rule out the search for a reasoned answer to the question of how we might discriminate between necessary and unnecessary desires and define the goal of right living for human beings. It seems to rule this question out, but in the end, I believe, we cannot and should not suppress it. It is true that the answer Socrates gives to the question is no longer available to us. We must find a different answer, one that is compatible with our commitment to individuality, the commitment that most profoundly separates his intellectual world from ours. Twenty-five centuries later, this still remains to be done. It remains a task before us. And though there is nothing in Plato's *Republic,* the wisest and most beautiful book we possess, that makes its distance from us as clear as Socrates' violent attack on democracy, there is also nothing that reminds us as forcefully of the question of reason's relation to freedom, a question that we, the sons and daughters of the modern world, shaped by Greek ideas as well as by the revelation that dispelled them, have yet to fully confront.

2

Lincoln and Whitman as
Representative Americans

DAVID BROMWICH

A way of life like American democracy has no predestined shape, and when we call historical persons representative, because they helped to make us what we are, we generally mean that in their time they were exceptional. Abraham Lincoln, a lawyer, state legislator in Illinois, and one-term congressman who became president, and Walter Whitman, a journeyman printer, newspaper editor, and journalist who became a great poet, were extraordinary in what they achieved. They were extraordinary too in the marks of personality that they left on their smallest gestures. Yet the thing about both men that strikes an unprejudiced eye on first acquaintance is their ordinariness. This is an impression that persists, and that affects our deeper knowledge of both. By being visibly part of a common world which they inherited, even as they were movers of a change that world had only begun to imagine, they enlarged our idea of the discipline and the imagination of democracy. But the accomplishment in all its intensity belongs to a particular moment of American history. The great works of Lincoln and Whitman begin in the 1850s — Lincoln's emergence as a national figure comes in the speech of 1854 on the Kansas-Nebraska Act; Whitman's self-discovery comes in 1855 with the first edition of *Leaves of Grass.* What was special about those years?

In the 1850s in America, the feelings of citizens were turned back with a shock again and again, to one terrible, magnetic, and central issue. This was the national argument — already in places a violent struggle — over the possibility of the spread of slavery. The future of slavery and freedom had been an issue from the founding of the republic, but it took on a new urgency in the 1840s, when people asked how to dispose of the lands taken in the war with Mexico — a debate in which Lincoln participated as a congressman, strongly and eloquently dissenting from the war policy of President Polk. The same issue confronted the nation again and more starkly with the Kansas-Nebraska legislation of 1854, which repealed the Missouri Compromise and opened free territories to the owners of slaves. All through these years, the free citizens of the Union had felt the weight of the Fugitive Slave Law, which required law-abiding persons in the free states to return escaped slaves to their masters. The law raised a question for the accomplice as well as the master and the slave. Am *I* free in a country that uses the power of the state to compel me to assist in the capture of a human being who has risked his life for freedom? These things were sifted deeply in those years. There has not been another time when so searching an inquest drew so many ingenuous minds to discuss the basis in law and morality of the life we Americans share.

Both Lincoln and Whitman were part of a radical current of opinion that started out in dissent. In reading about their lives, you sometimes sense a peculiar self-confidence, as of people who know they have company in their beliefs. You can feel it plainly when you read their writings, if you listen to the pitch of the words. Though the thunder comes when they need it, they are both of them, by practice and almost by temperament, soft-spoken writers. But they know that they are not alone; they know that someone is listening. A text from Whitman: "Whoever degrades another degrades me." And from Lincoln: "As I would not be a slave, so I would not be a master. This expresses my idea of democracy. Whatever differs from this, to the extent of the difference, is no democracy." The two statements have morally the same meaning. American slavery, they say, is a concomitant of American democracy and is its degradation and betrayal. The work of democracy in these years will be to resist that betrayal and save the constitutional system from destruction. In this contest the enemy is a selfishness so perfect that it would preserve a freedom to treat other persons as property. This then is the cause; but the motive of resistance is deeper. It comes from an idea of the self which — like the sense of property cherished by the slave power — could only have arisen in a democracy.

Both Lincoln and Whitman were familiar with an older and largely hostile tradition of response to the democratic character. Plato, who did not invent that tradition, gave it memorable formulation in book 8 of the *Republic* and elsewhere, and the echoes can be felt as late as Tocqueville's strictures on the propensity of Americans for bargaining and mutual adaptation. The typical dweller in a democracy is gregarious, good-natured, conciliatory, socialized, enormously apt in the use of language (perhaps in a way that cheapens language by rendering it always negotiable), self-absorbed yet commonly attuned to the pleasures and pains of others, full of seductiveness and a curious readiness to be seduced. This is a partial portrait, with enough truth to suggest a likeness in the personality of many Americans. And yet, whomever I call to mind as an example, I find on analysis that a part of me appreciates the very trait another part despises. The reason is that people in a democratic culture aspire to something besides democracy, something even beyond the fulfillment of the democratic character. This is a paradox of manners that Whitman and Lincoln know well. All of the people want to be respected *as* the people, yet each wants not to be known merely as one of the people. Huey Long, the governor of Louisiana during the Great Depression and an instinctive and brilliant demagogue, captured the sentiment exuberantly in the campaign slogan "Every man a king." Do we in no way agree? And if you think that the phrase is sheer sloganeering, consider the satisfaction we take in the sort of democratic scene Whitman describes in his introduction to *Leaves of Grass*. Speaking of "the common people," he praises "the fierceness of their roused resentment — their curiosity and welcome of novelty — their self-esteem and wonderful sympathy — their susceptibility to a slight — the air they have of persons who never knew how it felt to stand in the presence of superiors." Then, for illustration, he mentions a democratic custom: "the President's taking off his hat to them and not they to him." The people do not know what it is to stand in the presence of a superior; it seems to them a natural gesture when the president salutes them. They are the gracious equal to whom he owes an unquestioned deference.

It is an ideal scene: "the President's taking off his hat to them and not they to him" — none the less ideal for its origin in actual experience. But notice that it exhibits a practice of virtue (chivalric virtue) as much as it does a performance of equality in manners. Readers of *Democratic Vistas* — the prose work of social criticism that Whitman published in 1867 and 1868, in which on the whole he speaks as a friend of modernity — have sometimes wondered at the note of awe with which this modern author speaks of the Crusades. Maybe we have a clue in his appreciation of the president's taking off his hat to the people. The dignity, the generosity and sensitivity on points of honor, the sense of a grace of life that cannot be bought, all of which belong to chivalry, are to be transplanted into the New World as attributes of the people. The salute will not be exchanged between one exemplar and another of crusading valor, but between the representative of the people and the people themselves. The distance and deference and pride of station that went with the older virtues have all somehow been preserved. Whitman, who was a subtler psychologist than Huey Long, suggests that since kings are beneath us now, the ideal of democratic life may have become "Every man a knight."

Two traits, says Whitman, essential to the practice of democracy are individuality and what he calls "adhesiveness." We might translate his terms as self-sufficiency and a comradely sympathy; and under those names they sound like modern qualities. But the pervading virtues that will always accompany them — again, if we can judge by Whitman's examples — are the older virtues of gentleness and courage. It is because our aspirations have been raised so high that we fear the conduct of the people may grow vicious and their judgments corrupt. For the ruin of the people brings a disgrace more terrible than the ruin of kings. Lincoln, in a letter of 1855, looked at the swelling constituency of the anti-immigrant party of his day and found his thoughts drifting to a gloomy speculation. "I am not a Know-Nothing," he begins:

> That is certain. How could I be? How can any one who abhors the oppression of negroes, be in favor of degrading classes of white people? Our progress in degeneracy appears to me to be pretty rapid. As a nation, we began by declaring that *"all men are created equal."* We now practically read it "all men are created equal, *except negroes.*" When the Know-Nothings get control, it will read "all men are created equal, except negroes, *and foreigners, and catholics.*" When it comes to this I should prefer emigrating to some country where they make no pretense of loving liberty — to Russia, for instance, where despotism can be taken pure, and without the base alloy of hypocrisy.

So the Old World distrust of the tyranny of democratic opinion can be shared by even so democratic a character as Abraham Lincoln. A democracy, he says, may be as slavish as a despotism, but it has the added evil of hypocrisy.

Much of Lincoln's writing and speaking between 1854 and 1859 will turn on the question whether the moral right and wrong of slavery can be decided by the will of a majority of voters. He was moved to an unusual show of anger when he thought about Stephen Douglas's saying that the problem of slavery should be simply settled by the rules of popular sovereignty. Douglas liked to say, "I don't care if they vote slavery up or down," and as often as he said it, Lincoln would quote the words against him, with derision and a sense of baffled shame. *Can* the people do as they please in a matter of such interest to the conscience of human nature? Lincoln is compelled to admit that the majority can legally do so. But he thinks the constitutional founders were in principle opposed to slavery, and he finds his main evidence in the Declaration of Independence, in the words "all men are created equal." The will of the people at a given moment is not the standard of right and wrong. Whitman for his part shows the same readiness to criticize both the practices and the opinions of the majority. He writes in *Democratic Vistas:* "Never was there, perhaps, more hollowness at heart than at present, and here in the United States. Genuine belief seems to have left us." And again: "The depravity of the business classes of our country is not less than has been supposed, but infinitely greater." And: "The magician's serpent in the fable ate up all the other serpents; and money-making is our magician's serpent, remaining to-day sole master of the field." Lincoln and Whitman respect the people too much to want to flatter them. They agree that democracy — to remedy evils which it has itself brought into being — requires a self-respect more thoroughgoing than can be found in any other system of manners. The maintenance of democracy will be a task different in kind and harder than its founding.

Whitman traces the new democratic self-respect to "an image of completeness in separatism"; an image, he goes on (choosing his words awkwardly and vividly), "of individual personal dignity, of a single person, either male or female, characterized in the main, not from extrinsic acquirements or position, but in the pride of himself or herself alone; and, as an eventual conclusion and summing up, (or else the entire scheme of things is aimless, a cheat, a crash,) the simple idea that the last, best dependence is to be upon humanity itself, and its own inherent, normal, full-grown qualities, without any superstitious support whatever." If the equality of individuals is for Whitman the self-evident truth of democracy, it is a truth we all of us confirm every day by the link between body and soul. What does individual mean if not undividable? One body, one soul. "I believe in you my soul," Whitman writes in *Song of Myself,* "the other I am must not abase itself to you, / And you must not be abased to the other." The range of possible reference in these words is very wide. It is the body speaking to the soul — the body must not be pressed by the soul to ascetic torments, even as its sensualism must not tamper with the soul's steadfastness — but it is also a world of spontaneous impulse addressing a mind informed by high ideals.

In writing as he does about the integrity of body and soul, Whitman stands against a tendency that he calls realism. *Democratic Vistas,* in a surprising and memorable phrase, deplores "the growing excess and arrogance of realism." Evidently, Whitman has in mind the imperative to build a railroad and get rich fast, which finds its correlatives in our own day. Realism is the voice that tells you to specialize your habits and feelings, to ride your personality on the current of things as they are, to do anything rather than stand and think and look at the world for the sake of looking. By contrast the "unsophisticated conscience" — for it takes resolve to *shed* sophistication — is a result of prolonged and partly involuntary exposure to experience. Let me pause here to say a word for the kind of experience Whitman praises. It is the experience of a single person dwelling unseen among others—an experience, in fact, of anonymity. This condition ought to be a blessing in democracy, where it need not go with material deprivation, yet we are apt to regard it as a curse. Anonymity is a vital condition of individuality—perhaps the only such condition that requires the existence of a mass society. When, in section 42 of *Song of Myself,* Whitman hears "A call in the midst of the crowd" and feels that he is being summoned by name, and that he must deliver his message with "my own voice, orotund sweeping and final," it is a profoundly welcome moment because he is being called from an interval of non-recognition and his speaking now will derive power from the time when he was alone in the crowd. Such intervals are not a kind of apprenticeship. They are supposed by Whitman to recur in the lives of the renowned as well as the obscure, and their continual return is to him an assurance of sanity.

The voice of *Song of Myself* rises from anonymity to the speech of "Walt Whitman, an American, one of the roughs, a kosmos," but this is not to be conceived of as an ascent from a humble to an exalted station. It is an emergence of individuality that could only happen to someone nursed in anonymity, and the occasion prompts his speech only because he is sure of passing back to anonymity. During the Civil War, Whitman did not fraternize with the great, did not seek to interview and write up the sage and serious opinions of statesmen, generals, ambassadors. He visited the sick and wounded at New-York Hospital, and served as a wound-dresser in the military hospitals in Washington, D.C. He eked out a living in the years of war by clerical work in the U.S. Army Paymaster's office and clerkships in the Department of Interior and the U.S. Attorney General's office.

As it happened, he lived on the route that President Lincoln took to and from his summer lodgings, and in his book *Specimen Days* Whitman left a record of his impression of Lincoln. It stresses the commonness, almost anonymity, of the president as he passes by, but also his unsearchable depth.

> The party makes no great show in uniform or horses. Mr. Lincoln on the saddle generally rides a good-sized, easy-going gray horse, is dress'd in plain black, somewhat rusty and dusty, wears a black stiff hat, and looks about as ordinary in attire, &c., as the commonest man. . . . I see very plainly ABRAHAM LINCOLN'S dark brown face, with the deep-cut lines, the eyes, always to me with a deep latent sadness in the expression. We have got so that we exchange bows, and very cordial ones. . . . Earlier in the summer I occasionally saw the President and his wife, toward the latter part of the afternoon, out in a barouche, on a pleasure ride through the city. Mrs. Lincoln was dress'd in complete black, with a long crape veil. The equipage is of the plainest kind,

only two horses, and they nothing extra. They pass'd me once very close, and I saw the President in the face fully, as they were moving slowly, and his look, though abstracted, happen'd to be directed steadily in my eye. He bow'd and smiled, but far beneath his smile I noticed well the expression I have alluded to. None of the artists or pictures has caught the deep, though subtle and indirect expression of this man's face. There is something else there.

The life that Whitman always went back to, even in the presence of great events and characters, was the life of an observer, an onlooker, with the patience to catch a subtle and indirect expression glimpsed by no one else.

His manner of looking at others has everything to do with his attitude toward himself. "Trippers and askers surround me," he says in section 4 of *Song of Myself,* "People I meet . . . . the effect upon me of my early life . . . . of the ward and city I live in . . . . of the nation"; and he says of all these environing facts and circumstances, "They come to me days and nights and go from me again, / But they are not the Me myself." There follows an unusual self-portrait:

> Apart from the pulling and hauling stands what I am,
> Stands amused, complacent, compassionating, idle, unitary,
> Looks down, is erect, bends its arm on a certain impalpable rest,
> Looks with its sidecurved head curious what will come next,
> Both in and out of the game, and watching and wondering at it.

It is a self-portrait; but a portrait of what kind of self? Whitman has said that "the other I am" must not abase itself. But the person who lives as the crowd lives will always abase "what I am," which Whitman also calls "the Me myself," the self that stands apart from the trippers and askers, the pulling and hauling. Whitman's self therefore in this portrait stands apart from the work of pleasing others. He is, to repeat, a simple separate entity: *what I am.* The features of the portrait, which correspond to a pencil sketch that continues to appear in many editions of *Leaves of Grass,* have an expression of almost conscious aloofness. On the other hand, his clothes are plain and the tilt of his head is inquisitive rather than rakish. He is wondering about himself as much as he is about those who are in the game full time: the game of having things to do, titles to be known by, roles to be identified with. Being both in and out of it, he is sometimes able to stand and rest and watch.

Whitman claims, and he encourages us to find in ourselves, the irony of the person who is not one thing — who, even to his own understanding, is composed of unseen parts — who can imagine that an event or experience may possibly alter what he is. The sequence of adjectives describing "what I am" is fascinating: "amused, complacent, compassionating, idle, unitary." *Amused,* at what if not himself and at the likelihood, as he puts it elsewhere in the poem, that even now he discovers himself "on a verge of the usual mistake." But still, *complacent,* sufficiently pleased with his situation, not wanting to change it for another, and at this moment without ambition as a true observer must be. The game he is in and out of is filled with other people, their pleasures and pains: he is *compassionating* as one made what he is partly by susceptibility to them. And *idle* — a great theme of Whitman's — for to act in the world and seek an effect would be to blunt his finer sense of mobility and alertness. By the way that all these words round off the portrait, they explain the choice of the climactic word *unitary.* The poet has a special endowment — which yet he shares potentially with any democratic citizen — and that is to be known by himself. One body, one soul.

His great book was called *Leaves of Grass* through all its editions. The title comes from a question early in *Song of Myself* about the meaning of life: "A child said, What is the grass? fetching it to me with full hands; / How could I answer the child? . . . . I do not know what it is any more than he." As you know if you have ever watched children, the question is really (pointing to the grass) "This must *mean* something. (But what?)" The child assumes something that grown-ups also assume in their different ways. Because he plucked the grass, he is its owner; and an owner may create meaning; and the more meanings the better. And yet — we never stop being children — all of the meanings had better be specific. Whitman would like to cooperate and so he gives the child, gives us, a series of conjectures, which by their sheer variety confess that the truths they indicate will be partial. "I guess," Whitman says of the grass, "it must be the flag of my disposition" — whatever I feel is what I now make it be. Or the grass is itself a child, "the produced babe of the vegetation." Or it is an image and shadow of divine things, to be read as a message from the Lord. Or an emblem of democracy: "Growing among black folks as among white, / Kanuck, Tuckahoe, Congressman, Cuff, I give them the same, I receive them the same." This is a catechism strangely appropriate to the questionings of a child, who, when he asks *what,* also always wants to know *why* things are. For example, if they come to be, can they cease to be? Are some more important than others? And will this die, now that I have picked it?

Whitman begins to answer the last question with a haunting line, "And now it seems to me the beautiful uncut hair of graves." He continues in one of the greatest stretches of imaginative writing in our literature:

> This grass is very dark to be from the white heads of old mothers,
> Darker than the colorless beards of old men,
> Dark to come from under the faint red roofs of mouths.
>
> O I perceive after all so many uttering tongues!
> And I perceive they do not come from the roofs of mouths for nothing.

> I wish I could translate the hints about the dead young men and women,
> And the hints about old men and mothers, and the offspring taken soon out
>   of their laps.
>
> What do you think has become of the young and old men?
> And what do you think has become of the women and children?
>
> They are alive and well somewhere;
> The smallest sprout shows there is really no death,
> And if there ever was it led forward life, and does not wait at the end to
>   arrest it,
> And ceased the moment life appeared.
>
> All goes onward and outward . . . . and nothing collapses,
> And to die is different from what anyone supposed, and luckier.

He says it is lucky to die and means it is lucky to live — to know that one *has* lived, without scheme or plan, restrained but not cautious, unobtrusive, uninhibited. The good of death, not that it happens to us, but that it happens and we are part of a world of things that happen, comes then only to this, that one sort of life makes room for another while life itself persists. All goes onward and outward, nothing collapses.

This is Whitman's ethic of "inception" or beginnings: "Urge and urge and urge, / Always the procreant urge of the world. / Out of the dimness opposite equals advance . . . . Always substance and increase, / Always a knit of identity . . . . always distinction . . . . always a breed of life." We would rather be part of something vital than part of something inert. In this light his creed seems one of entire and omnivorous acceptance. That is what it is, a free acceptance both ideal and physical among free persons, and Whitman connects it with a knowledge of identity that never can be fixed. He makes us feel all this in his address to the ocean:

> You sea! I resign myself to you also . . . . I guess what you mean,
> I behold from the beach your crooked inviting fingers,
> I believe you refuse to go back without feeling of me;
> We must have a turn together . . . . I undress . . . . hurry me out of sight of the
>   land,
> Cushion me soft . . . . rock me with billowy drowse,
> Dash me with amorous wet . . . . I can repay you.
> Sea of stretched ground-swells!
> Sea of breathing broad and convulsive breaths!
> Sea of the brine of life! Sea of unshovelled and always-ready graves!
> Howler and scooper of storms! Capricious and dainty sea!
> I am integral with you . . . . I too am of one phase and of all phases.

A similar current of ecstatic power belongs to many parts of *Song of Myself*. The parts are almost self-contained, yet the whole is different and is greater than the parts. How often Whitman's ecstasy, his standing outside himself, becomes a standing in some other kind of being, or an inhabiting of a man or woman apparently far from him in society. His originality is to insist that such changes of feeling do not point to the inconsequence of a mind adrift. They offer occasions for a sympathetic imagining that is identical with self-invention.

Nobody would want to call Whitman a nationalist, in any but the most loose-fitting sense, but in *Song of Myself* he commemorates some heroic and singular deeds from American history. He does it unforgettably in the sections of the poem devoted to the Alamo and a frigate-fight of the revolutionary era; and again but more familiarly in domestic scenes like the one that shows him giving comfort to a runaway slave. These narrative or historical parts of the poem turn out to have a feature in common, namely that they are about self-sacrifice, and their nameless heroes are individuals who know how much they are giving up. They know that nothing is better than life. There is accordingly no bombast, no triteness of assurance. Whitman sums up the losses in the sea battle, its deaths and amputations, in words of a simple finality: "These so . . . . these irretrievable." He admires great actions and thinks that physical courage is to be prized, but seems to feel that in the presence of readers who know the full worth of life, the words of an elegy ought to be calm and unarousing. A life of independence and self-respect — that is the good to be sacrificed for, and not the honor of a glorious death. By the manner of his words about death in battle, Whitman finds a way of persuading us that this is so. It is a grace he shares with Lincoln — something I hardly need to say.

Often in the course of *Song of Myself*, the poet seems in contact with the reader. A critic said once about Whitman, and with perfect truth, "You feel that he is in the room with you." The alternation of his whispers and prayers and enticements, with the strenuous catalogues and shorter glimpses of rural and urban life, seen close up or in a medium shot or montage, "The blab of the pave . . . . the tires of the cars and sluff of bootsoles and talk of the promenaders, / The heavy omnibus, the driver with his interrogating thumb, the clank of the shod horses on the granite floor" — these blendings of energy give the poem its sweep and poise and its miraculous air of inclusiveness. Then come the closing sections, and we seem suddenly to have entered a different climate. Every reader has felt this. The poet turns and talks to us now in a daily voice, as a person might stop to exchange a few words with a passerby. He has said a moment earlier, "I concentrate toward them that are nigh" (meaning *us*) — "I wait on the door-slab" — and by the way what an amazing and evocative word that is, "door-slab": the passage into a new home, or into the grave.

Both meanings fit Whitman's conception that every life is the leavings of many deaths. But now, in the last verses of the poem, it is as if his death and our life were different names for the same occurrence.

He says a gigantic farewell with no more ceremony than nature itself; he speaks to us as air, as breath:

> I depart as air . . . . I shake my white locks at the runaway sun,
> I effuse my flesh in eddies and drift it in lacy jags.
>
> I bequeath myself to the dirt to grow from the grass I love,
> If you want me again look for me under your bootsoles.
>
> You will hardly know who I am or what I mean,
> But I shall be good health to you nevertheless,
> And filter and fibre your blood.
>
> Failing to fetch me at first keep encouraged,
> Missing me one place search another,
> I stop some where waiting for you.

This stop is not really an ending. A pause, rather, that awaits resumption in another voice akin to his. The poem remains as an incitement, in our own lives, ever to be re-begun. Whitman is telling us also that the author of *Song of Myself* was never the Walter Whitman who took out the copyright, who has renamed himself Walt and appeared just once, by that half-assumed name, in the middle of the poem. He has not said and did not mean to say, "This is *me*." The author becomes any of a multitude of people who learn what he means by asking, without external help or support, "What is the grass?"; fetching it to ask that question, as now we must fetch him from the knit of identity in which we know that we too have been woven. Different readers of a poem as long as this will choose different lines as their favorites, but a pretty irresistible candidate is line 577, which says in other words what Whitman's closing words have said: "Happiness, which whoever hears me let him or her set out in search of this day." The leaves of grass that are Walt Whitman, the flag of his disposition, out of green stuff woven, are, he says, to be discovered under our feet and in our lives, indeed they were there if only we thought to look. So the poem keeps its modest and extraordinary promise: "What I assume you shall assume." The signers of the Declaration of Independence, who were also interested in what they called happiness, really meant no less than that when they subscribed the mutual pledge of their lives, their fortunes, and their sacred honor.

The rules or observances that cement society are largely implicit in a democracy, far more so than they are in any more hierarchical way of life, and so the tacit need for shared assumptions becomes correspondingly sharp. Lincoln, more conspicuously than Whitman, turned for moral guidance to the Declaration of Independence. He thought one could see the highest idealism of American democracy articulated in the words "all men are created equal." Throughout his early political career, he faced, in arguments by the slaveholders and their apologists in Congress, the counter-assertion that the founders meant by those words "all white men are created equal." As Stephen Douglas put it — speaking as a centrist by the standard of that time and by no means an abject apologist for slavery — the nation was "established by white men for the benefit of white men and their posterity forever." Now Lincoln is often, and I think mistakenly, described as a centrist or a moderate or a skillful pragmatist. Bear those words by Stephen Douglas in mind as you listen to Lincoln in 1857, in his Speech on the Dred Scott Decision, offering his own interpretation of the well-known phrase. The signers of the Declaration of Independence, he says,

> defined with tolerable distinctness in what respects they did consider all men created equal — equal in "certain inalienable rights, among which are life, liberty, and the pursuit of happiness." This they said, and this they meant. . . . They meant to set up a standard maxim for free society, which should be familiar to all, and revered by all; constantly looked to, constantly labored for, and even though never perfectly attained, constantly approximated, and thereby constantly spreading and deepening its influence, and augmenting the happiness and value of life to all people of all colors everywhere. . . . They knew the proneness of prosperity to breed tyrants, and they meant when such should re-appear in this fair land and commence their vocation they should find left for them at least one hard nut to crack.

The politician like the poet is a worker in words, though it seems fair to say they aim at widely different effects: the one to imagine; the other to persuade. Still, let us not exaggerate the difference. The imaginative work that persuasion implied for a man with Lincoln's aims was immense, and it required him to help his listeners discover what it was that created the value of life for them. Most of us probably now agree with him on the meaning of the words in the Declaration. Few of those whom he spoke to could have been sure that they agreed. Those who were sure they disagreed felt no compunction in calling his interpretation perverse and heaping abuse on Lincoln for having even dared to venture it.

Hatred of violence and love of liberty are the clues to Lincoln's political character. He believed that the history of slavery, in fact, was a history of violence under one name or another; that the only dangerous divisions in the United States ever since its founding had come from the contest over slavery; and that the decision returning Dred Scott to his master, and the justification of it by the Supreme Court, were "an astonisher in legal history," a terrible extension of that violence. Nevertheless, Lincoln was for avoiding a war, the worst kind of violence because the most organized, a war whose result in any case could not be foreseen, so long as assurance was given that slavery would not expand and would be allowed to die a natural death. Until the firing on Fort Sumter by the guns of the confederacy, he reiterated his purpose of standing firm without surrendering persuasion to violence. "Where the conduct of men is designed to be influenced," he said in an early speech to a temperance society, "*persuasion,* kind, unassuming persuasion, should ever be adopted." But Lincoln's opposition to slavery was founded on something deeper than his reading of the constitutional framers; it came from a settled belief about the constitution of human nature: "I hold if the Almighty had ever made a set of men that should do all the eating and none of the work, he would have made them with mouths only and no hands, and if he had ever made another class that he intended should do all the work and none of the eating, he would have made them without mouths and with all hands."

Persuasion, however, as Lincoln knew well, does not operate just through fable or example or the counting of short- and long-term benefits. It requires that we place ourselves in the situation of the people whom we would persuade—however disagreeable that may be when it obliges us to admit the irrational influence of custom and training. "I have no prejudice against the Southern people," says Lincoln in his Speech on the Kansas-Nebraska Act. "They are just what we would be in their situation. If slavery did not now exist amongst them, they would not introduce it. If it did now exist amongst us, we should not instantly give it up." When Lincoln speaks like this, he is engaged in a disagreeable and necessary act of sympathy. He is seeking to conciliate, and he is also telling the truth as he sees it.

And here we come to an uneasy fact—uneasy for people who like to divide the political world between saints and sinners—namely that Abraham Lincoln was a politician. He was a man of strong beliefs, trying to change the thinking of people who began with very different strong beliefs, and his practical aim was to pull them to his side. He did not cherish a hope of converting them to all his opinions. The intensity of his dedication to this task at the peak of his powers is unimaginable. It had to happen for us to imagine it. In 1857 and 1858, even before the famous series of debates, Lincoln tramped up and down the state of Illinois in the footsteps of Stephen Douglas, arriving in a town sometimes a few hours and sometimes a few days after Douglas spoke. He would set right the people whose judgment Douglas was trying to bribe. For he believed that by obtaining the passage of the Nebraska act, Douglas had sold out the constitutional principle that slavery is the enemy of freedom. Yet

Lincoln knew that many who agreed about this would disagree with the abolitionists that slavery was so intolerable an evil that it ought to be abolished at
once. They would also disagree with him, and among themselves, about the
appropriate policy to adopt toward the slaves once freed.

Some well-known words of his, taken in their full context, show as well as
anything could what persuasion in politics means. Truly persuasive words
always imply a kind of dialogue between our ideal views and the existing
opinions of people whose starting point is quite unlike our own. Here, then, is
Lincoln in the Speech on the Kansas-Nebraska Act, asking what will be the
relation between black and white races once slavery has been abolished. He
has begun by rejecting colonization for the time being as impracticable; and as
he goes on, we can hear him thinking aloud—a practice in which he excelled
every politician who ever lived. "What next?" he asks in this speech of 1854:
"Free them, and make them politically and socially, our equals? My own
feelings will not admit of this; and if mine would, we well know that those of
the great mass of white people will not. Whether this feeling accords with
justice and sound judgment, is not the sole question, if indeed, it is any part
of it. A universal feeling, whether well or ill founded, cannot be safely dis-
regarded." So he leaves himself and his audience with a perplexity that is to be
worked on. A profound central truth of democracy is that slavery is wrong—
Lincoln once wrote that "if slavery is not wrong, nothing is wrong"—but
when pressed to say what will follow once slavery is abolished, he confesses
that he does not know.

His hope, before the war changed everything, was to put slavery "in course of
ultimate extinction"—a phrase he repeated again and again with little variation. It took the coming of the war, on terms that made the president appear a
constitutional leader and not a fanatic, and it took the visible contribution on
the Union side of black soldiers against the slave power, to move what he had
called a "universal feeling" opposed to racial equality a long way toward the
acceptance of former slaves as fellow citizens. The record of the extent of that
change is eloquent in the Thirteenth, Fourteenth, and Fifteenth Amendments to
the Constitution. But it would not be right to conclude that the war and its
necessities alone changed the shape of the nation's self-understanding. When
we look closely at Lincoln's speeches and writings of the 1850s, what we are
seeing is the persuasive conduct of a man who is already a leader. Though out of
office, he is already preparing the minds of his fellow citizens for a momentous
change. And he contrives to do so even while serving as a publicist of the
principles of his party.

This is the pattern of Lincoln's speeches, letters, and occasional and com-
memorative statements throughout the 1850s. He uses, for example, the

occasion of a festival in Boston honoring the birthday of Thomas Jefferson, which he cannot attend, to compose a public letter in praise of Jefferson. He asserts in this letter of 1859 that the Republican Party of his day has become the true successor of the Democratic Party of earlier years, since the Democrats now hold the liberty of one man to be "nothing, when in conflict with another man's right of *property.* Republicans, on the contrary, are for both the *man* and the *dollar;* but in cases of conflict, the man *before* the dollar." It is a catchphrase and a good one, but it conceals a radicalism stronger than we may recognize at first. Really to put the man before the dollar would be to admit the wickedness not just of slavery but of the factory system and the ethic of money-making whose effects we have heard Whitman testify to a few years after the war.

There came a time before the war itself when Lincoln felt it necessary to speak of slavery from the point of view of the slave. He is at his firmest again in the Speech on the Dred Scott Decision, where, for the first time, he asks his white listeners to imagine the slave not as an other, but as another self — a "Me myself" or "what I am," to borrow Whitman's language — subject to a degradation without end, trapped by wheel within wheel of legal mystification and political compromise, a soul forever cut off from a body's experience of freedom. "All the powers of earth seem rapidly combining against him. Mammon is after him; ambition follows, and philosophy follows, and the Theology of the day is fast joining the cry. They have left him in his prison-house; they have searched his person, and left no prying instrument with him. One after another they have closed the heavy iron doors upon him, and now they have him, as it were, bolted in with a lock of a hundred keys, which can never be unlocked without the concurrence of every key; the keys in the hands of a hundred different men, and they scattered to a hundred different and distant places." In listening to these words, the free man or woman is asked to feel with the slave by virtue of nothing but a common humanity.

Look far ahead now to the middle year of the war — six years is not a long time, as we normally reckon, but in 1863 the world had been turned upside down — and hear Lincoln as he utters the other half of the same appeal. The occasion is an open letter to a group of antiwar Democrats, whose real objection is not to the war but to the Emancipation Proclamation. The abolitionist cause has now become an almost self-evident argument against white people who cannot admit a common humanity with the slave. "Peace," writes Lincoln in a letter to James C. Conkling on August 26, 1863, "does not appear so distant as it did. I hope it will come soon, and come to stay; and so come as to be worth the keeping in all future time. . . . And then, there will be some black men who can remember that, with silent tongue, and clinched teeth, and steady eye, and well-poised bayonet, they have helped mankind on to this great consummation; while, I fear, there will be some white ones, unable to forget that, with malignant heart, and deceitful speech, they have strove to hinder it." Lincoln describes the value of individuality and solidarity by showing what they are not.

Yet the anti-slavery principle is not the central element of Lincoln's thought. More primary and more radical is the principle that was called in his time "free labor" — the name of a political movement and also of a commonsense demand, that every man and woman should be accorded the power of obtaining adequate pay for work of any kind. The end in view is a society where one moves from working for someone else to working for oneself and to employing others in turn. This is the promise of democratic activity — we might say of democratic energy — and Lincoln goes out of his way to associate it with education. A speech given in 1859 about the ethics of labor directs itself against the so-called mud-sill theory of the inevitability of a degraded work force. Lincoln rejects the assumption that labor is not compatible with education. He was largely self-educated and knew the value of genuine learning, as he did of energetic labor. He had worked his way from the humblest trades to achieve the highest office in the land. The subject understandably provokes him to rewrite his fable of the body. With the slave and the master, the fable had told of the hands and the mouth. Now, with labor and education, it is the hands and the head: "Free labor argues that, as the Author of man makes every individual with one head and one pair of hands, it was probably intended that heads and hands should cooperate as friends; and that that particular head, should direct and control that particular pair of hands." The result of cultivating thought in the worker will be what Lincoln calls "*thorough* work." Every man and woman will become a virtuoso whose virtue is a particular kind of job well done. Word for word perhaps, Lincoln's Second Inaugural Address is as great a work in writing as democracy has to show, but no piece of it is more characteristic than the phrase "let us strive on to finish the work we are in." War, we know, presents a field of exercise that by a forced collaboration may bring out the best in the energies of men. Peace offers a scene of labor more naturally suited to equal division. Command and performance in time of peace can be a thorough product of consultation and of free discussion.

Lincoln — it comes as a constant surprise in so melancholy a man — was a great believer in human progress. But he asks us to beware of our inventions and our inventiveness. As he noticed once in a speech on discoveries, slavery too was a human invention, a saver of time and maker of leisure for some, but not for that reason worth all the evil it brought. In every epoch we need distinctive moral helps to fortify us in the battle against the evils of that epoch.

The mere belief in progress is not enough. "History," observes Whitman in *Democratic Vistas,* "is long, long, long. Shift and turn the combinations as we may, the problem of the future of America is in certain respects as dark as it is vast." This feels equally true if we read it today as a sentence about ourselves. And not to be tricked by any afterglow, we must not let the optimism of Lincoln and Whitman make us forget the despair that shadowed all their utterances, a despair that was the ground note of the time in which they lived. But as heroes go, persons distinctive of an age and yet beyond it, their peculiar quality is to give encouragement. There is a prejudice, still common among educated people, against the very idea of personal heroes, but it seems to me fundamentally mistaken. The unmasking of great men and women, true as a tactic, is false as a discipline. By proving you contingently superior to the most admirable examples from the past, it deprives you of a weapon of criticism and a wellspring of hope. It fosters not the love of perfection but moral snobbery and self-satisfaction, and only adds to the growing excess and arrogance of realism. Can we express the morality of true democracy better than Whitman and Lincoln did? "Whoever degrades another degrades me." "As I would not be a slave, so I would not be a master. This expresses my idea of democracy. Whatever differs from this, to the extent of the difference, is no democracy."

3

Public Emblem, Private Realm:
Family and Polity in the United States

NANCY F. COTT

Prescriptions for upholding the political order in the United States often look to family life, assuming that certain family characteristics are needed for democratic citizenship. Observers may be far apart on the political spectrum yet still agree that citizens are made in families; family character therefore determines the capacities of the sovereign people as a whole. A couple of contemporary examples illustrate this point. The feminist political theorist Susan Okin, justifying her focus on the family in a book on democratic justice, explains that justice cannot be achieved without moral development in citizens, and that "it is within the family that we first come to have that sense of ourselves and our relations with others that is at the root of moral development." Far to the right of Okin on most political issues, the conservative journalist David Frum stands with her on this point. "The family is where we learn to be human and to be citizens," he writes in an editorial opposing Vermont's legal recognition of same-sex marriage.[1]

Okin and Frum take part in a long tradition making family life relevant to American democratic citizenship. They could have taken their cues from statesmen of the era of the American Revolution. In his diary in 1778, John Adams recorded his belief that "the foundations of national Morality must be laid in private Families."[2] His comment expressed views of human nature and its political possibilities that were common among the founders of the

American republic. Concern for the stability of their new government drew the attention of American revolutionaries to marriage and family. Revolutionary leaders believed that the character of the citizens mattered far more in the republican political experiment of the new United States than in a monarchy. Because the people were sovereign in the United States, the government's success would depend on the people's virtue. American revolutionaries derived this premise from the political writings of the French thinker Baron de Montesquieu. Understood to be the very spring of republican government, "virtue" among the people connoted not only moral integrity (as in Adams's diary entry) but also public-spiritedness. Selfish, small-minded individuals narrowly seeking their own advancement would not do: citizens in a republic had to appreciate civic obligation and take to heart the collective good of the polity.[3]

Marriage and family were assumed to play an important part in making republican citizens suitably virtuous. Literate Americans at the time of the Revolution generally believed that the most reasonable and humane qualities of human beings arose in sociability. They learned this in part from Montesquieu and also from the later eighteenth-century Scottish moral philosophers, who contended that human beings were not isolates by nature, but rather sought companionship and defined themselves in relation to others. The family setting created by marriage was a basic site for sociability and care for others. Marriage played a salutary part because it served as a "school of affection" where citizens would learn to be solicitous of others. A 1791 essay in the *New-York Magazine,* for example, praised love for enabling a man to subdue selfishness and egotism: "In detaching us from self, it accustoms us to attach ourselves the more to others. . . . Love cannot harden hearts, nor extinguish social virtues. The lover becomes a husband, a parent, a citizen."[4] Family life in its collective intimacy would provide training grounds for citizens, then, and would serve the aim of bringing the best capacities of citizens to the fore.

Today we don't ordinarily think of love, or marriage, or family relations, as leading directly to robust citizenship. At best the relation between family life and the health of the polity is invoked as a vague and general principle. We may even assume that concern for intimates leads away from civic commitments. Political leaders of the past connected these arenas more directly. At the turn of the last century, President Theodore Roosevelt believed as the 1791 essay writer did that "the first essential for a man's being a good citizen is his possession of the home virtues." Roosevelt associated the capacities for good citizenship and good government with "the qualities that make men and women eager lovers, faithful, duty-performing, hard-working husbands and wives, and wise and devoted fathers and mothers."[5]

Roosevelt thus continued the deep-lying Revolutionary political discourse linking family life to citizenship. The habit of connecting the two had grown in prominence in the mid-nineteenth century, in response to a direct challenge from a new religious group, the Church of Jesus Christ of Latter-day Saints. From their settlement in the Utah territory, the Mormons announced in 1852 that divine instruction had led them to take up polygamy. Their revelation sparked a forty-year campaign by the United States Congress, successive presidents, and the United States Supreme Court to extirpate this heterodox practice. The belief that American representative democracy depended on monogamous families, which had been implicit in Revolutionary republicanism, emerged loudly in political opposition to Mormon polygamy.

Consider the pronouncements of Francis Lieber, a major political thinker of the time. Lieber imagined the Mormons corrupting the United States utterly if polygamous Utah were accepted into the Union as a state. In his view, monogamy was "the foundation of all that is called polity." It was not only the basis of "domestic being and family relation" but also "one of the primordial elements out of which all law proceeds," a "psychological condition of our jural consciousness, [and] of our liberty." He saw monogamously based families as intrinsically linked to political liberty — and polygamous families just as necessarily tied to coercion.[6] This contrast, aligning monogamy with a government based on consent and polygamy with despotism, had begun a century before during the European Enlightenment (Montesquieu was one of the first to give it prominence). Lieber was no maverick but rather the man generally credited with founding American political science. His major works, especially his treatise *On Civil Liberty and Self-Government* (1853), were standard American college texts in the nineteenth century and were read and quoted for many decades by politicians, lawyers, and judges. Like Lieber, in championing monogamy over polygamy American political thinkers thought they were endorsing representative government over tyranny.

One enduring result of Lieber's writing about monogamy was its enshrinement in the first, controlling, precedent of American jurisprudence on religious freedom. This Supreme Court decision of 1878, *Reynolds v. United States,*[7] arose because Mormons challenged a new federal law criminalizing polygamy in the territories of the United States. The Mormon defendant argued that the law abridged his First Amendment freedom of religion. The Supreme Court, unpersuaded, said that the First Amendment protected freedom of religious *belief* but did not cover *actions* that were contrary to law and public policy. Marrying — or cohabiting with — more than one wife was such a criminal action. The Court cited and quoted Francis Lieber's view that polygamy was incompatible with representative democracy. The Court later let stand federal laws that disfranchised polygamous Mormons and eventually expropriated the Mormon Church.

The longevity of Lieber's line of argument against the Mormons can be seen in David Frum's editorial of January 2000. Without acknowledging it, Frum was charting a lineage of ideas descending from Montesquieu when he asserted that "Americans have understood until now . . . that heterosexual monogamy is the only form of sexual organization consistent with republican self-government." He quoted approvingly from a United States Supreme Court decision of 1885 (validating disfranchisement of polygamists) that "no legislation can be supposed more wholesome and necessary in the founding of a free, self-governing commonwealth . . . than that which seeks to establish it on the basis of the idea of the family, as consisting in and springing from the union for life of one man and one woman in the holy estate of matrimony." This same 1885 sentence was quoted on the floor of Congress in 1996 by one of the co-sponsors of the Defense of Marriage Act, which allows states not to recognize same-sex marriage authorized outside the state. The Court's 1885 opinion went so far as to say that it was appropriate for legislatures to make marital status "a condition of the elective franchise," even to "declare that no one but a married person shall be entitled to vote."[8]

With this long introduction I hope to make the point that conceptions of family have figured centrally in the history of thinking about American representative government. Although common wisdom roots American democracy conceptually in individualism, with a political genealogy indebted to the social contract theory of John Locke and his fellow liberals, there is at least equal evidence for a political genealogy leading from Montesquieu and the Scottish moralists to root American representative government in a family unit based on monogamous marriage. Even Alexis de Tocqueville, who most famously cited individualism as characteristic of American democracy, actually placed the "individual" in family surroundings. In the chapter of *Democracy in America* called "Of Individualism in Democratic Countries," Tocqueville gave meaning to the word "individualism," which was new at the time in both French and English. Individualism, in Tocqueville's view, was not a "blind instinct" like selfishness, a "passionate and exaggerated love of self, which leads a man to connect everything with himself and to prefer himself to everything in the world." Individualism was rather "a mature and calm feeling, which disposes each member of the community to sever himself from the mass of his fellows and to draw apart with his family and his friends, so that after he has thus formed a little circle of his own, he willingly leaves society at large to itself."

Tocqueville invoked the word "individualism" not to praise the phenomenon but to worry about it — to express doubt and alarm about the American society he saw. He criticized the individual's severing himself, drawing apart, from the collectivity — but Tocqueville did not sketch an atomistic individual. He described a male adult who lived with a family around him, who was a head of household, with a wife and children (and perhaps others too) as dependents, when he accused the individual of "draw[ing] apart with his family and his friends." His implicit assumption that the "individual" was a male household head is typical of contributors to the Western political tradition. The implied actor is an adult male — the observations and theories really fit only a citizen who is a man of a particular sort, the head of a family household.[9]

Tocqueville indicted individualism for distancing the individual *and his family* from civil society. He concluded the chapter called "Democracy's Influence on the Family" with a similar sentiment. "Democracy loosens social ties, but tightens natural ones," Tocqueville wrote; "it brings kindred more closely together, while it throws citizens more apart."[10] This hypothesis of Tocqueville's accorded with his worry that what he called "individualism" in America produced families as insular units in society. It suggests a more positive point as well: in the social order of the United States, Tocqueville saw "natural" bonds — those built from family and kinship — taking the place of the established social hierarchies he was accustomed to seeing in a monarchy. If we read Tocqueville to say that family bonds substituted for other social ties in anchoring individuals and stabilizing society, thus making government workable in the United States, then he was positing that the family is a linchpin of public order. This proposition is not so far from John Adams's rumination — "the foundations of national Morality must be laid in private Families" — and not so far from politicians' assertions about "family values" today.

Even as we commonly refer to family life as "private" life, families have been expected to serve a preeminently public goal — the very health of the nation. There is a paradox here, an *apparent* contradiction that can be understood by recognizing the doubled, private *and* public, meanings of the relation between families and the polity. In his diary entry, John Adams used the adjective "private" to modify "families," in contrast to "national" (or, we can assume, "public") morality — suggesting that he himself saw this paradox and embraced it. Constitutional government in the United States, which makes the preservation of individual liberties a central premise, has always assumed that families are "private" ventures because familial conduct has been seen as an extension of individual conduct (rather as the acquisition of "private property" has been). Yet the vitality of these "private" entities is essential to public order, as Tocqueville explicitly noticed.

The relation between "private" families and the public interest has been continuous in American history, though its particular forms have changed over time, as would be expected, because conceptions of liberties, rights, public interest, and public order have themselves changed over time. The political and military demands of World War II and the early Cold War stepped up national rhetoric on the relation of families to the polity, intensifying the public weight given to the "private" realm. A global event of unprecedented magnitude, World War II brought enormous consequences on the home front. War production and the mobilization of 12 million men into the armed services caused immense movement among the population. The infusion of federal dollars into war production ended the unemployment and the economic despair of the Great Depression. Military service and jobs in the defense industry drew people away from their homes to distant locations. Far from the eyes of watchful neighbors, Americans mixed together in new locations, with strangers of different regions, religions, and ethnic derivations. This fostered both a new cosmopolitanism and new group allegiances. A rhetoric of racial and religious tolerance and cultural pluralism came to the fore from official sources, championing the diversity of America's population in contradistinction to Nazi "racial" distinctions.[11]

While millions of men went into military service and bore the heroic burdens of the war, manufacturers welcomed women into what had formerly been seen as men's jobs. With so many men away, the doors of higher education institutions and the professions also opened much wider to women. The employment of women — especially of wives and mothers — reached dramatically new highs. Attention to the tremendous numbers of women in civilian industry outweighed the impact of a small number of women serving in their own new branches of the military, though that too was a very important benchmark of women's integration as full citizens.

Upheavals in family lives and gender roles caused immense controversy. Alarmists lamented that young people had too much freedom; that servicemen adopted a live-for-the-day attitude; that women working in the war industries were unwilling to embrace home duties, and that juvenile delinquency loomed among the "latchkey children" whose mothers were at work. Although wartime changes might have spurred reassessment of the differences between the sexes as conventionally understood, public discourse tended to sidestep that result. Both government and industry encouraged women to contribute to war production and applauded them for doing so. At the same time, both stressed that women workers were replacing men only "for the duration" of the war.

Pathbreaking jobs for women workers did not have to challenge long-held convictions about women's essential identities as sweethearts, daughters, wives, and mothers, if the innovations were suitably framed.[12] As women stepped partway into men's shoes — and took home man-sized pay envelopes — they were constantly reminded to retain their femininity, meaning their appeal to men.

The historian Robert Westbrook has argued persuasively that government mobilization of patriotism and self-sacrifice during wartime relied on appeals to defend individuals' private rights and rewards, more than on strictly public allegiances. American democracy in the mid-twentieth century could more plausibly mobilize male citizens to risk their lives for love, marriage, and home than for abstract democratic ideals. While waging war, the United States government used visions of women's attractiveness to bolster servicemen's morale and to imply that long-held views of sexual difference and expectations of family roles were firmly in place. The government cooperated with Hollywood to scatter "pin-ups" of movie stars over the field of war. Millions of photographs of female stars were distributed, coming to adorn the walls of barracks, bulkheads of ships, and fuselages of planes. Wives and sweethearts back home eagerly participated by sending "pin-up" poses of themselves to the men at the front. A wartime bargain between American men and women was being struck: women at home would retain their femininity and attachments to domesticity, while men at war would fight to defend their rights to those comforts of femininity, home, and prospects of fatherhood.[13]

The war rhetoric of the United States dwelt on the intimate and familial aspects of the American way of life, centering on heterosexual love and marriage, while championing democratic freedom against Nazi aggression and Japanese imperialism. For example, the federal government produced and broadcast on all stations in 1942 a radio program called "To the Young." It featured a young male voice saying, "That's one of the things this war's about." A young female voice responded, "About us?" The man affirmed: "About all young people like us. About love and gettin' hitched, and havin' a home and some kids, and breathin' fresh air out in the suburbs . . . about livin' and workin' decent, like free people."[14]

Government recruitment efforts, Hollywood, and the War Advertising Council harmonized as one on this theme. So precious was the private experience of marriage and family that it composed a public necessity worth fighting for. This message was addressed both to men and to women. Ads from the Union Central Life Insurance Company, for example, pictured the war as a "fight to keep our country a safe place for the wives we love, a place where our children can grow up free and unafraid." The Eureka vacuum cleaner company assured women war workers that they were fighting "for freedom and all that means to women everywhere. You're fighting for a little house of your own, and a husband to meet every night at the door . . . for the right to bring up your children without the shadow of fear."[15] In popular culture and widespread sentiment, family ties signified and virtually constituted the American way of life. The Academy Award for Best Picture of 1944 went to the film *Since You Went Away,* described on screen as the story of that "unconquerable American fortress, the American Home." That same year, a United States Supreme Court decision first discerned a "private realm of family life which the state cannot enter" and spoke of parents' direction over their children as "sacred private interests, basic in a democracy."[16]

This sacralization of the privacy of the home, linked directly to the political system of democracy, continued into Cold War politics. In confrontations with the Soviet Union and its socialist allies, American politicians emphasized that marriage, family, and the emotional and material comforts of home were private freedoms and, at the same time, were public emblems, essential to the existence, image, and defense of the United States, as they had been during the world war. Vice President Richard Nixon epitomized this point of view in his famous "kitchen debate" with Soviet premier Nikita Khrushchev. This exchange took place in Moscow in 1959, at the opening of the American National Exhibition, which showcased recreational and consumer goods. A six-room, furnished, and well-equipped ranch-style house was on display. Leaning into the kitchen, Vice President Nixon contended with Khrushchev over the virtues of American washing machines for housewives' comfort and leisure. The vice president made clear that freedom to pursue the good life at home was what the United States had to offer the world.[17]

In the second half of the twentieth century, public insistence on the importance of families for the polity has never flagged, and public policy interventions into families have increased, without unseating, or much complicating, assumptions that family interactions are "private life." The Supreme Court set the linkage between family, privacy, and polity into constitutional interpretation not long after Nixon's kitchen debate. Justice William O. Douglas wrote a very telling opinion in 1961, in a case brought purposely to dismantle Connecticut's longstanding prohibition on the use of contraceptive methods. The details of the case, which was called *Poe v. Ullman,* need not be discussed here. The Court's majority declined to hear it, ruling that the case did not call for constitutional decision making because of the particular circumstances of the original plaintiffs.

Justice Douglas dissented. He thought the Court should act to overturn the antiquated Connecticut law, which stipulated criminal punishment for "any person who uses any drug, medicinal article or instrument for the purpose of preventing conception." Douglas's reasoning was novel. By criminalizing the behavior of a wife or husband who *used* a contraceptive, the law reached into "the intimacies of the marriage relationship," Douglas wrote; the law's arm entered the "innermost sanctum of the home" and violated "the privacy that is implicit in a free society." Douglas's link between "privacy" and "a free society" was crucial to his reasoning. The "privacy" of the marital relationship "emanated from the totality of the constitutional scheme under which we live," he wrote, the "regime of a free society." A law that would punish a husband or wife for using birth control was not appropriate in a polity based on constitutional liberty; it was "congenial only to a totalitarian regime." The term "totalitarian," used in the 1940s to refer to both fascism and communism, had become a virtual synonym for Soviet communism by the time Douglas wrote this dissent in 1961.[18]

By fusing the protection of marital intimacy to the political principles of constitutional democracy, Douglas initiated postwar constitutional doctrine on privacy rights. In his view, marital and domestic privacy stood for the people's liberty and identified the United States as a free nation. His dissent foreshadowed the Supreme Court's holding four years later in *Griswold v. Connecticut*. In this 1965 case the Court did strike down Connecticut's prohibition on contraceptives, because it invaded "the sacred precincts of the marital bedroom." The Court's 1965 opinion found that the Constitution's guarantees of liberty implied "fundamental" rights of privacy, marital choice, and family creation.[19]

Because privacy rights are linked to liberty of person, which is a basic and revered goal of our constitution, the potential scope of family privacy as a constitutional right is large. The line of Court decisions descended from the *Griswold* case has altered the landscape of Americans' personal lives while extending the legal principle of privacy from a protection of family intimacy to freedom of *individual* choice in intimate matters. The most controversial extension has been *Roe v. Wade* (1973), which ended state restrictions on abortion in the first trimester of pregnancy. In *Roe*, the Supreme Court's majority held that fundamental rights of privacy were "implicit in the concept of ordered liberty" even if not explicit in the Constitution, and it ruled that "a woman's decision whether or not to terminate her pregnancy" was included.[20]

Emphasis on familial freedoms and privacy as emblems of democracy has led to consequences unanticipated during the World War II era, including recent legal arguments on behalf of same-sex couples who want to marry. An Alaska judge in 1998, for example, called the "right to choose one's life partner" constitutionally "fundamental," a right of privacy that deserved governmental protection even for choosing a partner of the same sex. Positing that "government intrusion into the choice of a life partner encroaches on the intimate personal decisions of the individual," he underlined the association between free choice in marriage and individual liberty.[21]

In this line of privacy-based Supreme Court decisions stemming from *Griswold v. Connecticut*, as well as in common parlance, privacy seems essential to the family. Constitutional emphasis on the marriage relationship as an intimate consensual zone embodies one conception of the values of democracy: that is, what democratic government exists to protect. Yet thinking of the family as simply private provides only a partial view. The family is historically a system of governance. Traditionally, the husband and father governed his wife and their children just as the king ruled his subjects. "Such duty as the subject owes the prince / Even such a woman oweth her husband," Shakespeare's title character Kate concedes at the end of *The Taming of the Shrew*. Not all members of the family were equal. Liberty for the male household head could easily mean constraint for his wife or children.

Modern ideas and legal doctrines have moderated the husband and father's position as "lord and master," of course. We assume today that family members deserve more equal status and freedom than in Shakespeare's time — yet just how equal remains a question without a consistent answer. Where the old maxim "A man's home is his castle" implied that the husband and father governed all within his walls with impunity, recent legal developments have drawn public attention and government regulation to conflict within the family. Pressured by feminist advocacy and dire revelations of abuse, states by the 1980s made domestic battery and rape criminal offenses and began prosecuting wife-abusers and child-batterers. Criminalization of these offenses expresses and symbolizes the current limits on individuals' power and freedom within the family.

"The family itself is not beyond regulation in the public interest," said the United States Supreme Court in 1944, in the very same decision that recognized a "private realm of family life which the state cannot enter."[22] Governments at all levels in the United States have always taken strong interest in family forms and vitality. Family roles endow their holders with public and legal obligations, and with concomitant government-authorized status and benefits. Shaping families to favor "the public interest" is a constant public project, which can take numerous forms. Local, state, and national governments have always stepped inside some families whose members do not appear to be fulfilling their obligations. State laws allow government authorities to place children in foster homes, for instance, and to compel fathers to provide for their children. Interventions into poor and needy families have been common throughout American history. Surveillance and regulation have come along with any form of public assistance, whether the poorhouse, the asylum, or monetary "relief." The federal government has been involved in the family since the time of the Civil War, when authorities examined the circumstances of widows of Civil War pensioners to make sure they were suitable recipients of federal aid. From then through twentieth-century expansions and contractions of public assistance to the needy, those who obtain government aid have not been able to insulate their family lives from public scrutiny and interference. They have been required to conform to government expectations. To welfare clients under Aid to Families with Dependent Children in the 1960s or to Temporary Assistance to Needy Families recipients today, the pronouncement of a "private realm of family life which the state cannot enter" rings hollow.[23]

In the long history of American public endorsement of families as a linchpin of the republic, one doesn't find precise profiles of the "home virtues" (to use Theodore Roosevelt's words). Despite rhetorical claims that good families will sustain a sovereign people in a stable republic, there are only general assumptions, not detailed blueprints for family life. There are no precise specifications for the relation of family nurture to "national Morality" (John Adams's concern). What are the family interactions that will create citizens capable of sailing the ship of state? Are familial transactions supposed to look like those of representative government? Should family members decide their members' relative statuses, conduct their relationships, and make decisions on the "one person one vote" model? Or should family relationships, being trained in the "school of affection" rather than in objective judgment, differ qualitatively from those of public life, the very different values of the "private" arena somehow favoring the healthy development of the public?

That last model, Lockean liberalism, which distinguishes the "natural" character of familial relations from the contractual, consent-based transactions of public authority, is the political tradition on which the United States government is based. Most Americans probably incline toward believing that intimate family relationships do, and should, differ qualitatively from governmental ones. Most would shun making an exact analogy between representative democracy and the family, where unequal earning power and parents' authority over children are basic facts. Yet there are also expectations that the "little commonwealth" of the family will mirror to some extent the values desired for the larger commonwealth, the public at large. As early as the time of the American Revolution, and perhaps even earlier, prescriptions for appropriate family conduct in the United States accorded with the values of representative government, finding reasoned governance and a sense of explicit mutual obligation, rather than strict hierarchy, desirable in the relationship between parent and child and between husband and wife. Tocqueville claimed that relationships between fathers and sons were noticeably more egalitarian in America than in France in 1830, and he attributed this greater balance to the influence of the political model.[24]

Popular conviction and political rhetoric continue to insist that the family is a "private" arena — *the* private arena for self-expression and choice despite public regulation of the form of marriage and all the rules and incentives of the tax and welfare systems. Family forms and conduct have been less self-chosen than the rhetoric of privacy would suggest. Governmental demands have helped shape the families that Americans make and approve of. The assumption that citizens are best nurtured in monogamous, male-headed, two-parent families often remains implicit, while it structures basic provisions such as the income tax, social security, veterans' benefits, and immigration preferences, and can be punitive toward outliers, whether single mothers or resurgent polygamists. With unusual explicitness, the Bush administration's initiatives in 2002 to give "marriage education" to recipients of public assistance brought this assumption to the surface.[25] While "privacy" appears to rule over a vast terrain of conduct and ethics in the family, public demands are omnipresent. This twisted strand of public and private construction of family is not likely to unravel soon.

Notes

1. Susan Moller Okin, *Justice, Gender, and the Family* (New York: Basic, 1989), 14; David Frum, editorial, *Weekly Standard*, January 2000.

2. Entry of June 2, 1778, in *Diary and Autobiography of John Adams*, ed. Lyman Butterfield (Cambridge: Harvard University Press, 1962), 4:123.

3. See Anne M. Cohler, *Montesquieu's Comparative Politics and the Spirit of American Constitutionalism* (Lawrence: University Press of Kansas, 1988), esp. 12–17; Gordon S. Wood, *The Creation of the American Republic* (New York: Norton, 1969).

4. "On Love," *New-York Magazine*, June 1791. On sociability, see Henry F. May, *The Enlightenment in America* (New York: Oxford University Press, 1976), 282, 342–47; Jay Fliegelman, *Prodigals and Pilgrims: The American Revolution against Patriarchal Authority* (New York: Cambridge University Press, 1980), 24; Diana J. Schaub, *Erotic Liberalism: Women and Revolution in Montesquieu's "Persian Letters"* (London: Rowman and Littlefield, 1995), 25–31; Jan Lewis, "The Republican Wife: Virtue and Seduction in the Early Republic," *William and Mary Quarterly*, 3d ser., 44 (October 1987): 689–721.

5. Theodore Roosevelt, *The Free Citizen*, ed. Hermann Hagedorn (New York: TR Assoc., 1956), 30–31.

6. Francis Lieber, "The Mormons: Shall Utah Be Admitted into the Union?" *Putnam's*

Monthly 5 (March 1855): 234; and see Nancy F. Cott, *Public Vows: A History of Marriage and the Nation* (Cambridge: Harvard University Press, 2000), 20–22, 114–16.

7. 98 U.S. 145 (1879).

8. Frum, editorial; *Murphy v. Ramsay*, 114 U.S. 15, 43, 45 (1885); Dave Weldon of Florida, *Congressional Record,* 104th Congress, 2d sess., vol. 104, pt. 2, July 12, 1996, p. 7493.

9. Alexis de Tocqueville, *Democracy in America,* trans. Henry Reeve, ed. Phillips Bradley (New York: Vintage, 1945), 2:104; on the individual as male, see Susan Moller Okin, *Women in Western Political Theory* (Princeton: Princeton University Press, 1979).

10. Tocqueville, *Democracy in America,* 2:208.

11. See Lewis A. Erenberg and Susan E. Hirsch, *The War in American Culture: Society and Consciousness during World War II* (Chicago: University of Chicago Press, 1996).

12. See Susan M. Hartmann, *The Home Front and Beyond: American Women in the 1940s* (Boston: Twayne, 1982).

13. See Robert Westbrook, "'I Want a Girl, Just Like the Girl That Married Harry James': American Women and the Problem of Political Obligation in World War II," *American Quarterly* 42 (December 1990): 587–614; and Robert Westbrook, "Fighting for the American Family: Private Interests and Political Obligation in World War II," in *The Power of Culture,* ed. Richard W. Fox and T. J. Jackson Lears (Chicago: University of Chicago Press, 1993), 195–221.

14. Quoted in Elaine Tyler May, "Rosie the Riveter Gets Married," in *The War in American Culture: Society and Consciousness during World War II,* ed. Lewis A. Erenberg and Susan E. Hirsch (Chicago: University of Chicago Press, 1996), 137.

15. Quoted in Westbrook, "Fighting for the American Family," 201–2.

16. *Prince v. Massachusetts,* 321 U.S. 158, 166 (1944).

17. Elaine Tyler May, *Homeward Bound: American Families in the Cold War Era* (New York: Basic, 1988), 16–18; see also Sonya Michel, "American Women and the Discourse of the Democratic Family in World War II," in *Behind the Lines: Gender and the Two World Wars,* ed. Margaret Randolph Higonnet et al. (New Haven: Yale University Press, 1987).

18. *Poe v. Ullman,* 367 U.S. 497, 519–22 (1960).

19. *Griswold v. Connecticut,* 381 U.S. 479, 486, 495 (1965) (Justice Goldberg, concurring). See Thomas C. Grey, "Eros, Civilization, and the Burger Court," *Law and Contemporary Problems* 43, no. 3 (1979–80): 83–100.

20. *Roe v. Wade,* 410 U.S. 113 (1973). The constitutional rearticulation of marriage as a fundamental right in *Griswold v. Connecticut* formed an important background to an equally historic case two years later, *Loving v. Virginia,* 388 U.S. 1 (1967), which closed the long history of race-based prohibitions on marriage by striking down Virginia's law that made it a felony for a white person and a nonwhite person to get married. Equal protection of the laws, rather than marital intimacy, was the deciding point in *Loving,* but the opinion reiterated clearly that marriage was a "fundamental freedom."

21. *Brause v. Bureau of Vital Statistics,* 1998 WL 88743 (Alaska Super. Ct.).

22. The Court ruled in this case against a parent's claim to the religious and familial freedom to have her child selling religious newspapers on the street, in violation of child labor laws. *Prince v. Massachusetts,* 321 U.S. 158 (1944).

23. See Cott, *Public Vows;* Gwendolyn Mink, *The Wages of Motherhood: Inequality in the Welfare State, 1917–1942* (Ithaca: Cornell University Press, 1995).

24. Tocqueville, *Democracy,* 2:204–08, and Fliegelman, *Prodigals and Pilgrims;* cf. John Demos, *A Little Commonwealth: Family Life in Plymouth Colony* (New York: Oxford University Press, 1970).

25. See "Welfare Chief Is Hoping to Promote Marriage," *New York Times,* February 19, 2002, A1, A15; Gwendolyn Mink, "Violating Women: Rights Abuses in the Welfare Police State," *Annals of the American Academy of Political and Social Science* 577 (September 2001): 79–93.

4

Can Religion Tolerate Democracy?
(And Vice Versa?)

STEPHEN L. CARTER

Not everything is science. Not everything is art. Not everything is politics. So much of life is faith. Against all predictions, against all odds, faith abides. Just about a hundred years ago, a prominent Pennsylvania pastor named George Ferris, preaching on the theory of evolution, insisted that scientific progress left Christian morality undisturbed:

> It may be that back in the mists somewhere the greatest of our grandfathers was just a shapeless jelly-like bit of digestive incoherence. For this reason must we lose our reverence for the moral grandeur of a Paul . . . ? It may be that our arms and hands are merely the evolution of wiggling antennae on the surface of a moving sponge. Does this fact remove the grandeur and beauty from the pen of a Whittier or the brush of a Raphael? And yet, there have been multitudes who have allowed a secret scorn of religion to creep into their souls, while reading evidence to prove that it originated in ancestor-worship, or in the dread of some mighty Caliban who rattles in the thunder, or shouts in the surge of the sea.[1]

Ah, the secret scorn of religion! So long has it characterized Western thought. And sometimes the scorn is not so secret. One is reminded of Voltaire's dream of strangling the last king with the intestines of the last priest. Or of Jefferson's dismissal of traditional Judaism as "fumes of the most disordered imaginations" — and of traditional Christian teachings about Jesus as "the follies, the falsehoods, and the charlatanisms which His biographers father on him."[2] A few historians go so far as to suggest that concern about the anti-Catholicism rampant in the colonies during the eighteenth century was one reason for Canada's refusal to join the American Revolution. In short, many a democratic hero has been villainous in attitude toward religion.

And what about religion's attitude toward democracy? Nearly every religion on earth could fairly be described as compatible with democratic institutions,[3] but one will search very hard to find a religious tradition that takes the view that democracy is ontologically entailed. True, all through the nation's history, there have been Christian preachers who have argued that *America* is ontologically entailed, that it is the New Jerusalem, the light to lead the nations to righteousness, a history to which we will shortly return. But to claim for your nation a special status in God's eyes is no new thing, and many religious people have done it over the ages, and some do it today; indeed, the identification of a "people" according to their faith and the guidance and protection of their god is evidently far older than the identification of a "people" as residents, subjects, or citizens of a particular nation-state.

We must therefore be careful not to make the mistake of thinking that theologians or preachers who see the United States itself as specially favored of the Lord are also necessarily contending that democracy is specially favored of the Lord. Heaven, after all, is no democracy.

We also must avoid a parallel mistake: supposing that democrats who proclaim themselves in favor of religious freedom are therefore in favor of religion. One might carve out a space for people to indulge their primitive superstitions while, at the same time, hoping that they will one day grow out of them.

In both cases, the most we can reasonably conclude is that people go with what they've got. A democracy must deal with religion because it has within its borders religious citizens. A religion must deal with democracy if that is the form of government within which its followers reside.

I begin this way because I think it is useless to think out the relationship between religion and democracy in theoretical terms, but useful to consider it in practical terms. Most contemporary theorists of democracy would probably conclude that democratic politics and democratic life could proceed just fine if, tomorrow, no one in America woke up believing in God. Most believers who happen to live in America would probably insist that they would believe in the same God, in the same way, were they to awaken tomorrow in a land in which nobody believed in democracy.

In this sense, we might say that democracy, in the abstract, probably would find religion dispensable; and that religion, in the abstract, probably would find democracy dispensable; and the fact that some of us would describe ourselves as committed deeply to both democracy and our faith does not change the fact that neither commitment entails the other.

If both religion and democracy likely could exist without the other (or think they could), it is scarcely surprising that each works constantly to press the other into a mold it finds useful. After all, from the point of view of democratic theory, religion possesses no independent importance. From the point of view of religion, democracy possesses no independent importance either. Theorists of democracy nowadays complain bitterly about illiberal religions, and some of them have written about how to try to tame those religions they like least, usually through the education of the children of the parents whose beliefs are objectionable.[4]

Similarly, many religious believers level accusations against a culture that is, they insist, unfriendly to religion, or, at least, unfriendly to those religious believers who are sufficiently sincere about their faith to place allegiance to God before allegiance to the state. Many have pushed for changes in law or practice to move the nation in a direction more sympathetic to the world they want to build.

This tension is natural and, I would suggest, quite healthy. Democracy and religion should never quite be happy with each other. Thus a polemicist like Edmund Burke led the rest of us down a dangerous road when he lauded religion because, he claimed, it trained people to be good. Like contemporary "defenders" of religion who insist that faith is good because it molds better citizens, he conceptualized religion as a servant of the needs of the state.

Religion and democracy need not be at war, but they cannot quite be at peace. If they manage to live as though at peace, the reason should be that they have found a modus vivendi, not that one has triumphed: for the triumph of one will likely be the destruction of the other. And here, again, we see the tension itself. The committed democrat, forced to choose, will say it is better for faith to die and democracy survive; the committed believer, faced by the same choice, will say it is better for democracy to die and faith to survive.

In the United States, we like to say we have worked out a uniquely American solution we call the separation of church and state. We talk a lot about the "principle" of separation of church and state, or the "constitutionally mandated" separation of church and state. But, when we talk that way, we talk unrealistically and dangerously.

The separation of church and state is not a principle. It is not a rule of constitutional law. It is not an abstract theory of an ideal relationship and is, emphatically, not the precious invention of the wise founders of the republic.

It is, for lack of a better way to put the matter, a contract . . . or, to use what might be a better metaphor, a treaty. A peace treaty.

The separation of church and state certainly has a normative dimension, but its normativity stems entirely from its origins. We tend to miss this point and thus place on the back of separation a weight it cannot bear. One learned article after another proclaims the separation of church and state to be an indispensable constitutional protection for religious minorities. It is not any protection at all. Religious minorities lose out in America all the time, and neither courts nor legislatures do very much to help. Neither more separation of church and state nor less would do religious minorities any good, because the separationist tradition has nothing to do with the problem. Similarly, one learned article after another proclaims the separation of church and state to be a fundamental principle of liberal democracy, but few other liberal democracies have seen any compelling reason to copy the American design. Nor is there any reason that they should, because the separation of church and state, for all of its glories, is our peace treaty, not someone else's; it is an American solution, deeply Protestant in character, linked to our history, and thus not necessarily an approach that would appeal to another culture with a history of its own.

The legal scholar Michael McConnell has recently put the point this way: "Separation of church and state was a reality long before it was an idea."[5] His reference is to the experience of the early Christian church, which learned the hard way, and more than once, about what happens when the state becomes dominant over the church. Early Christians, existing in a decidedly inferior position, had no particular reason, other than faith, to thrust themselves forward. To be known as a Christian often meant imprisonment, torture, and death. In 1868, Bishop J. B. Lightfoot of the Church of England wrote of the leadership of the early church: "Ambition of office in a society where prominence of rank involved prominence of risk was at least no vulgar and selfish passion."[6]

The European church of the Middle Ages had a rather different view, and it sought to build what the historian Paul Johnson has labeled "a total Christian society" — a culture in which every aspect of every life was governed by the teaching of the church. Whatever the theology of this effort, history has not been kind to it on practical grounds: human beings seem wired to aspire to more than being told what to do, whether the one doing the telling is benign or malign in intent, and efforts to build total societies, whether inspired by love of God or by love of a political idea, have always ended in oppression and murder.

What is striking about American-style separationism, however, is that it owes a good deal less than is commonly thought to some supposed dread of religious warfare. The founders of the republic did not believe that religious warfare was a very big risk. The last European religious war of which they would have been aware ended in 1648, and the Continent suffered wars aplenty, none of them religious, in the century and a quarter that followed.

The separation of church and state is not, in any interesting sense, a product of the Enlightenment. Neither Hobbes nor Rousseau believed in it. Each wrote, unambiguously, of the need to subordinate the church to the state, so that the first loyalty of every individual was not to divine command but to the will of the sovereign. They wanted, in effect, to build the total society of the medieval church, but without the church.

James Madison's famous "Memorial and Remonstrance," drafted in 1785 in a successful effort to oppose a mandatory assessment in Virginia for the support of the clergy of the established Anglican Church, is cited as a crucial document in understanding the separation of church and state. I am among those scholars who believe that the Supreme Court's heavy reliance on the elitist Madison to explain the First Amendment is a bit of a stretch, but even Madison offered what amount to Christian reasons against the tax: "Whilst we assert for ourselves a freedom to embrace, to profess and to observe the Religion which we believe to be of divine origin, we cannot deny an equal freedom to those whose minds have not yet yielded to the evidence that has convinced us. If this freedom be abused, it is an offense against God, not against man."[7]

This was the common view of the founders. Even if, as most historians believe, Madison was more influenced by the Enlightenment than by Christianity, few of his fellow citizens were likely of the same mindset. As the historian Harry V. Jaffa has recently reminded us, if Americans from very early on accepted, with enthusiasm, the separation of church and state, "it was because they were persuaded that the true teaching of the Gospel required that, as in the ministry of Jesus, no political rewards or punishments influence the soul in its contemplation of the requirements of eternal salvation."[8]

One simply cannot make the case, historically, that the nation wanted to limit the church to a small and harmless sphere while exalting the power of the state. No, American-style separationism owes its origins to a sense, not of the dangers of religion, but of its importance. The Protestant tradition, especially as brought across the ocean by the Puritans, taught of the two great powers that God ordained on earth, the church and the state. Separate they were, but not because religion was a power to be pent up. They were separated because their tasks, although quite important, were also quite different, and the mixing of the two had a tendency to corrupt the true faith. The church had the role of preparing men and salvation; the state of keeping order while the church did its work. Neither church nor state should dominate the other, but both were subservient to the same God.

The particular metaphor of a wall of separation between church and state we owe, of course, to Roger Williams, who, having fled what he considered the oppressions of Puritan New England, strove to create the proper Christian state instead in Rhode Island. For Roger Williams, all the earth was either garden or wilderness, and a high hedge or wall separated the two. The garden was the place of the people of faith, who nurtured one another in their understanding of what the Lord demanded of them; the wilderness was the un-evangelized world, a place of danger and temptation to the faithful. The wall did not protect the wilderness from the garden; it protected the garden from the wilderness. The risk, for Williams, was that the un-evangelized wilderness might interfere with the work of the people of the garden. That was the reason for the wall.[9]

The wall emphatically did not exist in order to keep the people of the garden out of the wilderness. On the contrary, Williams believed that it was the obligation of the believers, responding to divine call, to go out into the garden to preach and teach. The wall of separation was, for Williams, the peace treaty. It confined the different authorities to their different tasks but did not interfere with God's plan, which involved, ultimately, the evangelization of the entire wilderness.

Now, before we go any further, we have reached an interesting place to stop and take stock. If the wall of separation, in its American usage, began as a metaphor for the protection of the church, which would then go out and try to change the world, then what possible protection would it ever provide for the religious dissenter? How does the minority religion benefit from the separation of church and state? What about the atheist, or the agnostic, or the individual who, for whatever reason, would rather just not be bothered?

The answer Williams would have given, I think, is that the protection is of a particular kind, and none other: because the wilderness is not to impinge on the garden, the religious dissenters can set up any religion they wish, with no interference from the state. The state cannot impose on them a requirement to join any faith or profess any creed.

But what about one of our contemporary bugaboos: the provision of tax dollars to, say, religious schools? Here Williams has a further bit of teaching. He did not believe it proper for the state to coerce individuals to act contrary to their consciences or to pay for what they, in conscience, believed they should not. The sole exception he drew was for the funding of those things needed to enable the state to survive.

It was for this purpose that Williams deployed his famous metaphor of the "ship of state." The ship, Williams wrote, carried many different people, of many different views. None could force the others to do anything that the others, in conscience, refused to do; except that everyone, even dissenters, could be required to perform those tasks, or pay for those things, that were essential in order to keep the ship afloat.

One might reasonably argue, then, that tax dollars for religious schools would be prohibited under Williams's vision of separationism: how, after all, can religious schools be essential to keeping the ship afloat? But it is important to remember how broad the metaphor is. Williams's concern was for conscience. He did not say that nobody should be forced to support anything religious to which he or she had a conscientious objection; he said that nobody should be forced to support anything to which he or she had a conscientious objection. Thus if Citizen A could object to the use of his tax dollars for religious schools, because conscience intervened, then Citizen B could object to the use of her tax dollars for abortion services, because conscience intervened. Williams's metaphor provides no basis for distinguishing between the two.

It is striking, at this late date, that just about every industrialized nation other than ours has in place a program of public support for at least some forms of religious education, even states, like France and India, which have in their constitutions enshrined principles of the separation of church and state. Even as the world embraces, with astonishing rapidity, fundamental principles of democracy, we have not succeeded in persuading the world that our vision on the question of religious education is the right one, and we do not even try very hard. So far, no American presidential administration has sought to cut off aid to regimes that engage in the putatively undemocratic practice of using tax dollars to fund religious schools—a wise choice, as it would cost us nearly every ally we have in the world. Perhaps this wisdom supports the proposition that the separation of church and state, as we have come to understand it on these shores, is less a fundamental democratic principle than a distinctly Protestant, or perhaps Puritan, artifact of our peculiar history.

I do believe, however—even though I am sure that Williams himself would not—that the original separation metaphor provides a firm ground for opposing organized classroom prayer in public schools. Why? Because, in the public schools, the state, largely run from the wilderness, is seeking to mold the youth, many of whom are from various gardens. By teaching them how to pray, the state does precisely the work that the garden has reserved for itself, and thus impermissibly breaches the wall of separation of church and state. I am constrained to add, however, that any effort in the public schools to teach morality is properly subject to the same objection, whether the curriculum is for the purpose of enhancing tolerance or inculcating the values of the free market. Teaching right and wrong is the task of the garden; protecting that teaching is the purpose of the high wall.

Consequently, when religious parents — or, for that matter, nonreligious parents — object to a feature of the school curriculum on the ground that they wish to teach their children something different, they are not being intolerant. They are simply demanding that the state remain on its side of the wall. How we should handle such objections when they arise is a nice problem, and one on which the courts, struggling to make sense of a nearly unreadable set of constitutional rules on church and state, so far have messed up horribly; but that is a subject much picked over in the scholarship, and one that need not detain us here.[10]

Let it suffice here to emphasize that in the terms of Williams's original metaphor, the development of conscience — that is, the teaching of morality — is the task of the garden, not the wilderness. Thus one might reasonably argue that when the state, acting through its schools, seeks to teach morality, it breaches the high hedge wall between church and state. And if, as I have suggested, American-style separationism is best understood, not as a rule of law, but as a peace treaty, or a contract, the state is in breach. And we are seeing in our politics, in the still-rising tide of activism among religious conservatives, a significant subset of the American population that seems to think that the state has indeed broken the contract and that the church, as a result, is no longer bound.

(One would of course exclude the religion or denomination that finds separationism theologically compelling. But, even then, as we shall see, the state has arguably broken the bargain; and, certainly, a theological compulsion is not, under the contract, one the state should ever be able to enforce.)

It is easy to see why the state would want to breach the wall that Roger Williams built. The state would prefer to behave as though there were no wall for the same reason that many religions would like to do the same thing. There is a sense in which the state and the religions are in competition to explain to their people the meaning of the world.[11] When the meanings provided by the one differ from the meanings provided by the other, it is natural that neither will quite be content with the peace treaty. The treaty might make both sides feel like losers: the state upset with those dissenting, mischievous religionists who refuse to give up their illiberal ways; the religionists refusing to accept a state that teaches a meaning they consider ungodly. Feeling like a loser, each might do what it can to become a winner. Often, especially in today's mass-produced world, characterized by the intrusion into every household of the materialist interpretation of reality, religions are just overwhelmed, which leads some of them to change and many of them to die.[12]

But more subtle tools are available in the assault on religious meaning.[13] All through history, the state has tried to domesticate religion, sometimes by force, simply eliminating dissenting faiths; sometimes through the device of creating an official, "established" church, which then places reliance for its continued survival in the state instead of its vision of the divine; and some-times — as in the twentieth-century American experience — through the device of reducing the role of religion by confining its freedom within a state-granted, state-defined, and state-controlled structure of constitutional rights.[14]

Religion, however, is no idle bystander. If the state tries to domesticate religion, its most powerful competitor in the creation of meaning, authentic religion tries simultaneously to subvert the state. Democracy often seems to see this tendency as one of religion's dangers. Actually it is one of religion's virtues. A great gift that religion gives to democracy is dissent, especially moral dissent, and the gift has been given, repeatedly, all through the nation's history. There have of course been many moral dissenters who would not think them-selves not religious, and many of them, like many of the religious, have deliv-ered as their particular gifts to the nation great sacrifices in the cause of princi-ple. It has been a sad characteristic of democracy, as of every other system of governance, to try to force the dissenters into a non-dissenting mold.[15] In the United States, for example, we condition the receipt of tax-deductible status for churches on the agreement of their pastors not to endorse candidates for office from the pulpit. If you think about this widely accepted rule, you begin, I hope, to see the problem: the state is reaching into the garden to try to limit what religious leaders may talk about.

The wall of separation between church and state, one might think, exists precisely to prevent that result. The state should not be pressing a religion to change its ways. The state should not be using the tax code or the zoning laws or any other device to pressure the people of the garden to interpret divine command in a particular way. Of course, as the church and the state are in competition to provide meaning, we should not be surprised when the state behaves as though the wall does not exist; we should simply be equally un-surprised when the religions do the same thing.

Very well: Let us return to the peculiarly American experience of the separa-tion of church and state. We sometimes talk and write as though it has long been an American understanding that the separation of church and state means that openly religious argument has no place in our political debates. We might say that intolerance of religion is the homage that the state pays to the wall of separation: so much do we love religion that we will turn Roger Williams's hedge into a barbed wire escarpment, with the barbs facing inward, lest those pesky religionists manage to climb over.

Actually, American democracy has never embraced that model, which is a fortunate thing for our democracy. Democracy needs its dissenters, for it is courageous acts of dissent that spark the dialogue through which, in a truly democratic polity, we are most likely to advance. The dissenter needs courage because he or she is a resister, insisting that the meanings prevailing in a given day are not necessarily the right ones, even when the state supports those meanings with the rather persuasive arguments of attack dogs and shotguns and prison cells.

Religion, at its best, is a vital source of dissent. "The religions," writes the theologian David Tracy, "live by resisting."[16] Religion, to be sure, has often in history been simply a defender of the status quo, especially when successfully domesticated. Informal establishment may be enough: in the late years of the nineteenth century and the early years of the twentieth, we saw, in America, the informal establishment of the Protestant mainline as the nation's quasi-official church, and the predictable result was that church and state tended to act as one. The notable exceptions, such as prohibition, tended to be populist movements, a point of some importance.

Prohibition was supported almost entirely by evangelical Christians; the mainline churches mostly opposed it. I mention evangelicals explicitly for a reason — and not simply because I am one. Given recent political history, it is terribly easy to forget that a powerful strain in evangelical thought has long counseled avoidance of the contagion of politics. Like the preachers of the First Great Awakening back in the eighteenth century, many evangelical leaders of the twentieth urged their followers to ignore elections and instead use their energies preparing for salvation. As late as the 1960s, millions of Christians of traditional views did not even bother to use their votes, and America, in its traditional reciprocity, did not even bother to care. Among the evangelical clergy urging followers to stay away from the polling place was the pastor of the Thomas Road Baptist Church in Virginia, a man by the name of Jerry Falwell.

There was even an unspoken, but very satisfactory, peace treaty between the evangelicals and the mainline, subsidiary to the treaty we have already discussed, a treaty going all the way back to the original battle between fundamentalist and modernist Protestants at the end of the nineteenth century and the early years of the twentieth: "We'll leave you alone if you'll leave us alone."

The 1908 sermon by George Ferris that I quoted to open the lecture occurred toward the end of this battle: Ferris contended that Christians had nothing to lose by embracing modernity. Fundamentalists believed that they had a great deal to lose: in particular, their souls.

That was the era in which what have come to be known as the mainline Protestant churches, fired by the ideology of Progressivism, began chipping away at the authority of the Bible and other traditions that seemed to them not to fit the needs of a modern, more professional society. As the historian Nathan O. Hatch has pointed out, even the fight over biblical interpretation mirrored the battle between Populists and Progressives. The Progressives believed in expertise, and so, naturally, understanding the Bible became the province of wise theologians with advanced university training. The Populists believed in the masses, and so, naturally, understanding the Bible was equally the province of everybody (they usually said "every man") who happened to own one.

As the century swept on, the alliance of Progressivism and the mainline churches won major legal battles, which was not a surprise, as the same belief in professional expertise is reflected in the legal system, where constitutional interpretation is ultimately the province of wise judges with professional training — in other words, an elite — rather than of the people as a body.

The battle over evolution, a battle not yet ended, features precisely these battle lines. On the one side are the devotees of expertise; on the other, the celebrants of populism. The experts say, first, that the theory of evolution is the best account of the origin of humanity and, second, that the Bible, understood properly, is not inconsistent with the theory. The populists reply, first, that the creation account in Genesis is the best account of the origin of humanity and, second, that the theory of evolution is hopelessly inconsistent with Genesis because the Genesis account is literally true.

We tend to treat this battle as possessing constitutional magnitude, and the Supreme Court has weighed in twice. But the real struggle is less legal than epistemological. Creationists, as the populists in this argument have come to be called, do not insist on their vision because they want the state to advance their religion. They insist on their vision because they believe it to be true. By their lights, the state, by teaching revolution in its public schools, is doing two bad things, at least one of them forbidden by the church-state peace treaty. The first bad thing is teaching their children lies. The second bad thing — the one that violates the wall of separation, in their view — is teaching particular lies that will wean the children from their parents' religion. One need not share the theology of creationist parents to see why they would think it is the state that has broken the pact, and why efforts to gain "equal treatment" for creationism, or even to ban evolution from the classroom, are seen by the parents as simply a response to the attack.

Of course, the most profound of the battles was probably the elimination of organized classroom prayer in the public schools, which was won by the elite, not by the people, a majority of whom, according to public opinion polls, remain unhappy with the result to this day. The end of organized classroom prayer (alongside, it must be conceded, the integration of the public schools, which white evangelicals largely opposed) hastened what had been a more gradual evangelical retreat, not only from politics, but even from contact with the larger secular society. The rise of the Christian school — the evangelical alternative to both public and Catholic schools — dates largely from this era. More and more evangelicals decided that what they wanted most from America was the opportunity to live their own lives, build their own communities, and raise their children in their own way as they waited on the Second Coming.

Through this retreat, the evangelicals built their own wall of separation between church and state, theologically and culturally, struggling to banish from the lives of their families the changes they hated in the country they loved. They were no more successful than King Canute was against the rising tide, and the ultimate recognition of their failure, particularly in the wake of the Supreme Court's 1973 abortion decision, *Roe v. Wade*,[17] helped reverse the separatist trend. In 1976, the votes of hundreds of thousands, possibly millions, of evangelical voters, many of whom had never before been inside a polling place, helped to elect Jimmy Carter. Four years later, of course, white evangelicals largely deserted the Democratic Party, largely because of the so-called social issues, and, ever since, they have been a solidly Republican constituency (although there is some debate among experts over just how solidly).[18]

Similarly, we find the organizations of what is sometimes called the Religious Right rising — and sometimes falling — around the same set of events. Moral Majority was founded by the Reverend Jerry Falwell in 1980 and folded about a decade later. The Christian Coalition was founded in 1989 by the Reverend Pat Robertson and is still in existence, although most experts think it is struggling, and it probably fell far short of its stated goal of training ten political activists in each of America's 175,000 electoral districts by the year 2000. But the trend for conservative religious organizations is not necessarily downward, for other groups, such as the Eagle Forum, Excellence in Education, and, especially, Focus on the Family, remain quite dynamic. Their profiles are lower, and they have little interest in electoral politics, and there, perhaps, is the secret of their survival. For one thing that history teaches us is that when religious organizations get into electoral politics, they tend to lose their focus on the divine, muting or even altering certain aspects of their teachings in order to further the fortunes of the candidates or parties they happen to support.[19] The conservative religious groups that have ignored this wisdom have usually come to grief.

It is a commonplace in public dialogue to describe such organizations as these as involved in an assault on basic freedoms or on our democratic heritage — everybody in this room knows the words by rote. But, on most issues, the groups are in retreat, fighting at best a holding action. More important, from the point of view of Christian conservatives, the first shot that ended the peace treaty came from the wilderness, not from the garden. One does not have to agree with many or any of their positions to see how, from their point of view, today's breach in the wall of separation is not of their making.

In what we like to think of as the modern age, democratic governments have grown increasingly scientistic — that is, the production of policy has more and more become an instrumental exercise, in which governments seem less interested in seeming wise than in seeming well informed. Policy is ideally guided, in this technocratic era, not only by expertise but by expertise that is, or at least sounds, scientific in nature. Regulations that cannot plausibly be cast as resting on the latest expert learning begin to look somewhere between stuffy and malign.

Religious believers who have clambered over the wall into the realm of the wilderness, even if they have been drawn by what they consider the need for self-defense, have been infected by this scientistic disease. That is why evangelical parents who believe the Genesis story to be literally true describe their worldview as scientific creationism. That is why religionists who believe abortion to be murder search out medical evidence on the beginning of human life. And why supporters of vouchers feel compelled to present data purporting to show that students in religious schools perform at least as well on tests as do public school students. As policy advocates, religionists perhaps can do no other. But scientistic religion, as the legal scholar Steven Goldberg has pointed out in a recent book, is rarely a showcase for religion at its best.[20]

Revealed religion is not necessarily inconsistent with modern science, but also must not make the mistake of supposing that scientific truth is all the truth there is. In the Western tradition, the Creator — God — who made and rules the universe has created moral facts as well as scientific ones. The religionist who is true to the tradition does not exalt the material over the spiritual, and thus cannot exalt science over morality. In other words, if it can be "true" that the earth goes around the sun, it can also be "true" that sex outside of marriage is wrong. A scientistic approach to governance can accept the first but must leave the second to the free choice of individuals, as there is no technological means for testing its truth. The traditional religionist who believes in the Creator-God cannot concede that epistemological point because material revelation is not all the revelation there is. In fact, the revelation of the observed world is, in the Western tradition, inferior to — less important than — the revealed Word as passed on from God and through the generations.

This might be another good reason for the people of the garden to stay out of the wilderness: some deep truths of the garden are inexpressible in a wilderness grown so scientistic that it risks becoming morally illiterate. On the other hand, we do not show our love of our neighbors by denying them access to the great truths of the universe. The same impulse that makes the secularist want to teach modern science to the children of the religionist might make the religionist want to teach traditional morality to the children of the secularist. The necessary epistemological neutrality of the wall of separation between the garden and the wilderness means that our great peace treaty can offer no basis for preferring one set of teachings to the other. All the wall can tell us is that either side would understandably view the other's victory as a breach.

My suggestion is not that either side's epistemological vision is "truer" than the other, only that the peace treaty manifested in the wall of separation tells us not to prefer one in a way that harms the ability of the faithful (the faithful of science or the faithful of religion) to pursue the other. Science will never accept that revealed religion is as useful a source of truths as observation and experiment in the material realm; but revealed religion will never accept that science is as useful as the Word.

The social theorist Isaiah Berlin argued long ago that the most dangerous enemy of the Enlightenment was not religion but the skeptical tradition that stretches back to the ancients. If we view scientism as the unexpected inheritor of Enlightenment liberalism, then skepticism is the cynical uncle who thought he should have had the family fortune. All day long he carps and criticizes. Nothing the heir does is ever good enough, simply because the heir was undeserving in the first place.

It is striking that religion more and more sides with the heir instead of the uncle. Striking, but not surprising, because if skepticism is the enemy of liberal rationality, it is even more the enemy of revealed religion. The skeptical tradition, if one thinks of, say, Voltaire or Hume, may be said to have cut its eyeteeth in the struggle against the organized church. It is that tradition that we honor (if that is the word) when, in our own era, we meet the truth claims of the faithful with a sullen *Sez who?* The notion that my truth is every bit as good as yours (and that it is intolerant of you to suggest otherwise) degrades not only religion but Enlightenment liberalism as well. Democracy need not rest on a skepticism about moral truth, although we sometimes pretend that it does; but it must rest on a willingness to permit others to organize moral life within communities that demonstrate diversity in epistemology.

There is a tendency toward imperialism in the way the faithful on either side of the wall look at the truth-claims of the others; all of us seem to want to educate those with differing worldviews into our own. Small wonder that we battle so hard over school curriculum, for what is at stake in the education of children is often a dream of conquest, a taming of the wildness on the other side of the wall. Yet the faithful on either side of the wall continue to profess astonishment when the objects of their dreams prefer to stay wild.

But we have been speaking of dissent as a vehicle to change, and it is here, perhaps, that we can both illustrate the working of the separation of church and state as originally understood and get a sense of the manner in which religion and democracy, with their competing claims of meaning, might continue to coexist, in a relationship less mutually tolerant than mutually respectful.

American history is of course full of important episodes of religious activism as a vehicle for change. The evangelical, almost fundamentalist Christianity of an activist like Fannie Lou Hamer was not the whole of the Civil Rights Movement, but the movement is unimaginable without her, without the Reverend Dr. Martin Luther King, without the religious leadership that believed itself to be on a religious crusade to change for the better the world that the Lord created and his creatures so sullied. Their faith gave them the strength to sacrifice, to stand up for their beliefs when something was at stake, and it was the power of their sacrifices, as much as the power of their arguments, that finally moved a nation.[21]

Or we might consider the labor movement. Much of what we have long come to accept as fundaments of fair labor-management relations — collective bargaining, reasonable wages, protective legislation for children, higher levels of safety in the workplace — maps precisely onto the platform of the Men and Religion Forward movement, which fought for labor rights during the early years of the twentieth century.[22] Pope Leo XIII, in his 1891 encyclical *Rerum Novarum,* caught the separationist nuance perfectly. He warned that "greedy" employers had a responsibility to pay their workers wages adequate to support families, lest they be tempted into sin.[23] All power, he argued, was God-given, and must therefore be used according to God's ordinances. Thus those who ran both the country and the factories should not create conditions in which it would be harder for workers to lead Christian lives. The traditional Catholic position on church-state relations was more complex than the Williams model we have been discussing, but the encyclical did not violate the separation of church and state even as understood by Protestants, because the pope was simply calling upon the people of the wilderness to stop interfering — in this case, through conditions in the factories — with the work of the garden.

Imagine for a moment the America of the late nineteenth and early twentieth centuries, the swift transition, over a period of perhaps thirty years, from a nation in which nearly everybody worked the land in one way or the other to a nation in which the defining form of labor was working for a wage in the factory. Small communities that had preserved their values for centuries were shattered as the young began to wander to find work. The great industrial cities were built around the great factories, and suddenly, for the first time in American history, great masses of strangers lived crowded together in tenements. Many were immigrants from the farms; many more were immigrants from abroad. Women and children worked as well, often for pennies a day. In the tenements, there was neither decent sanitation nor running water. In the factories, there was dangerous work under oppressive conditions, but whenever the workers tried to organize unions, the police, private detectives, even the armed forces, were called out to put a stop to the attempt.

The churches could hardly have stayed silent if they wanted to. And, although there were many preachers on behalf of the status quo, the situation of the workers inspired many others to challenge, publicly, the policies of both business and government. And they were hardly alone. The nineteenth century flowed into the twentieth on the cusp of the Progressive Era, in which — at least according to popular history — the states and, later, the federal government adopted a number of statutes and regulations aimed at curbing what were viewed as the abuses of an unfettered laissez-faire economy.[24] Whatever the softness of the popular history, nobody denies that the reformers in the pulpit were prominent and provocative players in the political drama of the age.

Consider the contemporary complaint that the late years of the twentieth century saw the government abandon most efforts to rein in business excess, as long as prosperity reigned for most Americans. The complaint turns out to be as old as preaching — the great biblical prophets regularly issued injunctions against the rich who despised the poor — and it is certainly as old as America. Thus the rector of a Philadelphia church lamented on All Saints Day in November 1914: "Our leading business men value tariff laws more highly than the Sermon on the Mount."[25] American business, he argued, preferred to make the Gospel "just the kind suitable for American business conditions." He added: "Wall Street has always kept tight hold of the Church, so the Church would not let Christ do any damage among stocks and bonds. Christianity, if allowed full swing anywhere, will, at times, close the stock exchange."[26]

Bishop Charles D. Williams of Michigan argued in 1917 that the Gospel required the development of a new social conscience. Altering the course of law to enable it, he insisted, was a Christian obligation, a part of the Great Commission to evangelize the world (Matthew 8:16–20). Poverty and inequality of wealth, according to Williams, were the enemies of the Gospel: "There are everywhere in our modern world economic, industrial and social conditions which make the Christian life practically impossible. Is it not the business of religion to deal directly with those conditions and try to make the environment at least more favourable to the regenerate life? Our concern is with the soil as well as with the seed in our sowing of the Word." In other words, if the conditions of the workers were not improved, there would be no rich soil in which the Word could take root.

The more radical of the preachers, not content to worry about the salvation of the souls of the workers, challenged industrial capitalism itself. One vehemently anti-capitalist preacher, David C. Reid of the Congregational church in Stockbridge, Massachusetts, published a book in 1910 titled *Effective Industrial Reform.*[27] Living and working in the Berkshires, he saw around him the hovels of the working class and the grand villas of the wealthy. It was not only the patent inequalities that disturbed him, but the effect of the economic system on the family, and thus on the faith. (One of his examples was that the wage-labor system forced women into the workforce and children into daycare, where they could not receive proper moral instruction.)[28] His solution was to "release these wives and mothers from work in the factory," so that they might "go where their hearts are, and where they of right ought to be — into their own homes with their own children; and all these evil conditions will be changed."[29] Christians, Reid argued, were obliged to pursue "Christ's ultimate aim," which was "to transform human society itself." Jesus, Reid insisted, envisioned "not only regenerated men and women, but also perfected institutions and laws."[30] He was prepared to fight for constitutional amendments, if necessary, to accomplish his plan.[31] And Reid, like Williams, saw socialism (although, he emphasized, not Marxism) as the only available system that would offer those "perfected institutions and laws."

As with the conservative Christian movements that are with us today, it does not matter whether one agrees with any part of the message of the anti-capitalist and pro-labor preachers of a hundred years ago. The point is that, from their point of view, silence was impossible. The conditions in which the workers were required to live raised fundamental questions about the justice of the world that created those conditions. The world was the wilderness, and it was breaching the wall, for the moral teachings of its economic structures were bound to affect the consciences of the people of the garden. Thus there was no real choice for the people of the garden but to fight back. They did not cause the breach in the wall (or the contract, or the treaty — pick the metaphor that pleases you). But, once the breach occurred, it was hardly the place of the world to tell the people of the garden that what was happening was none of their business.

Let me pause here and say a word about the title of this essay. I ask in the title whether religion can tolerate democracy, and vice versa. When I use the word "tolerance," I have in mind its traditional sense. We also have a casual, sloppy, modern sense of the word that drains it of interesting moral content: the sense in which, if you criticize my behavior or my ideas, you are said to be intolerant of me. In the old days, this was called disagreement, and that is all we should call it today.

Tolerance in the traditional sense — let us say the Lockean sense — was morally robust, on both sides of the matter. When Locke wrote of the need to tolerate religions other than officially recognized Protestant Christianity, he had in mind a vision of tolerance almost like what we would now think of as the tolerance of the body for disease, the ability to include within the community a thing the community finds unpleasant. His vision of tolerance did not in any sense place the thing tolerated beyond criticism. Here is why his vision is more morally robust than ours: the larger society, required to tolerate, does not lose the moral faculty of judgment; and the small dissenter, faced with criticism, develops the backbone to stand for unpopular ideas. Thus neither side yields on its principles, and, for just that reason, we can envision the possibility of a productive dialogue somewhere down the democratic road.

Thus, when I ask whether religion can tolerate democracy, and whether democracy can tolerate religion, I am not in the last concerned over whether either one criticizes the other, even harshly. Criticism is not intolerance — not in any morally significant sense. I am interested, rather, in the way they actually live together, whether as symbiotes, as parasites, as diffident neighbors, as friends, or even as enemies . . . enemies who might perhaps require a treaty of peace. But we have to be crystal clear about the terms.

Today, we often hear the wall of separation described as though it is, in reality, a kind of moral soundproofing, the purpose of which is to make the voices of the nation's religious traditions impossible to hear outside the garden, at least when those voices are raised in dissent. Williams's bold metaphor is used as a conversation stopper, a command to the church to shut up and go away.

The separation of church and state as we nowadays too often envision it has an eerie echo in perhaps the most important era of religious activism in the nation's history: the campaign to abolish slavery. That campaign, largely led by clergy (at least within white America) was, by its own lights, carried on quite within the bounds of the separation of church and state.

Let us begin by considering an important legacy of the wall of separation as traditionally understood: the Christian duty of obedience to constituted authority. A prominent North Carolina clergyman, not long before the Civil War began in 1861, warned his flock: "The general sentiment of our country, and I believe of christendom [*sic*] is, that politics are not a proper subject for the pulpit, and the exhibitions made by those who act on the opposite view, are not such as to recommend either their practice or their principles. Loyalty to government, respect for existing institutions, these are christian [*sic*] graces, earnestly inculcated in the New Testament; but what is the best kind of government, and which the most rightful and expedient institutions, are matters as to which it is profoundly silent."[32] The preacher, that is, should stay away from the business of governance and stick to the business of tending souls. In the words of the pastor of the Presbyterian church of Norfolk, the extent to which slavery should be allowed "is a purely political question," meaning that "the discussion of it, in the pulpit and on the Sabbath, is as much a desecration of holy place and holy time, as would be a discussion of the 'tariff question' for 'the distribution of public land.' "[33] A clergyman, he added, does not give up the role of citizen, and may, in that role, discuss whatever he wishes. But to hold forth on a political issue from the pulpit on Sunday is "a profanation of the holy Sabbath."

The antislavery side in part agreed with this proposition, but gave it an importantly different spin. Wrote a commentator on Mark's Gospel in 1859: "It is the binding duty of every Christian, and every good citizen, to render by act, and by word, and by every other lawful influence, respect and obedience to the constitutional laws of the land, so long as the laws remain unrepealed, and we recognize our allegiance to the Government that ordains them." To this statist sentiment (which would no doubt have warmed the heart of the current Supreme Court) the commentator added that every Christian shared nevertheless in the obligation "to use his utmost endeavors, to heal, purify, and preserve in its integrity this great Nation, that, united and harmonious, is so soon to give laws to the whole earth."[34]

This is the forgotten piece of the separationist sentiment. The reason the believer can respect the wall of separation, in the traditional understanding of the Protestant theology that produced it, is that church and state are both ordained by God. Both fall under divine law. When the state varies from God's law, it is the responsibility of the believer to try to alter the laws of the state until, once more, the two abide in harmony. Only then can the believer rest.

In the middle of the nineteenth century, the notion of obligation to improve the fallen world was tied in the minds of American Protestants to a sense of the United States as the New Jerusalem, which would lead the world toward righteousness. This sentiment made the Civil War possible. The Reverend James Lyon, whose commentary on the relationship of the church to the civil laws we have been following, concludes with the proposition that "this united, homogeneous, christian [*sic*] Government" must be "the great Evangelizer which is to give, not only law, but the Gospel to the world!" Therefore, he asks: "How can we regard the enemies of the Union in any other light than as the enemies of God, the enemies of a pure church, and the enemies of the human race!"[35]

And there we have the separation of church and state, as understood by Protestants for much of the nation's history. Far from defeating the ideal of a Christian nation, separationism, in the American understanding, was deeply tied to the idea of a Christian nation. Were the state less Christian, less pure, the hoped-for separation would not be possible; not, at least, until the believer worked to get the state's laws back to where they should be.

That is why the religiously inspired abolitionist Salmon P. Chase could, at the same time, articulate the view that the Unite States was a Protestant republic and proclaim himself a strong supporter of the separation of church and state. Chase, who would go on to serve as secretary of the treasury and chief justice of the Supreme Court, saw no inconsistency. It was Chase who first had the legend "In God We Trust" embossed on the nation's coins, lest a future generation, excavating the ruins of ours, should imagine that we were a "heathen" people; and it was Chase, too, who insisted time and again that church and state were forever separate. The separation did not, for Chase, mean that the state was not under God's guidance. On the contrary: the state was ordained by God and required to follow God's laws. If it failed to do so, then it was in breach of the peace treaty.

The abolitionist preachers were explicit on this point. It was right to fight for freedom for the slave because the nation that held them captive could not be the New Jerusalem, the light of the world, and therefore was, in a sense, not deserving of the separation of church and state.

The New York abolitionist preacher Seth Williston—who, like many nineteenth-century American Protestants, saw the United States as the New

Jerusalem — called for an end to slavery, but not at the cost of warfare: "If [America] has war, it should be from invasion, not from her own citizens. We are required to pray for the peace of Jerusalem, accompanied with an assurance that they shall prosper who love her."[36] On the other hand, the abolitionist Henry Darling suggested that the war was God's way of purifying a nation that had sinned mightily, and in many different ways. But, once the war began, Darling argued, there was no choice but to fight it to a conclusion, for the war, if won, would make the New Jerusalem what it ought to be. Thus, in response to efforts to negotiate an end to the war that would allow slavery to continue, he offered withering contempt: "Are other demons to be exorcised from our body politic, and this one to remain? Is God bringing us through this terrible baptism of blood, to cleanse the white robe of our national purity from a few of its minor impurities, but yet to permit this deepest, darkest stain to remain? That would be a strange teleology, indeed, that would lead any to such a conclusion."[37]

Even the abolitionist preachers who eschewed the violence of Turner and others embraced activism in the cause of making God's will a reality out in the un-evangelized wilderness. They did not believe that their advocacy of the abolitionist cause breached a barrier that should remain pristine. An 1859 sermon by Nathaniel Hall was explicit: "I undertake to say that there was never a more senseless assumption put forth in all Christiandom, — one more to be resisted, if need were, to the very death — than that the pulpit, standing as the visible exponent of God's truth and law, should have nothing to say in reference to the fact that millions of human beings, in the nation in which it stands, are forcefully deprived of their natural rights, and crushed beneath the heel of lawless oppression."[38] Like the famous abolitionist Theodore Parker, Hall came close to calling for violent warfare: "With the North should be the unalterable decision, We will no longer be partners in the upholding and cherishing of this accursed barbarism. We will no longer be tied up to a complicity in this intolerable outrage and affront to Christianity and the age."[39]

And, lest his audience think he was simply speaking of ending the union, Hall ended his sermon with a telling biblical quote: "Wherefore, put on the whole armor of God, that ye may be able to stand in the evil day, and, having done all, to stand."[40] (It is worth noting that this sermon followed Hall's sermon of the previous week, occasioned by the execution of John Brown, in which he lauded Brown, despite his violence, for sacrificing to battle a violent institution. Hall implied, although he did not actually say, that "aggressive force," as he called it, was appropriate in ending oppression, and pointed out that Americans of his day [like those of our own] tended to applaud the use of force in causes with which they agreed — at least when the violence succeeded.)[41]

Other abolitionists managed, rather cleverly, to hide a call for violent warfare inside a call for peace. One, the Reverend Charles E. Hodges, in a tract titled *Disunion Our Wisdom and Our Duty,* conceded the claim of the proslavery forces that the Constitution itself protected the institution. Therefore, Hodges explained, Christians were required to view the Constitution as immoral and because "it is wrong to sustain sin," to work for the end of the Union—a result, as everybody knew but Hodges failed to mention, that could hardly be brought about peacefully. "Can you do otherwise," he demanded, "than commit yourself to this cause . . . ?"[42] It is unlikely that Hodges had to point out to his readers that a commitment to the cause of abolishing slavery by abolishing the Constitution was, in the politics of the time, little different from a call for civil war.

The abolitionist preachers did not think it possible to confine their vision of justice to a narrow, walled-off region called "church"; they considered action in the world not only justified but imperative. The Reverend Ezra Gannett explained that the survival of the institution of slavery "is not purely a political question." Why not? Because "it has its moral side, and religion and Christianity are entitled to examine it as entering within their domain."[43] That which touches morality, in other words, is precisely that which religion is "entitled" to examine; no argument about separation of church and state can prevent the church from protecting its own side of the wall. One might reasonably ask, of course, what falls on the church's side of the wall—what aspects of life religion is entitled to "examine"—but Gannett, like other abolitionists, seemed quite sure that the question of the size of religion's sphere was one for religion, not the state, to decide. And, having made its decision, said Gannett, religion had to act in the world. Those who oppose slavery on religious grounds, he argued, "may take all constitutional and lawful methods for securing an abrogation of those enactments, and of those provisions of the fundamental law [he meant the Constitution], which offend our moral convictions."[44]

This is, indeed, the very point of the change in the American Protestant understanding of the believer's obligation during the early nineteenth century. The Christian, many and perhaps most pastors were by this time preaching, was to work for the betterment of God's creation—especially in a nation that was, in the minds of many Protestants, a nation specially favored by God to lead the world to truth and justice. That special land, the preachers believed, had to be made fit to live in.

Many abolitionists believed the land would be more fit when it was more Christian, and they supported abolition largely as a tool for evangelizing. It was imperative to convert the slaves to Christianity, as it was imperative under the Great Commission to convert everybody, but the effort to evangelize the slaves was that much harder, wrote one abolitionist preacher, because of "the heathenism of oppression" created by enslavement.[45]

Of course, not every preacher was persuaded of the unfitness of the New Jerusalem in the first place. Public preaching on the question of slavery was by no means limited to those who opposed it. On the contrary: there is no reason to suppose, especially during the first half of the nineteenth century, that anywhere near a majority of the American public opposed slavery. Even among those who did not happen to like it, few were, so early, willing to see young men fight and die in order to end it. And then there were many people, including many clergy, who believed that slavery — in particular, African slavery — was simply the will of God.

The historian Jon Butler has shown how an entire theology of authority and obedience was worked out in the colonies (especially in Anglican Virginia) in order to justify and reinforce the dominance of master over slave.[46] Although many Southerners, as the historian Don Fehrenbacher puts it, went through the motions of complaining of the unfortunate necessity of slavery, the truth was that it was defended, from an early moment, with all the available arguments, secular and religious, that the slave-owners and their tame clergy could muster.[47] During the eighteenth century, as American slavery grew progressively more violent, and thus less like slavery in most of the rest of the world, slave revolts (often led by Christian slaves) grew more frequent.[48] In response, the defense of the practice on Christian grounds grew ever more didactic: accepting the Gospel truth might make men free, but that freedom, argued the proslavery clergy, was only spiritual, not political.[49]

Again and again the proslavery preachers accused their abolitionist foes of breaching the wall of separation, but the accusation was wrong. Perhaps, as Thomas Jefferson believed, the wall of separation meant the president of the United States could not proclaim a national day of prayer (although he did, as governor, proclaim statewide days of prayer). But the metaphor has never meant, and could not sensibly be made to mean, that the people of the garden are in breach when they try to repair the wilderness.

The point of this extended history is that the separation of church and state did not mean, either to those who developed the metaphor or to those who, over the first century and a half of the nation's life, had to breathe life into it, that the people of the garden were uniquely disabled, among all the many competing factions in the American democracy, from pressing their views in politics, and even beyond. On the contrary: the separation of church and state was the tool that enabled them to have the freedom to build conscience without the interference of the state, so that they could go out into the wilderness and try to work a change.

Many people have worked to change America, of course, and not all of them have acted — at least as far as they knew — from religious inspiration. But the activism of the religious often brings into our public life what activism of a more explicitly secular sort might not. What makes religious voices in public life objectionable to some observers is exactly what makes them attractive to so many others: their tendency to focus on transcendence, on our obligations to a higher calling than the everyday striving for advantage that characterizes so much of American life.

Political theory has not in recent years been kind to religious voices in public life, proposing that the proper democratic project is to develop a kind of common language in which we can discuss whatever needs discussing, without reference to truths that seem inaccessible or to principles not widely shared. One could offer an empirical response: much of the language of religion is far more widely shared than some of the admirable principles on which theorists seem to think our dialogues should rest. One could also offer thoughtful theoretical responses, as a large literature of admittedly inconsistent quality has tried to do. But my response is historical, practical, and, perhaps, theological.

If, as I have argued, the separation of church and state represents a kind of treaty that neither side is supposed to breach, then it will do us no good to talk about the needs of liberal democracy as though those needs self-evidently trump the claims of religionists. The metaphor's history does not support an interpretation that keeps religion out of public life, although it does support an interpretation that keeps the state's nose out of religion. Had we followed, in the nation's stormy past, the dialogic rules so many theorists set for us now, our public conversation would have been impoverished, not enriched.

I think we have little option, in public life, but to do what we have been doing for more than two centuries, to throw the gates of dialogue open to any person who wants to argue. If it happens that the argument proceeds from premises I find inaccessible — either because I do not share the religion of the speaker or because I do not share her philosophy — then the likelihood is that she will fail to persuade me. But that likelihood does not justify a rule against allowing her to speak out in the first place.

It is often asserted, quite grandly, that the nation is more religiously diverse today than it was, say, during the abolitionist era, and that this diversity itself is an argument against religious voices in public life. There are reasons to doubt the underlying claim — the nation might well have been more religiously diverse at the dawn of the nineteenth century than it is at the dawn of the twenty-first. But there is a richer response. Let us take it as given that we find ourselves in the midst of a gloriously diverse conversation, in which, very often, disputants or even allies will, literally, not speak the same language.

Why is this a problem? Let all who wish to come, come, and let all who wish to speak, speak, and if we are generous and charitable in our dealings with others, then we will have a conversation across our differences; and if we are mean-spirited and arrogant in our dealings with others, then no rules sketched to govern dialogue will enable us to do much more than call our opponents nasty names and assure our friends that they can get away with anything as long as they stay on the right side of the issues.

If religious voices are to be as welcome in public life as other voices, the metaphorical separation of church and state provides the tool for ensuring that they are nurtured and preserved. If we return to the image of the garden, we can see how religious difference is created: within a place that is shielded, at least to some extent, from outside forces.[50]

The shielding is of course incomplete. Nathan Hatch has documented, for example, how the very ideology of democracy has come to predominate in every Christian denomination after its arrival on these shores. The same is true for many non-Christian traditions. Even traditions that are, elsewhere in the world, hierarchical in nature, come to reflect, in America, an individualist commitment, in which the believer can state, quite seriously, that he is firmly committed to the faith, and yet feels free to make up his own mind about what the faith means. Moreover, if traditional leaders ignore the calls of the faithful to alter the content of doctrine, they are said, even by many of their own followers, to be out of step with the era.

Culture has many ways of slipping past the wall of the garden. One need not be a follower of, say, Theodor Adorno to see how rapidly changing technologies of communication make it ever easier for cultural messages to slip past the earnest guard of protective families, so that adults and children alike begin to see the world as different from the world as the tradition might teach it.

Nevertheless, many religious families understandably try to strengthen the wall of separation, to preserve the garden from the incursions of the wilderness. To the extent that we value diversity and dissent, we should exalt the efforts of families and even communities to nurture children independent of the world's influence. Those children might well be tomorrow's religious dissenters, who go out to try to improve God's creation, and win or lose in the effort, but, either way, provide the nation with much-needed alternatives to the dominant meanings of the day.

The temptation of power is always to shut down dissent — in particular, to shut down dissent about fundamental questions of meaning. That is why my late colleague Robert Cover was absolutely right in arguing for the preservation of nomic communities — communities of sense and value — even if we find what they believe in abhorrent. Power wielders must resist the temptation to decide that they are so utterly inerrant that they should be building the "total society" that eluded the medieval church, which pursued the same goal: the society in which every institution reflects a commitment to the same unshakeable set of values.

Democracy in particular must resist the temptation to totalize, precisely because most of its ideas are so attractive. Thus it makes sense to entertain as a serious proposition, rather than an occasion for sloganeering, the possibility of providing public funds to assist poor and working-class parents who prefer to send their children to religious schools. Religious education (which the nation funded for most of its history but has also occasionally tried to destroy) can be a vital element in the efforts of the people of the garden to preserve their dissenting tradition against the incursions of the wilderness.

Leaving private education to one side, we might also rethink certain aspects of public education. The more we believe in separation of church and state, the less we should want explicit moral teaching of any kind in the public schools, for, as we have seen, the state is otherwise in breach. Moreover, parents who raise objection to aspects of the curriculum should perhaps have a very strong right to keep their own children shielded from what they do not like, in order to preserve, even within public education, some semblance of the garden.

Perhaps you do not believe parents should have a right of the sort I have just described. One can oppose it for a thousand reasons, from a concern that parents have too much influence over their children to a fear that the nation will wind up without the well-educated workforce it needs. I do not find these reasons compelling; you might. If you do, however, simply bear in mind that you are supporting another breach in the peace treaty, a rejection of the wall of separation between church and state. You are allowing the state to enter what was, when the treaty was laid down, widely understood to be the sphere of the church. You might respond that "we" no longer view matters that way, but the suggestion that this changing interpretation matters is nevertheless a proposal to tear down the wall.

The point is really quite simple: if the state decides to break the treaty, because of its own understanding of what the future requires, nobody should be surprised if the church decides that it, too, is no longer bound by the treaty.

I have suggested, thus far, that the separation of church and state serves democracy by creating communities of dissenting meaning that will tilt against the culture, bringing about a healthy democratic tension. But suppose you happen to disagree with the religion that is out there trying to alter the shape of the wilderness to fit its picture of what God wants? Let us put aside the previously discussed problem of the use of tax dollars to support this or that. Let us think instead of the problem of a religious believer, coming out of the garden into the wilderness, calling for a new law, say, that will, she believes, create a world closer to what God intends it to be. And let us further hypothesize a dissenter who is not a follower of her religion, and who objects to what she is trying to accomplish. Does the peace treaty between church and state help us resolve this problem?

The answer is yes, although not in the way that popular misunderstanding of the separationist metaphor often suggests. There is not, nor is it clear how there could be, any sort of right of one citizen to be free of another's religious motivation. In other words, if you and I both come before the bar of politics to argue, you may earnestly believe that my argument, because it rests in whole or in part on my religious beliefs, is entitled to less weight than yours, but your belief is only that — a belief — and politics will have to provide the resolution of our conflict. Separation of church and state has nothing to say on the matter, not unless we want to place on it, once more, weight that it cannot bear: a principle established in order to protect the garden in its work of nurturing the religious conscience is not readily transformable into a principle that protects the wilderness instead.

Does this mean that the dissenter who rejects the believer's faith is stuck, without recourse? Of course not. The fact that the separation of church and state offers no guidelines does not mean that no guidelines exist. Once we recognize that no citizen's rights are violated by the religious motivation of another citizen, we see the shape of a solution: in order to defeat the proposal the religionist is pressing, we must look at its substance rather than the reason for it.

This is a distinction that matters. Consider, once more, the case of public school classroom prayer. There are social science data (although they are far from undisputed) suggesting that people who pray regularly lead healthier lives than those who do not, are less likely to commit crimes, rarely use drugs, and tend to have happier marriages. All of these are goals that a secular state might pursue. Thus, we might plausibly imagine a state legislature that decides for these secular reasons to require, or at least encourage, students to pray. The legislative motivation would not be religious at all: the representatives might just want youngsters to lead happier, healthier lives. Yet the installation of classroom prayer would still be objectionable, for it would still represent an incursion by the wilderness into the garden. Nothing in the metaphor turns on why the breach has occurred.

A proper understanding of the separation of church and state does not enhance the power of the state, and therefore is unlikely to threaten the rights of dissenters. It limits the influence the state is able to exercise over the garden, which is a very good thing. It does not change the way our democracy does its business, for religious voices have always been present in the public square, and are not about to disappear — unless, of course, the garden itself disappears.

Now, having said all this, I must add that I do not believe that the voices of the people of the garden, simply because they happen to be religious, are therefore voices we obviously should follow. Nothing in history teaches us that those who claim to speak to God are frequently correct in their claim. Great good has been done in the name of religion; so has great evil. That does not distinguish religion from ideology or nationalism or a simple belief in one's own rightness: all of these have been forces for good and ill, and their interplay will continue to characterize our society, I hope, for a very long time. Meanwhile, there are urgent issues facing us to which religious voices might draw attention in a way that secular voices have failed to do. The plague of poverty has all but vanished from our electoral politics: neither Democrats nor Republicans seem to think it an issue of first importance. Nor the resurrection of our cities. Nor the plague of consumerism, the ethic of "me," that characterizes everything from the way we advertise products to the way we drive cars. The call of faith is the call of transcendence, the call to move beyond everyday striving. At its best it can move us to do great things, often providing language and inspiration that less passionate, more abstract forms of argument do not. Democracy without it would be a dreary and vulgar thing.

Yet faith without democracy can, in this sad, broken world, be a dreary and vulgar thing as well. The tension that democracy provides, the tension that the ideal of the two kingdoms, the two powers, the two sides of the wall tries to mediate is a healthy one for religion. Because religion, like any other force, is also prone to all the temptations of power. It is so hard to inspire people to do what is right; it is so tempting to force them instead. In times of emergency, all of us yield to the temptation to coerce, as perhaps we should. What all of us, secular and religious and whatever lies between the two, must resist is the smooth, seductive voice of the little devil sitting on our shoulders, whispering to us that all of our beliefs are emergencies.

Let me close, then, by repairing once more to the words of the Reverend George Ferris, with whose sermon I began this lecture. Said Ferris: "Whatever our idea as to how things came to be, or whether a certain transaction did or did not happen, many years ago, we cannot speak of the Force that keeps us from burrowing like worms in the soil of selfishness and greed, that holds us back from making prey of the wounded like a pack of wolves on the plains of Siberia, without calling it 'Divine.'"[51]

Sometimes, in our religious and secular selves, the choices we confront are that stark: we can be the worms who think only of our own needs, we can be the wolves, we can make prey of the wounded. Or we can march off to struggle sacrificially for what is the truest and the best. The peace treaty that keeps church and state separate cannot determine for us what is truest and best. It can, if we nurture it, help create the space in which to decide when to march.

Notes

1. Evolution and Religion: Sermon Preached by Rev. George H. Ferris, D.D., in the First Baptist Church in Philadelphia on Sunday, February 28, 1909 (unpaginated, undated).

2. Thomas Jefferson to William Short, Aug. 4, 1820, in William B. Parker, ed., Letters and Addresses of Thomas Jefferson (Buffalo, N.Y.: National Jefferson Society, 1903).

3. See, for example, some of the papers in Peter L. Berger, ed., The Desecularization of the World: Resurgent Religion and World Politics (Washington, D.C.: Ethics and Public Policy Center, 1999).

4. See, for example, the discussions in Stephen Macedo, Diversity and Distrust: Civic Education in a Multicultural Democracy (Cambridge: Harvard University Press, 2000), and Amy Gutmann, Democratic Education (Princeton: Princeton University Press, 1987). Although the concern over parents teaching children illiberal values is commendable, seeking to solve the problem through coercive authority raises democratic questions that I discuss below. See also Ira C. Lupu, "Home Education, Religious Liberty, and the Separation of Powers," Boston University Law Review 67 (1987): 971.

5. Michael McConnell, "Religion and Constitutional Rights: Why Is Religious Liberty the 'First Freedom'?" Cardozo Law Review 21 (2000): 1243, 1245.

6. J. B. Lightfoot, The Christian Ministry (1868), ed. Philip Edgecumbe Hughes (Wilton, Conn.: Morehouse-Barlow, 1983), p. 82.

7. James Madison, "Memorial and Remonstrance against Religious Assessment" (1785), in Arlin M. Adams and Charles J. Emmerich, A Nation Dedicated to Religious Liberty (Philadelphia: University of Pennsylvania Press, 1990), p. 104.

8. See Harry V. Jaffa, A New Birth of Freedom: Abraham Lincoln and the Coming of the Civil War (Lanham, Md.: Rowman and Littlefield, 2000), p. 141.

9. For a recent and very interesting treatment of Williams, see Timothy L. Hall, Separating Church and State: Roger Williams and Religious Liberty (Urbana: University of Illinois Press, 1998). The classic "resurrection" of Williams, still delightfully readable although marked with some historical flaws, is Mark De Wolfe Howe, The Garden and the Wilderness: Religion and Government in American Constitutional History (Chicago: University of Chicago Press, 1965).

10. See, for example, Nomi Maya Stolzenberg, " 'He Drew a Circle That Shut Me Out': Assimilation, Indoctrination, and the Paradox of Liberal Education," Harvard Law Review 106 (1993): 581.

11. For an argument that the free exercise clause of the First Amendment should be explicitly understood to foster a plurality of meanings, in order to avoid state hegemony, see Bette Novit Evans, Interpreting the Free Exercise of Religion: The Constitution and American Pluralism (Chapel Hill: University of North Carolina Press, 1997).

12. For two quite different accounts of the process of that change, see Harold Bloom, The American Religion (New York: Riverhead, 2000), and Nathan O. Hatch, The Democratization of American Christianity (New Haven: Yale University Press, 1989). Bloom argues that all religions in America eventually (perhaps inevitably) become gnostic, personal, mysterious. Hatch insists that they tend to lose the hierarchical structures characteristic of many European traditions. I hope Bloom is wrong; I am fairly sure Hatch is right.

13. I readily acknowledge that my discussion of the competition between religion and the state to explain the meaning of the world is greatly influenced by the work of the sociologist Peter L. Berger, especially The Sacred Canopy: Elements of a Sociological Theory of Religion (New York: Doubleday, 1967).

14. I discuss the problem of domestication through the granting of rights in greater detail in Stephen Carter, "Religious Freedom as if Religion Matters: A Tribute to Justice Brennan," California Law Review 87 (1999): 1059.

15. I explore this proposition in detail in Stephen L. Carter, The Dissent of the Governed: A Meditation on Law, Religion, and Loyalty (Cambridge: Harvard University Press, 1998).

16. See David Tracy, Plurality and Ambiguity: Hermeneutics, Religion, Hope (San Francisco: Harper and Row, 1987).

17. See Roe v. Wade, 410 U.S. 113 (1973).

18. I discuss these data in Stephen L. Carter, God's Name in Vain: The Wrongs and Rights of Religion in Politics (New York: Basic, 2000).

19. I discuss a small part of this history in Carter, God's Name in Vain. For a similar argument by conservative evangelicals who have been involved in electoral politics but now counsel staying away, see Cal Thomas and Ed Dobson, Blinded by Might: Can the "Religious Right" Save America? (Grand Rapids, Mich.: Zondervan, 1999).

20. See Steven Goldberg, Seduced by Science: How American Religion Has Lost Its Way (New York: New York University Press, 1999).

21. For a commentary on the relationship of the Civil Rights Movement to the separation of church and state, see Anthony E. Cook, The Least of These: Race, Law, and Religion in American Culture (New York: Routledge, 1997).

22. See Harry Lefever, "The Involvement of the Men and Religion Forward Movement in the Cause of Labor Justice," Labor History 14 (1973): 522. The effort by the Men and Religion Forward movement to present the values of trade unionism as central to the work of the church aroused "considerable enthusiasm." Ken Fones-Wolf, "Religion and Trade Union Politics in the United States, 1880–1920," International Labor and Working Class History 34 (1988): 39. It must be noted, however, that the movement generally discouraged strikes and other forms of direct action.

23. Pope Leo XIII, Rerum Novarum — Encyclical Letter on the Condition of Labor (1891; authorized translation) (Washington, D.C.: National Catholic Welfare Conference, 1942).

24. The text describes only the popular history. Like the regulatory triumphs of the twentieth century, the free market of the nineteenth tends to be overstated. The innovative regulatory forms of the Progressive Era were frequently cloaks for cartelization. Licensing statutes for the professions provide the usual example: described as laws to

protect the public, they had the effect (and still do) of limiting entry to a field, thus enabling those in the profession to raise their prices. Moreover, these new regulatory forms were quickly subjected to another innovation known as regulatory capture — the tendency of regulators to become advocates for rather than watchdogs of the industries they regulate — has been studied by economists for decades. The classic economic argument was presented in George Stigler, "The Theory of Economic Regulation," Bell Journal of Economic Regulation 2 (1971): 3. For an early analysis of how licensing statutes can serve as a form of capture, see Edmund W. Kitch, Marc Isaacson, and Daniel Kasper, "The Regulation of Taxicabs in Chicago," Journal of Law and Economics 14 (1971): 285. But it has never been any secret to serious historians, either. An early work is Gabriel Kolko, Railroad and Regulation, 1877–1916 (Princeton: Princeton University Press, 1965).

25. Rev. George Chalmers Richmond, The Open Altar: The Sermon Preached Sunday Morning, November 1, 1914 (Philadelphia: The Vestry, 1915), p. 7.

26. Ibid., p. 17.

27. David C. Reid, Effective Industrial Reform (Stockbridge, Mass.: David C. Reid, 1911).

28. Here is what Reid wrote on the subject of women in the workforce: "It means the destruction of the home among the lower one-third or one-half of human society. It means the creation of a soil in which human character cannot grow. It means the growing up of children on the streets, with no mother's care or uplifting influence surrounding them." Ibid., p. 256.

29. Ibid., p. 257

30. Ibid., p. 247.

31. Ibid., p. 221.

32. Rt. Rev. Thomas Atkinson, On the Cause of Our National Troubles: A Sermon Delivered in St. James' Church, Wilmington, N.C. (Wilmington: n.p., 1861), p. 6.

33. George D. Armstrong, D.D., Politics and the Pulpit: A Discourse (Norfolk, Va.: J. D. Ghiselin, 1856), pp. 33–35.

34. James A. Lyon, A Lecture on Christianity and the Civil Laws, p. 22.

35. Ibid., p. 29.

36. Seth Williston, Slavery: Not a Scriptural Ground of Division in Efforts for the Salvation of the Heathen (New York: M. W. Dodd, 1844), p. 24.

37. Reverend Henry Darling, Slavery and the War (Philadelphia: Lippincott, 1863), p. 4.

38. Nathaniel Hall, The Iniquity: A Sermon Preached in the First Church, Dorchester, on Sunday, Dec. 11, 1859 (Boston: John Wilson and Son, 1859), p. 8.

39. Ibid., pp. 17–18.

40. Ibid., p. 19.

41. Nathaniel Hall, The Man, The Deed, The Event: A Sermon Preached in the First Church, Dorchester, on Sunday, Dec. 4, 1859 (Boston: John Wilson and Son, 1859), p. 31 and passim.

42. Rev. Charles E. Hodges, Disunion Our Wisdom and Our Duty (New York: American Anti-Slavery Society, [undated, but internal evidence suggests c. 1860s]), p. 12.

43. Ezra S. Gannett, Relation of the North to Slavery: A Discourse Preached in the

Federal Street Meetinghouse in Boston on Sunday, June 11, 1854 (Boston: Crosby, Nichols, 1854), p. 6.

44. Ibid., p. 16.

45. Williston, p. 12 and passim.

46. See Jon Butler, Awash in a Sea of Faith: Christianizing the American People (Cambridge: Harvard University Press, 1990), pp. 130–51.

47. See Don E. Fehrenbacher, Slavery, Law, and Politics: The Dred Scott Case in Historical Perspective (Oxford: Oxford University Press, 1981), pp. 55–57.

48. See, for example, the discussion in Albert J. Raboteau, Slave Religion: The "Invisible Institution" in the Antebellum South (New York: Oxford University Press, 1978).

49. As the historian Edmund S. Morgan has shown, prior to the 1660s, it was common for slaves in Virginia to convert to Christianity in order to take advantage of laws prohibiting (or at least making difficult) the holding of Christians as slaves rather than as indentured servants; and they were often set free as a result of the conversion. See Edmund S. Morgan, American Slavery, American Freedom: The Ordeal of Colonial Virginia (New York: Norton, 1975), pp. 329–32. See also Butler, Awash in a Sea of Faith, especially p. 138. The question of Christianity and slavery was also debated on the floor of Congress. See the discussion quoted in William Lee Miller, Arguing about Slavery: The Great Battle in the United States Congress (New York: Knopf, 1996).

50. I have said little in my text about the protection of the garden as a matter of constitutional law, not least because I am skeptical that the world of secular courts will ever show very much interest in protecting it. (It hasn't so far.) Perhaps the wall might be better understood by the judges in the wilderness if they came to view the people of the garden as groups rather than as individuals — that is, if they saw the element of "groupness" in religion as an additional reason for protection. For an argument in favor of religious liberty as a group or communitarian right, see Frederick Mark Gedicks's very fine book The Rhetoric of Church and State: A Critical Analysis of Religion Clause Jurisprudence (Durham, N.C.: Duke University Press, 1995).

51. Ferris, Evolution and Religion.

5

Taking Democracy to School

RICHARD H. BRODHEAD

In our world, the notion that the prospects for democracy rest on the health of the education system has the status of a self-evident truth. A person my age won't have known a time when the fate of democracy was not felt to be riding on developments in the schools. The year I started fifth grade, I listened every morning to radio news of the struggle to integrate the public schools of Little Rock, Arkansas — news that made the schoolhouse, unremarkable scene of my own daily life, the site of the war against systematic inequality in America. Later that year, when Russia launched the first space satellite *Sputnik,* I learned that the fate of world democracy hinged on figuring out why Johnny can't read and Ivan can. In more recent times, before it was overshadowed by concern for homeland security, education had emerged as something like the problem in chief in American political discourse. During the 2000 presidential election, there was virtually no problem that failing schools were not alleged to have caused, as — paradoxically, given that no one would say a good word for this institution in its current form — there was virtually no ill for which the reformed school was not proposed as the cure.

As these examples suggest, modern democracy tends to regard schooling not as a social process among others but as the very source of civic strength. So inevitable does the interdependence of democracy and education seem that two points might be worth making as correctives. The first is that this link is not a transcendental given. The ideas of democracy and the schooling needed to support it have no fixed shape: they have evolved over time, elaborated in changing ways by the larger action of social history. The other is that if this link has not been immutable, it has also not been straightforward or trouble-free. The demands that democracy has made on schooling have carried not only all the idealism but also all the variegation and latent contradiction that characterize that complex term, so that the history of democratic education has been the history of the puzzles of democracy quite as much as of its aspirations and successes. This essay looks at the history of democratic schooling partly to understand why that history should be problematic and partly to underline that those problems do indeed have a history — that they are in some cases far older and more enduring than modern consciousness might suppose.

It is well known that this nation's founders looked to Old World philosophers for their theory of representative government. It is not always remembered that those same philosophers also had ideas about education, which were imported together with their political thought. John Locke, the author of the *First and Second Treatises on Civil Government,* was as familiar in America for his work *Of Education,* which urged the freeing of education from physical coercion. Noah Webster's 1787 essay "Of the Education of Youth in America" cited Montesquieu to the effect that while despotic governments would want to give little or no education to the people, a republican government would need for education to be widely available, since it would require "every class of people [to] know and love the laws." But if government by the people and schooling for the many were linked ideas, it would be a mistake to think that universal public education existed at the time of this nation's founding or that this idea figured in any prominent way in the early national agenda. In the late eighteenth century, most schooling was rudimentary and irregular, and education was by no means thought of as the monopoly of the schools. Family, church, and workplace were still the primary scenes of education in the early United States, with school serving as an occasional supplement.

One of the earliest elaborations of a democratic plan of schooling comes from Thomas Jefferson. Jefferson's draft legislation of a "Bill for the More General Diffusion of Knowledge" dates from the time just after the Continental Congress and the Declaration of Independence, when he returned to Virginia to undertake the revision or "revisal" of fundamental laws. Jefferson's revisals are an attempt to change the deep organizing structures of social life so as to generate a new social reality, the free, self-governing people of the Jeffersonian dream. His first proposed measure, the abolition of the laws of primogeniture and entail, aimed to break the means by which the passage of land

and wealth perpetuated a hereditary ruling class. His second, a bill for establishing religious freedom, aimed to break the citizen's subordination at the level of inward conviction or belief. Jefferson's third revisal aimed to dismantle the mechanism by which those equipped with wealth and status won superior access to knowledge and the power knowledge brings: their privileged access to schools.

Jefferson's proposal envisioned a state-sponsored system that would make education available at three levels: the local elementary school, the regional grammar school, and the university. But the plan's most striking feature is not its integrated systematic organization, an idea unheard of in its time, but its fusion of this system with a sense of school's social mission. Jefferson's plan aims to create a political community in which the whole people, "every individual who composes their mass," will "participate of ultimate authority." Through their participation in the political process, citizens will be able to play the role of "guardians of their own liberty," watching for and warding off the degenerations Jefferson believes will result if power is allowed to pass from the people to their rulers. (Like that of all early republicans, Jefferson's thinking is fraught with a sense of the fragility and vulnerability of the republican enterprise.) To equip citizens for the task of keeping their collective liberty safe, Jefferson writes, "their minds must be improved to a certain degree": in short, democratic government requires watchful citizens, and this requires a democratization of learning. It is noteworthy that Jefferson's scheme removes the Bible from elementary schooling and installs lessons in Greek, Roman, European, and American history in the first level of instruction. To Jefferson's mind, the one thing needful for future citizens is a working knowledge of political history, so they can spot the signs of government degeneracy or decay.

To fit Virginia's citizens for the work of citizenship, Jefferson proposes to establish a local school every five or six miles, where all children will be guaranteed three years' schooling at local taxpayers' expense. To equip especially capable pupils for future careers as public leaders, he plans a selection mechanism to give the most gifted access to further schooling "without regard to wealth, birth, or other accidental condition or circumstance." In order to "avail the state of those talents which nature has sown as liberally among the poor as the rich," at the end of three years of universal public education Jefferson would "chuse the boy, of best genius" in each school "of those whose parents are too poor to give them further education" and send him at public expense to one of twenty grammar schools to be founded throughout the state. After a year or two of trial at this level, "the best genius" at the new school would be chosen to receive a free six-year course of grammar school education. At this point, half the students would be qualified to be teachers and their education would be discontinued, and the half "of still superior parts" would be sent on to the College of William and Mary.

This blueprint is a brilliant work of civic imagination, but Jefferson puts deep paradoxes of democratic education on display in the act of unfolding a democratic educational vision. We could start with the fact that Jefferson's scheme was not adopted. It failed partly because Virginia voters were unwilling to entrust their local schools to a statewide system, an unimaginably remote and unreal entity at this time, but largely because they refused to assume the tax burden the scheme would entail. This would not be the last time that financial considerations would trump civic ambitions in the history of American schooling: this episode reveals that that tension between dreams and costs is endemic to democratic education, having been present since the creation. But what is most interesting about the fate of Jefferson's plan is not that it shows public high-mindedness at war with public tightfistedness but that it reveals contradictions within the concept of "the democratic" itself. Jefferson's scheme was democratic in one sense of the word. It created equal access to school without regard to family income or status. Its defeat was democratic in another sense of the word. It resulted from the action of majority rule, government by the consent of the governed. This early chapter teaches that "democracy" encompasses not one but many different values, including — as here — directly competing ones; and that education can bear the weight of these plural goals only at the cost of making school the place where conflicts among democratic values are fought out.

A second paradox of Jefferson's scheme is even more flagrant to modern eyes. Jefferson would make school the great equalizer, *the* tool for neutralizing differences of income and family standing, but there are striking limits to the equality it creates. Slaves are not included in the people the school serves, and we can further note that the unspecified children who go to grade school silently metamorphose into the "boy" who might be chosen to go on. These are the habitual discriminations of an older world, but Jeffersonian selectivity does not stop there. His whole three-tier apparatus is an elaborate sorting device, a mechanism for separating out the person of superior parts and blessing him with further advancement. When Jefferson speaks of best geniuses being "raked from the rubbish," the limits of his egalitarianism come clear.

Jefferson's vision displays one of the most vexing contradictions that has attached itself to democratic education, the way an educational system designed to negate received social hierarchies can end up generating new inequalities of its own. This problem again derives from the tension between democratic values — here, democracy as the equalization of social lots and democracy as the creation of individual opportunities. In this case, the conflict is intensified by the fact that school reinforces democracy's egalitarian *and* anti-egalitarian or individualistic programs through its very structure. On the one hand, school as Jefferson conceives it equalizes opportunity. If there are enough schools and the public will pay the teacher, then everyone can learn literacy and civics. On the other hand, the essential nature of school in Jefferson's idea is that it plots a progression from lower to higher learning and measures and rewards differences of achievement as students struggle up this ladder. As long as school has the function of discriminating superior from inferior performance and aiming those with different school records toward different social fates — an idea deeply rooted in the idea of school to this day — then formal education can be only an ambiguous ally to the democratic project: an instrument for neutralizing inequalities of station and wealth in some measure but the potential creator of new differences in their place, differences based this time on educational performance itself.

Nothing remotely resembling Jefferson's plan came into being during his lifetime. By the end of the eighteenth century some states had made preliminary moves toward establishing universal education — in 1795 Connecticut voted to sell off the state's land claim in Ohio (the so-called Western Reserve) and invest the proceeds for the support of public education. But sixty years after Jefferson wrote his revisal, American schools were still haphazard and chaotic, as measured by the fact that toddlers were sometimes dumped into the same schoolroom as older children and teachers taught reading from whatever different books their pupils' families happened to own. The great push for systematized public education came from the generation of school reformers active in the North and Midwest in the 1830s and 1840s, the so-called Common School Movement. This group envisioned and won public and legislative support for "school" as Americans have known it since: something open to all children, paid for by public taxes, running for set terms, with pupils divided into progressive grades, taught by professionally certified instructors, under local control, but governed by state norms overseen by a state board of education.

It is important to remember that what the Common School Movement envisioned was only gradually enacted. Though its plans were fully articulated by 1840, it was decades before what it promoted came to full reality even in states where progress was most advanced. But if this movement eventually succeeded, as it did, it was because it fused a detailed plan for a school system with a persuasive theory of this plan's social value. Horace Mann was not the only effective advocate of this cause, but he was its most skilled rhetorician. A crucial part of Horace Mann's work as secretary of the Massachusetts State

Board of Education was to fashion a rationale for the new common school and render it publicly compelling. The Annual Reports that Mann wrote between 1837 and 1848, one of the great contributions to the literature of democratic education, elaborate a far richer role for schooling in democratic culture than what Jefferson had proposed sixty years before.

In these reports Mann repeats, but marks as trite, the thought that people need education in order to play their political role in a republic. This is already a truism by Mann's time, and he hastens to supplement it with new rationales. This argument is joined on one side by a theory that school's real work is the psychological formation of the young, and that the service the school can render the republic is less to teach civics lessons than to instill the inward dispositions of republican civic character — especially the habit of self-government, which equips children (in the Ninth Annual Report's words) to be "a constituent part of a self-governing people."

Elsewhere, Mann devises an economic argument for the need for schooling in American democracy. In the Annual Report of 1848 Mann looks across the ocean to an England convulsed by the strife brought on by industrial and capitalist development, the Britain of the Chartist Movement and Friedrich Engels's *The Condition of the Working Class in England*. Reflecting that Massachusetts is the lead site for these developments in America, Mann asks: What can prevent our being visited by the same destructive disparities of wealth and power? The answer (as always for Mann!) is common school education. If education is universally available, then Americans need not be mere wage slaves at the mercy of the owners of great capital. They will be skillful, inventive, productive contributors to the process of development. Fueled by this mass brainpower, American society will not collapse into class war over a static pot of wealth. The spread of knowledge will create an ever-expanding economy, and so an ever-expanding world of opportunity in which all can win advantage. "Knowledge and abundance sustain to each other the relation of cause and effect," Mann writes in a memorable passage. "Intelligence is a primary ingredient in the Wealth of Nations."

Mann here develops the notion that democratic citizenship requires not just participation in the political process but also participation in a growing economy, an economy fueled by the intellectual capital its members share. Elsewhere he finds an argument in the heterogeneity of the American population, which permits him to propose yet another role for schools in a democracy: as the creator of a common culture for a people of mixed origins. Mann's First Report contains a surprisingly early reflection on the problem of private schools. The parents in any elementary school, Mann reflects, will likely contain two elements: the apathetic, those who care too little about what's going on in their kids' school, and the heavily invested, those who care, if anything, too much. (Who was it who said that the only new history is the history we have forgotten?) Rather than subject their children to the low average of the whole group's expectations, he reasons, these parents will want to pull their children out of the common school to give them superior advantages elsewhere. But when they send their kids to private school, parents will also shift their interest to the new place ("the heart goes with the treasure"), leaving the public school further impoverished by the withdrawal of their commitment and concern. The whole voucher debate is here in embryo.

Writing at the very birth of mass immigration as a feature of American life, Mann is already foreseeing how school could become the site for the sorts of social separations our later history has made all too familiar. But as usual with Mann, if school is part of the problem, it is the whole of the solution. Because of the tendency to social segregation in American life, Mann writes, it is more important than ever that elementary schools draw in the whole population. The goal of the common school is to be the thing people have in common, to *create* the experience of living together and knowing each other that may be lacking in the so-called community outside its walls. "It is on this common platform, that a general acquaintanceship should be formed between the children of the same neighborhood. It is here, that the affinities of a common nature should unite them together so as to give . . . a stable possession to fraternal feelings, against the alienating competitions of subsequent life."

One thing I have learned from the study of Horace Mann is that as the public school system has been elaborated over the course of American history, school has been asked to take on more and more problems and become the solution to more and more social ills. It might occur to us that one reason schools succeed imperfectly in teaching things like reading or math is that such instruction is the least of what modern democracy asks them to accomplish. Mann was the great seeker-out of problems the school could volunteer to shoulder, and the mark of his and his colleagues' success is that, for all its limits, the school they designed continues to be a key symbol of democratic hope. When I edited the journals of Charles W. Chesnutt, the chief African-American writer of the post–Civil War generation, I learned that the first thing the freed blacks of Fayetteville, North Carolina, did when the Civil War ended was to buy a plot of land with their own funds to build a public grade school on the New England model. (By means of this investment, black children in Fayetteville had public grade schools before their white contemporaries.) Their choice says what this school had come to symbolize: the way to knowledge, freedom, and full civic enfranchisement.

But like Jefferson's, this ideal carries tensions within it, two of which might be quickly mentioned. Seen one way, the school of the Common School Movement is the dream agent of democracy, creator at once of individual enablement and social community. But looked at in another light, it would appear to foster a very different social reality: systemwide regulation, the reign of standardized ordering devices — the school day, grades, teacher certification, the state board — the whole panoply of modern bureaucracy. Though they can be separated in theory, in actual history the democratization of schooling and the bureaucratization of schooling formed parts of a single process in America. We know the consequence: we sometimes get the democratic yields schooling promises, but we always get the bureaucratic ones, and the more inspiringly democratic a reform is made to sound, the more we can fear that its leavings will be bureaucratic. In the most recent national debate, who would not favor tests and mandated standards if they keep schools from passing off an inferior education in socially disadvantaged areas? This has been tolerated far too long, and there is obvious sense to the thought that the way to address unequal social fates in later life is to provide more equal educational enablement in early life: to leave no child behind. But given that only the bureaucratic part of this program — the newly mandated tests — will be enforceable, it will require special effort to be sure that we get the reality of new enablement, and not just a new mass of official exercises and quantifying instruments.

On another front, Mann's school promises the creation of a common culture, but it is easy to suspect that this culture may be more common to some than to others. It is fascinating to watch Mann maneuvering against all the foes lined up against the common school and threatening to fracture his community of the whole: the private school with its limited class audience, the parochial school with its limited religious audience, the partisan school with its limited political audience, and so on. Over against these foes Mann labors to imagine things we could all be taught together, lest we be condemned to live in separate camps and at the mercy of the strongest faction. Since it is easy to underestimate the challenge he is facing, I find this part of Mann's work intelligent and even moving, but for all that, the "we" he proposes fits some groups very differently from others. His culture of self-government will fit us fairly comfortably if "we" have grown up in the antebellum American North, with its heavy promotion of internalized self-discipline, but if we have just "made a voyage across the Atlantic," as a hundred thousand Irish did in the year this line was written, we will have been "dwarfed under the despotisms of the Old World" and will need to have our deep character structures made over. (More work for the common school!) So too the nondenominational religious teaching he favors may seem of universal value to us if we are Christian and more particularly Protestant but will read like coercive proselytizing if we are from another faith.

We can fault Mann for the limits of his toleration, and we could all name schools that have favored children of some origins and marked others as inferiors to be made over. But the problem here is not a function of some person's or some institution's failings: it derives in part from a problem with the idea of democratic education itself. That idea is extraordinarily inspiring, but the moral glow it casts tends to conceal the fact that this term contains different and even opposite meanings, all of which have their legitimacy but not all of which tend to be held in mind at once. Mann gives prominence to the idea that democratic education needs to create an ethos that provides for collective agreement about collective rights. If we doubt that this is important, we should reflect that where such agreement is lacking, individuals and groups are wide open to violation by those who despise them. On the other hand, when we criticize Mann's enforced monoculturalism we are giving priority to an equally central democratic value: the right of the minority not to be victimized by the majority and the right of individuals not to have their beliefs constrained by the state. The harder Mann pushes for a culture of the whole, the more he calls up the critique of the whole's coercions of other cultures. Historically, the movements to protect children from victimization by schooling conducted in English or in an alien faith were contemporaneous with the Common School Movement and products of its success, and modern arguments for bilingual education and against secular humanism can be found virtually fully formed in the mid-nineteenth century. (Catholics of that time resisted the enforced culture of the public schools long before Protestant fundamentalists did, and the people pushing for public education in their own tongue were not Hispanics but Germans and Norwegians.) Here and not only here, a common problem of democratic education is that those who embrace it can become so enthusiastic about one of its values as to be oblivious to the fact that they are negating another. The solution can't lie in simplifying the problem, whose complexity is the essence of its reality. It can only lie in being aware of the plurality of goods to be served and mediating thoughtfully among them.

Over the last century, primary school has continued to supply the main arena for staging democratic education's new ambitions and fighting out their attendant conflicts, but in the twentieth century it has been joined by other venues. The most salient development of American education in the last hundred years has been the increased schooling of the population — by which I mean both the incorporation of the whole school-age population into school and the extension of time normally spent in school. The historian David Tyack

estimates that the average American had only five years' formal education in
the year 1900. By 1940, however, a number approaching 50 percent of American children had been to high school, the novel invention of the post–Civil
War years. And since World War II, in a development that would have been
unthinkable a hundred or even sixty years ago, the notion of adequate education has expanded for a larger and larger sector of the population to include
the idea of college. Higher education has been the great growth sector in the
postwar educational economy. Something like 2 million Americans went to
college in 1951, but the number had grown to four million by 1961, and the
Chronicle of Higher Education reckons that that number stood at more than
15 million by the year 2001 — with 11.8 million in public and 3.4 million in
private colleges and universities; 9.3 million in four-year and 5.8 million in
two-year institutions.

In the context of this essay, the meaning of this growth will I trust be clear. In
our lifetime, higher education, for centuries an arcane domain for the few, has
been annexed to the expanding empire of mass educational opportunity. And
as college has become the great new site of democratic opportunity, it has also
become a new object of public fixation and vexation, the new place for democratic controversies to be fought out.

I can only gesture at the factors that have driven the expansion of higher
education. The first are those changes in the modern economy that continue
ever more sharply to stratify employment opportunities and the educational
attainment they require. This under-analyzed development has worked to re-
value high school education, a relative rarity and a badge of advanced training
a century ago, into a minimal preparation for most jobs and an insufficient
qualification for a good one. This change has created a need and an ambition
for higher education where none had previously existed; and other developments have allowed this need to be much more widely met. I have in mind the
rapid growth of the higher education system, which created millions more
places for possible students, and the not-unrelated growth of the economy
itself, which created billions more dollars to pay for this new necessity.

In modern times, the conjunction of these new social facts has created two
quite different consequences: first, massive new enrollment in many parts of
the higher education system and, second, massive new competition for places
at certain schools. At selective institutions, increased external demand has
meshed with an internal development that was by no means inevitably linked
to it (Nicholas Lemann's *The Big Test* is the best chronicle of this development): conversion to an admissions system that gave much more weight to
scholastic aptitude and academic performance. To oversimplify a little, in
America's leading private universities, gentlemanly accomplishment had long

been the main qualification for admission, with intellectual ability and attainment welcomed in appropriate measure but not by any means the dominant criterion. In the 1930s, in the middle of the Great Depression, Harvard president James Bryant Conant instituted an increased emphasis on intellectual aptitude in admissions, but as usual the change worked its way through the system fairly slowly. At first, Lemann shows, Harvard used its new meritocratic academic criteria to judge the admission only of scholarship students. It took three decades for the new admissions calculus to thoroughly succeed in delegitimating and replacing the older standards at Harvard and schools of its sort.

The more academically oriented admissions system was devised in quite a different world than the one in which it triumphed — really, it is a late creation of the Progressive Era. Once embraced, it served an increasingly important intra-university function: as universities began their evolution into the scenes of specialized knowledge-creation they are today, this admissions policy supplied a new, more intellectual breed of student for a new, more professionalized breed of professor. But though it was devised for other occasions, in the late 1950s and 1960s this new admissions system came under the pressure of a new social development. Admissions policy at selective schools was not the Civil Rights Movement's principal target, but in the changed world that the Civil Rights Movement created, selective universities became inevitably more conscious of and more embarrassed by everything that seemed to make them agents of discriminatory privilege. The fortuitous conjunction of these developments produced the great admissions revolution that we are on the far side of. I speak as one who lived through this change. In 1964 I entered a Yale College that was consciously increasing its outreach to public high schools but that was still — and still congratulated itself on being — all male. In 1968 I graduated from a Yale College that had made a decisive shift away from recruitment at feeder schools and was on the verge of announcing that it would admit women. In 1972 I started teaching at a Yale College where the students were men and women from many different backgrounds and where students showed far more interest in their studies than had been the norm so short a while before — not surprisingly, since the democratization of admissions and the academicization of admissions criteria formed part of a single process.

But I have been arguing that democratization brings expanded controversy together with expanded opportunity, and so it has proved in this case. As *The Big Test* establishes in fascinating detail, when President Conant became interested in the Jeffersonian project of opening education to merit irrespective of family circumstance, as the means to calibrate merit he chose an intelligence test that measured scholastic aptitude — the dreaded SAT. As it has grown to its current massive use, the SAT has been essential to the opening of opportunity, giving the mentally adept a way to demonstrate their prowess and win advancement independent of family status. But when an instrument was adopted that seemed to yield a standardized, nationwide measure of objective merit, that same instrument could then create other, unforeseen consequences, ones we know well.

The SAT registered differences of performance between white and African American students at all income levels, thus creating a quandary. If test disparities were allowed to stand uncorrected, then this measure could supply a new basis for group discrimination, a new means to enforce exclusions from high-level social opportunity. Given this country's painful racial history and the role schools have played in the enforcement of American racial inequality, these outcomes were unacceptable to large sections of the public and virtually all universities. Like other sites of opportunity, school systems devised ways to mitigate the pure rule of test scores so as to produce a result more adequately inclusive of the social whole—a democratic (i.e., equalizing, inclusionistic) corrective to the antidemocratic action of a democratic (i.e., meritocratic, individual-opportunity-creating) instrument.

But once this move was made, the test could cut the opposite way. As Lemann notes, when there was no uniform measure of merit, there were no grounds to document one person's unfair treatment for someone else's advantage. But a scheme that required objective tests but then corrected the results with affirmative action protocols created a rich new ground for grievance and resentment. The Supreme Court's *Baake* decision gave tenuous legitimacy to a policy of mediation among the different democratic imperatives that came into collision over affirmative action, but twenty years later that mediation has produced no secure consensus. This issue is still the subject of constant court battles, and we seem to have arrived at a new historical turn in which the SAT itself, unwitting "cause" of so much contention, seems about to become the agreed-on victim for all sides' collective wrath. In the winter of 2001 Richard C. Atkinson, the president of the University of California system, called for the abolition of the mandatory SAT I in admissions consideration, and Lemann makes a similar case in the conclusion to *The Big Test*.

When I hear proposals of this sort, I feel powerful sympathy with the frustration that fuels them, but I can't help suspecting that frustration is generating the fantasy of a simple solution: kill the evil test and the good democratic world will return! The charges against the SAT are now well known. Every newspaper reader or TV watcher knows that, taken in large aggregates, student scores on this test rise with parental income, and that the better off can afford prep courses that artificially enhance their children's appearance of brilliance. Further, as President Atkinson has emphasized, this test can corrupt schooling by leading teachers to teach too exclusively toward this one fateful event. (Atkinson claims that California eighth graders now spend school time drilling thought patterns like "untruthful is to mendaciousness as circumspect is to caution": the source, no doubt, of the complex vocabularies for which Valley girls and boys are famous.)

These are weighty arguments, but a fair-minded person would want to post some items on the other side of the ledger. Given the perplexities of this moment, it is easy to forget that American higher education has in fact opened itself to talented individuals from a large variety of previously disparaged backgrounds in the last forty years, and that devices like objective test scores have played no small part — continue to play no small part — in establishing their claims to admission. These results are now taken for granted, but they would not be assured if the instrument that enabled them were to be discarded. In my view, it would be well to be frank about who is going to lose in the next change of standards as well as who will gain. It would be well to foresee, in other words, what new problem of democratic education this fix of the current one would cause.

In any case, unless selectivity itself (the real culprit) can be made to go away from college admissions, there will always be competition, and thus the need for some ground for choosing among well-qualified contenders. When the SAT is repudiated, what will take its place, and what will guarantee the superior fairness of its discriminations? Lemann proposes replacing the scholastic aptitude test with an achievement test that would measure mastery of things actually studied in the high school curriculum. That sounds reasonable; but if the current test offers a very partial index to intelligence, in what way will this new one be a fuller gauge, and how will it fend off covert social advantage? Won't students from strong school systems outperform those from weaker ones on such tests — and if they do, how much advantage should we tolerate before we take steps to correct it? Lemann is particularly upset by the fact that high-achiever parents are now desperate to pass on the advantage of superior education to their not quite so formidable children. (Horace Mann saw it coming.) But if overinvested parents have corrupted the old selection scheme, why would we assume they would give up in face of the new one, rather than hire even better tutors for the new big test?

On the other hand, if we replace a single test as a measure of an applicant's qualifications with (in the word of the hour) "holistic assessment," how are we to expect the public mad at "objective" standards to tolerate the subjectivity the new evaluation would require? And when one's child's whole personhood has been assessed and found wanting instead of just his or her scholastic aptitude, can we really expect the decisions to win a greater degree of public acceptance? Though current debate often overlooks the fact, selective private universities have always used a much broader form of evaluation in which the SAT scores are weighed as one item among many — without winning notably greater happiness with their negative decisions.

I am not speaking in defense of the SAT. After all these years its limits and usefulness are both well known. But I am speaking against the notion that the SAT is in any simple sense the heart of our problem. Our problem is not a flaw in the measuring tool and is not to be solved by rejiggering the instrument. It derives from the difficulty of deep questions about how merit itself should be defined for the purpose of university admissions and how this opportunity should be fairly distributed. These are not questions on which our society can be expected to come to easy agreement, but there will be no reaching even the most fragile solution except by engaging the real questions and exploring them in a searching way. In this struggle (should we be so lucky to have it), the helpful position will be one that acknowledges the authentic difficulty of the issues and recognizes the partial legitimacy of many competing answers.

To give a taste of the problem of judgment in this domain, I could say a word about the admissions philosophy of the school I know, which will find echoes at other selective colleges. Yale College looks for students with quick, inquiring minds. Such intelligence is the prerequisite for admission not because it is the only human value but because it has special relevance to the nature of such a school. Having amassed the resources of learning and inquiry, the university has a legitimate interest in sharing them with the students who will make the fullest use of these resources and contribute most vigorously to the unfolding of understanding. (This means that universities have legitimate interests that are not democratic interests.) But since the active, thoughtful play of mind is what this place requires, we do not measure intellectual potential mechanically. We look not just for dutiful accomplishment but for deeper traits of curiosity and mental independence, and we consult every available form of evidence — aptitude and achievement scores, grades, recommendations, the candidate's own writing — to help gauge this elusive potential. At the same time, a school that sees its mission as training students who will make constructive contributions to the world will look for many traits of character besides academic intelligence narrowly defined: traits like drive, commitment, the sense that gifts carry an obligation to use them well, a sense of the importance of living in and for a larger community.

Now, is this way of proceeding democratic? No, in that it rewards differences of gift and accomplishment; but yes, in that it opens doors for individual talent without regard to family background or ability to pay. No, in that we hope our students will distinguish themselves in later life; but yes, in that we hope that distinction will lie in their service to the social whole. No, in that we do not aim to "represent" the public through a fixed demographics in our student body. But yes, in that we actively seek talent from every sector of society and recognize that measuring differences of personal promise will require some reckoning of differences in advantages enjoyed. Adjudicating among competing values before the particulars of individual cases is the hard work of admissions. It is in the nature of things that neither the individual decisions nor the principles on which they are made can be beyond dispute.

When I call the attack on the SAT a false diagnosis of the college admissions problem, I mean that the real difficulty lies in agreeing on *what* is to be measured and *why*, not how. But I would also suggest that this attack may take attention away from other sides of the problem that are no less serious. First and most obviously, there is no point worrying about inclusiveness at the point of college admissions if we do not first make sure that many more people have a chance to be contenders for such admission. The scope of possible democracy in colleges will always be predetermined by the availability of excellent training before college, and this will require not just mastery of fundamentals — crucial though that is — but access to everything that provokes and expands the mind. Second, while controversies about tests and test scores have grabbed the headlines in recent years, there is reason to think that the real thing we should be worrying about is the money.

As Jefferson already recognized, the creation of educational opportunity requires someone to foot the bill. The past decades have witnessed two historically unprecedented developments in this area, the expansion of mass educational opportunity at relatively low cost at public colleges and universities and the adoption of need-blind admissions and need-based aid at the most selective private schools. But there is some danger that both of these may be coming under threat. Without much national attention, many states have moved to give students with good high school averages a free ride at a state college in hopes of keeping top students in the state. In practice this has rewarded students whose families could have paid the tuition while reducing admissions opportunities for the financially disadvantaged. But if "to those who have, much is given" becomes the implicit aid policy of public education, we could witness a restriction of opportunity at the financial end even as it is being nominally expanded at the level of official criteria. On the other side, recent financial aid improvements at a handful of wealthy private universities will increase the pressure on schools with smaller endowments to consider a return to merit-based aid if their competitive position erodes. But if need-blind admission and need-based aid should go by the board at a significant number of schools, then even more aid money will be chasing the well-to-do — a threat to democratic opportunity far graver than the choice of tests.

I have been focusing on college admissions, but my point applies to a far wider range of issues. I might state it this way. We do not do sufficient justice to the fact that the alignment of the words "democratic" and "education" is a fairly recent historical development. For centuries education had no democratic component or aspiration: the thought that schooling too should be of the people and for the people is a glorious invention of relatively recent times. But to say that it is glorious is not to say that it is unproblematic. Democracy in schooling means many things, not all of them achievable in full measure at the same time; and when schools inspire frustration, it is often not because they have failed their democratic mission, but because they have achieved some part of this mission at the expense of another.

Solving these conundrums — working through the difficulties in a thoughtful and constructive way — will be the ongoing task of every community that cares about democratic education. In this process, two things will always be of the essence: keeping alive a full, generous, expansive dream of what education itself could be; and taking pains to entrust the work of teaching to the most devoted and inspiring of our contemporaries, those best geniuses who can make education happen. There's plenty of work ahead.

Works Cited

Jefferson, Thomas, "A Bill for the More General Diffusion of Knowledge" and *Notes on the State of Virginia,* Query 14, reprinted in *Writings* (New York: Library of America, 1984).

Kaestle, Carl F., *Pillars of the Republic: Common Schools and American Society* (New York: Hill and Wang, 1983).

Lemann, Nicholas, *The Big Test: The Secret History of the American Meritocracy* (New York: Farrar, Straus and Giroux, 1999).

Mann, Horace, "Annual Reports to the Massachusetts Board of Education," 1837–1848, selections reprinted in *The Republic and the Schools: Horace Mann and the Education of Free Men,* ed. Lawrence Cremin (New York: Columbia University Teachers College, 1957).

Webster, Noah, "On the Education of Youth in America," in *Essays on Education in the Early Republic,* ed. Frederick Randolph (Cambridge: Harvard University Press, 1965).

6

The Misuse of Numbers: Audits, Quantification, and the Obfuscation of Politics

JAMES C. SCOTT, WITH MATTHEW A. LIGHT

Louisa had been overheard to begin a conversation with her brother one day, by saying, "Tom, I wonder" — upon which Mr. Gradgrind, who was the person overhearing, stepped into the light and said, "Louisa, never wonder."

Herein lay the spring of the mechanical art and mystery of educating the reason, without stooping to the cultivation of the sentiments and affections. Never wonder. By means of addition, subtraction, multiplication, and division, settle everything somehow, and never wonder.

—Charles Dickens, *Hard Times*

Would you please join me in a brief fantasy? The year is 2020. Richard Levin has just retired after a long and brilliant career as president of Yale University and has declared this "2020: The Year of Perfect Vision." Every last building is rebuilt and shining; the students are even more precocious, accomplished, and unionized than they are today; and *U.S. News and World Report* and *Consumer Reports* (now merged) have ranked Yale University number one across the board — up there with the very best hotels, luxury automobiles, and lawnmowers. Well — nearly across the board. It seems that the quality of the faculty, as reflected in the all-important rankings, has slipped. Yale's competitors are shaking their heads at the decline. Those who know how to read between the lines of apparently serene "Yale Corporation" pronouncements can detect a rising, but, of course, still decorous, panic.

One sign of concern can be read from the selection of President Levin's successor, Condoleezza Rice, the retired secretary of state who most recently led a no-nonsense, businesslike, streamlining of the Ford Foundation. Yes, she is the first woman of color to lead Yale. Of course, four other Ivy League schools are also headed by women of color. Not surprising, inasmuch as Yale has always followed the New England farmer's rule: "Never be the first person to try something new, nor the last."

On the other hand, President Rice wasn't chosen for the symbolism; she was chosen for the promise she represented: the promise of leading a thoroughgoing restructuring of the faculty using the most advanced quality-management techniques: techniques perfected from the crude beginnings of the Grandes Ecoles of Paris in the late nineteenth century; embodied in Robert McNamara's revolution in the Department of Defense in the 1960s and Margaret Thatcher's managerial revolution in British social policy and higher education in the 1980s; further developed by the World Bank, and brought to near perfection, so far as higher education is concerned, by the Big Ten universities; and making its way, belatedly, to the Ivy League.

We know, from confidential sources among the members of the Yale Corporation, how she captivated them in her "job interview." She said that she admired the judicious mix of feudalism — in politics — and capitalism — in financial management — that Yale had managed to preserve. It suited perfectly the reforms she had devised — as did Yale's long tradition of what has come to be celebrated as "participatory autocracy" in faculty governance.

But it was her comprehensive plan for massively improving the quality of the faculty — or, more accurately, for improving its standing in the national rankings — that convinced the Corporation's members that she was the answer to their prayers.

She excoriated Yale's antiquated practices of hiring, promoting, and tenuring faculty. They were, she said, subjective, medieval, unsystematic, capricious, and arbitrary. These customs, jealously guarded by the aging and largely white male mandarins of the faculty (whose average age now hovered around eighty), were, she claimed, responsible for Yale's loss of ground to the competition. They produced, on the one hand, a driven, insecure junior faculty who had no way of knowing what the criteria of success and promotion were beyond the tastes and prejudices of the seniors in their department and, on the other hand, a self-satisfied, unproductive oligarchy of gerontocrats heedless of the long-run interests of the institution.

Her plan, our sources tell us, was beguilingly simple. She proposed using the scientific techniques of quality evaluation employed elsewhere in the academy, but to implement them, for the first time, in a truly comprehensive and transparent fashion. The scheme hinged on the citation indices: the Arts and Humanities Citation Index, the Social Science Citation Index, and the granddaddy of them all, the Science Citation Index. Sure, these counts of how often one's work was cited by others in the field were consulted from time to time in promotion reviews, but, as President Rice, she proposed to make this form of objective evaluation systematic and comprehensive. The citation indices, she stressed, like the machine counting of votes, play no favorites; they are incapable of conscious or unconscious bias; they represent the only impersonal metric for judgments of academic distinction. They would henceforth be the sole criterion for promotion and tenure. If she succeeded in breaking tenure, the indices would also serve as a basis for automatically dismissing tenured faculty whose sloth and dimness prevented them from achieving annual citation norms (ACN for short).

In keeping with the neoliberal emphasis on transparency, full public disclosure, and objectivity, President Rice proposes a modern, high-tech, academic version of Robert Owens's factory scheme at New Lanark. The entire faculty is to be outfitted with digitalized beanies. As soon as they are designed — in Yale's distinctive blue and white — and can be manufactured under humane, non-sweatshop conditions, all faculty will be required to wear them on campus. The front of the beanie, across the forehead, will consist of a digital screen, rather like a taxi meter, on which will be displayed the total citation count of that scholar in real time. As the fully automated citation recording centers register new citations, these citations, conveyed by satellite, will be posted automatically to the digital readout on the beanie. Think of a miniature version of the constantly updated world population count once available in lights in Times Square. Let's call it Public Record of Digitally Underwritten Citation Totals (PRODUCT, for short). Rice conjured a vision of the thrill students would experience as they listened, rapt, to the lecture of a brilliant and renowned professor whose beanie, while she lectured, was constantly humming, the total citations piling up before their very eyes. Meanwhile, in a nearby classroom, students worry as they contemplate the blank readout on the beanie of the embarrassed professor before them. How will their transcript look when the cumulative citation total of all the professors from whom they have taken courses is compared with the cumulative total of their competitors for graduate or professional school? Have they studied with the best and brightest?

Students will no longer have to rely on the fallible hearsay evidence of their friends or the prejudices of a course critique. The numerical "quality grade" of their instructor will be there for all to see — and to judge. Junior faculty will no longer need to fear the caprice of their senior colleagues. A single, indisputable standard of achievement will, like a batting average, provide a measure of quality and an unambiguous target for ambition. For President Rice, the system solves the perennial problem of how to reform departments that languish in the backwaters of their disciplines and become bastions of narrow patronage. This publicly accountable, transparent, impersonal measure of professional standing shall henceforth be used, in place of promotion and hiring committees.

Think of the clarity! A blue-ribbon panel of distinguished faculty (chosen by the new criteria) will simply establish several citation plateaus: one for renewal, one for promotion to term associate, one for tenure, and one for post-tenure performance. After that, the process will be entirely automated once the beanie technology is perfected. Imagine a much quoted, pace-setting political science professor, Harvey Writealot, lecturing to a packed hall. Suddenly, because an obscure scholar in Arizona has just quoted his last article in the *Journal of Recent Recondite Research* (*JRRR*) and, by chance, that very quote is the one that puts him over the top, the beanie instantly responds by flashing the good news in blue and white and playing Boola Boola. The students, realizing what has happened, rise to applaud their professor's elevation. He bows modestly, pleased and embarrassed by the fuss, and continues the lecture — but now with tenure. The console on the desk of President Rice's office in Woodbridge Hall tells her that Harvey has "made it" into the magic circle on his own merits, and she, in turn, sends him a message of congratulations broadcast through the beanie by text and voice. A new, distinctive "tenure-beanie" and certificate will follow shortly.

Members of the Corporation, understanding instantly how much time and disputation this automated system could save and how it could catapult Yale back into the faculty-ratings chase, set about refining and perfecting the technique. One suggested having a time-elapse system of citation depreciation; each year's citations will lose one-eighth of their value with each passing year. An eight-year-old citation evaporates in keeping with the pace of field development. Reluctantly, one member of the Corporation suggested that, for consistency, there be a minimal plateau for retention, even of previously tenured faculty. She acknowledged that the image of a bent professor's citation total degrading to the dismissal level in the middle of a seminar is a sad spectacle to contemplate, another suggested that the beanie, in this case, could simply be programmed to go completely blank, though one imagines the professor could read his fate in the averted gaze of his students.

Thank you for indulging my fantasy. I think you see where I'm headed. I'm abandoning the fantasy but continuing with a polemic. The point I want to make is reasonably straightforward. It is that democracies, particularly mass democracies like the United States that have embraced meritocratic criteria for elite selection and mass opportunity are tempted to develop impersonal, objective, mechanical measures of quality. Why? The short answer is that few social decisions are as momentous for individuals and families as the distribution of life-chances through education and employment or more significant for communities and regions than the distribution of public funds for vast public-works projects. The seductiveness of such measures is that they all turn measures of quality into measures of quantity, thereby allowing comparison across cases with a single metric. Whether they take the form of the Social Science Citation Index, the Scholastic Aptitude Test (SAT), or cost-benefit analysis (CBA), they all follow the same logic.

I mean to sketch that logic and argue that it is irremediably and fatally flawed. The first and most obvious problem with such measures is that they are often invalid: that is, they rarely measure the quality we believe to be at stake with any accuracy. (This is what is known in social science jargon as a lack of "construct validity.") This issue, on which most ink has been spilled, will not detain us long.

The second and greatest flaw of these administrative techniques is that they function as a vast "anti-politics machine," sweeping vast realms of legitimate public debate out of the public sphere and into the arms of technical, administrative committees. Far from eliminating politics, such techniques merely bury a vital politics in a series of conventions, measures, and assumptions that escape public scrutiny and dispute. They stand in the way of potentially bracing and instructive debates about social policy, the meaning of intelligence, the selection of elites, the value of equity and diversity, and the purpose of economic growth and development. They are, in short, the means by which administrative elites attempt to convince a skeptical public — while excluding them from the debate — that they play no favorites, take no obscure discretionary action, and have no biases, but are merely making transparent technical calculations. At a larger level, I shall argue that these techniques are the hallmark of a neoliberal political order in which the methods of neoclassical economics, in the name of scientific calculation and objectivity, have replaced other forms of reasoning. Whenever you hear someone say, "I'm deeply invested in him/her" or refer to social or human "capital" or, so help me, refer to the "opportunity cost" of a human relationship, you'll know what I'm talking about.

The third fatal flaw is that even if the measure, when it was first devised, were a valid measure, its very existence typically sets in motion a train of events that undermine its validity. Let's call this a process by which "a measure colonizes behavior," thereby negating whatever validity it once had. A historical example will clarify what I mean. The officials of the French absolutist kings sought to tax their subjects' houses according to size. They seized on the brilliant device of counting the windows and doors of a dwelling. At the beginning of the exercise, the number of windows and doors was a nearly perfect proxy for the size of a house. Over the next two centuries, however, the "window and door tax," as it was called, impelled people to reconstruct and rebuild houses so as to minimize the number of apertures and thereby reduce the tax. What started out as a valid measure became an invalid measure.

This kind of policy and its perverse consequences are not limited to the windows of pre-revolutionary France. Similar methods of audit and quality control are now entrenching their dominance in the educational system, especially in the United States. I now turn to a discussion of several examples of this phenomenon: the Social Science Citation Index, the Scholastic Aptitude Test, and Britain's "Research Assessment Exercise." I will then leave the academy to explore similar abuses of quantification in other areas.

The Science Citation Index (SCI), founded in 1963 and the granddaddy of all citation indices, was the brainchild of Eugene Garfield. Its purpose was to gauge the scientific impact of, say, a particular research paper and by extension a particular scholar or research laboratory by the frequency with which a paper was cited by other research scientists. Why not? It sure beat relying on informal reputations, grants, and the obscure embedded hierarchies of established institutions, let alone the sheer productivity of a scholar. More than half of all scientific publications, after all, sink without a trace; they aren't cited at all, not even once. Eighty percent are cited only once, ever. The Science Citation Index seemed to offer an objective, accurate, and transparent measure of a scholar's impact on subsequent scholarship — a blow for merit. And so it was, at least initially, compared to the structures of privilege and position it was offered to replace.

It was a great success, not least because it was heavily promoted. Let's not forget that this is a for-profit business! Soon it was pervasive: used in the award of tenure, to promote journals, to rank scholars and institutions, and in technological analyses and government studies. Soon the Social Science Citation Index followed. After that, could the Arts and Humanities Citation Index be far behind?

But was it valid? What precisely did it measure? The first thing to notice is the computer-like mindlessness and abstraction of the data gathering. Self-citations counted, adding autoeroticism to the normal narcissism that prevails in the academy. Negative citations, such as "X's article is the worst piece of research I have ever encountered" also count. As Mae West said, "There's no such thing as bad publicity; just spell my name right." Citations found in books, as opposed to articles, are not canvassed. More seriously, what if *no one ever read* the articles in which a work was cited, as was often the case? Then there is the provincialism of the exercise; this is, after all a massively English-language, hence Anglo-American, operation. Eugene Garfield claimed that "French science is provincial because of its reluctance to accept English as *the* scientific language." In the social sciences, this is preposterous on its face, but it is true that the translation and sale of your work to a hundred thousand Chinese, Brazilians, or Indonesians will add nothing to your Social Science Citation Index standing unless they record their gratitude in an English language journal or one of the handful of foreign language journals included in the magic circle.

Notice, too, that the index must, as a statistical matter, favor the specialties that are the most heavily trafficked, that is to say mainstream research or, in Thomas Kuhn's terms, "normal science." Notice finally that the Social Science Citation Index lacks any acknowledgment of historical development. What if a current line of inquiry is dropped as a sterile exercise three years hence? Today's wave, and the index blip it creates, may still allow our lucky researcher to surf to a safe harbor despite her mistake. There is no need to belabor these shortcomings of the SSCI further. They serve only to show the inevitable gap between measures of this kind and the underlying quality they purport to assess. The fact is that many of these shortcomings could, at least in principle, be rectified by reforms and elaborations in the procedures by which the index is constructed. In practice, however, the more schematically abstract and computationally simple measure is preferred for its ease of use and, in this case, lower cost.

The anti-politics of the Social Science Citation Index consists in substituting a pseudoscientific calculation for a healthy debate about quality. The real politics of a discipline — its worthy politics anyway — is precisely the dialogue about standards of value and knowledge. I entertain few illusions about the typical quality of the dialogue. Are there interests and power relations at play? You bet. They're ubiquitous. There is, however, no substitute for necessarily qualitative and always inconclusive argument. It is the lifeblood of a discipline's character, fought out in reviews, classrooms, roundtables, debates, and decisions about curriculum, hiring, and promotion. Any attempt to curtail that discussion by, for example, Balkanization into quasi-autonomous subfields, rigid quantitative standards, or elaborate scorecards tends simply to freeze a given orthodoxy or division of spoils in place.

My fun at the expense of the SSCI may seem a cheap shot. The argument I'm making, however, applies to *any* quantitative standard, rigidly applied. Take the apparently reasonable "two-book" standard often applied in tenure decisions. Some scholars' single book or article has generated more intellectual energy than the collected works of other, quantitatively more "productive," scholars. The commensurating device known as the tape measure may tell us that a Vermeer portrait and a cow plop are both ten inches across; there, however, the similarity ends.

Once in place, any index used to distribute rewards or punishments begins to circle back and colonize behavior. Thus, I have been told that there are "rings" of scholars who have agreed to cite one another routinely and thereby raise their citation rating. Outright conspiracy of this kind is but the most egregious version of a more important phenomenon. Knowing that, like the "window and door tax," the citation index can make or break a career exerts a subtle or not-so-subtle influence on professional conduct: for example, the advantages of mainstream methodologies and populous subfields, the choice of journals, the incantation of a field's most notable figures are all encouraged by the incentives thereby conjured up. This is not crass Machiavellian behavior; I'm pointing instead to the constant pressure at the margin to act "prudently." The result, in the long run, is a selection pressure, in the Darwinian sense, favoring the survival of those who meet or exceed their audit quotas.

A citation index is not merely an observation; it is a force in the world, capable of generating its own observations. Social theorists have been so struck by this "colonization" that they have attempted to give it a lawlike formulation. Charles Goodhart's version is, "Any observed regularity will tend to collapse, once pressure is placed on it for control purposes." Another scholar reformulates it: "Every measure which becomes a target becomes a bad measure." Put succinctly, an authority sets a quantitative standard to measure a particular achievement; those responsible for meeting that standard do so, but not in the way that was intended.

Audits and Commensuration

How exactly did we develop the idea that quantitative indices and audits should form the basis of public policy? Originally, and literally, "a hearing," the audit was an oral account by a vassal or serf to the lord or his agent of the services and dues rendered. It came, later, to mean the checking of "accounts" — especially of quantifiable activity — against other documentary evidence (receipts, bills, tax statements, contracts) for accuracy. At the limit, it implied tracing every transaction back to its origin for verification. Audits, then, were from the beginning born of a fear of misrepresentation and fraud. As with other forms of accountability and quantification, they were, as Theodore Porter aptly puts it, "technologies designed to overcome distrust and distance." They serve the rhetorical and political functions of convincing a possibly skeptical outsider that the affairs of the party or institution are fairly represented here; the audit is a guarantee that supplements or, in some cases, substitutes for trust founded on reputation, kinship, religious ties, and friendship. Double-entry bookkeeping, a Renaissance innovation, was designed as much to improve the social standing of merchants — demonstrating their probity and professionalism — as actually to keep accurate records. Yet, for centuries the financial audit existed more in theory than in practice, even in the largest business enterprises of the time. (For example, the books of the British East India Company were kept only sporadically.) Auditing, as standard practice of enterprises and public bodies, came into its own with the modern corporation's separation of ownership and management and the rise of mass democracy. Interestingly, nineteenth-century American railroads, among the earliest large national corporations, were pioneers in the rise of modern financial accounting. Distrust and distance are at work here again.

Against this crude background, how might we explain the huge, one might say hegemonic, influence of quantitative representations of qualities, such as the SAT and cost-benefit analysis? Michael Power, a prominent student of this subject, attributes the rise of "an audit society" to the neoliberal politics of the 1970s and 1980s, as exemplified by Thatcher and Ronald Reagan. He notes these politicians' emphasis on "value for money" in public administration, their adulation of market structures, and their denigration of the state.

This approach ignores the long history of the politicized use of quantitative indices. Not only the SAT, but many other attempts to institutionalize quantitative indices such as cost-benefit analysis, predate the emergence of neoliberalism by many decades. Neoliberals, however one might define them, did not invent the practice of audit. Rather, they are only the latest to make use of it for their own ends. To the extent that neoliberalism and audit are indeed related, the connection may rather be simply that because neoliberals have been pursuing and, more recently, enjoying political power for the last several decades, it is they who have recently been in a position to implement auditlike policies.

On a broader view, the current prominence of quantitative measurements probably has many causes. We could chart the rise of audit by moving from the most general to the most specific causes. The prestige of numbers in Western culture has been growing for hundreds of years, in part because of the process of political democratization, with its rejection of status as the basis for authority and its demand for political control of administrative decisions. In addition, audits seem to be linked to the growth of large-scale business enterprises — the modern corporation.

At the same time, the United States seems to be something of an outlier in its embrace of audits and quantification. No other country has embraced audits in education, war making, public works, and compensation of business executives as enthusiastically as has America. Contrary to our self-image as a nation of rugged individualists, Americans are among the most normalized and monitored people in the world. This being the case, the rise of audit around the world may represent an extension of American influence, in the same way that English spread around the globe in the aftermath of the two world wars. Finally, there is Power's idea of the neoliberal onslaught. To the extent that disputes about evidence are one indication of political ferment, the current craze for audits may indeed represent, as Porter would have it, an attempt to undermine the political bases of the postwar welfare state.

But let us look more closely at the peculiarly American embrace of quantification. This seems to reflect a paradoxical requirement of democracy: the need to justify political decisions in a nominally egalitarian society drives decision makers to find — or invent — objective standards, which in turn obscure political decisions to profoundly undemocratic effect. Perhaps the most fundamental question of quantification concerns the use of evidence in political life. What kind of authority can justify formulating, implementing, and evaluating social policies? A political actor's success in discrediting the evidence offered by political opponents, and substituting its own, can be taken as both cause and consequence of a successful bid for power. However, perhaps the greatest triumph comes in the successful depoliticization of an issue.

The development of American politics has been shaped by the conjunction of high-modernist faith in the efficacy of scientific and technical management, on the one hand, and mass democracy, on the other. High modernism provides an ideological climate in which numerical assessments of quality and decision-making techniques, such as the SAT and cost-benefit analysis, can flourish. As a muscle-bound version of modernism, technical (not literary or artistic) high modernists believe that the great advances in science and technology provided unitary and, for the moment, definitive answers to the design of society, to social policy, to how a city ought to look and function, to how infants ought to be bathed, to how social rewards ought to be distributed, and to how crops ought to be grown. Nothing escaped the hubris of the high-modernist lens: neither the redesigning of *Homo sapiens* through eugenic laws nor the reshaping of the natural world through vast public works.

Applying scientific laws and quantitative measurement to most social problems would, high modernists believed, eliminate sterile debates once the "facts" were known. This lens-on-the-world has a deeply embedded political agenda. It proposes that there are facts (usually numerical) that require no interpretation. Reliance on such facts should reduce the destructive play of narratives, sentiment, prejudices, habits, hyperbole, and emotion generally in public life. A cool, clinical, and quantitative assessment would resolve disputes. Both the passions and the interests would be replaced by neutral, technical judgment.

High modernists aspired to minimize the distortions of subjectivity to achieve what Lorraine Daston has called "a-perspectival objectivity," a view from nowhere. The political order most compatible with this view was the disinterested, impersonal rule of a technically educated elite using its scientific knowledge to regulate human affairs. Partisan politics could only distort their wise decisions. Ultimately, rule on high-modernist lines would install a cosmopolitan ruling class that would, if they had them at all, set aside their nationalisms, their tastes, and their fears and perhaps even their scruples too, so as to govern scientifically. This aspiration was seen as a new "civilizing project." The reformist, cerebral Progressives in early-twentieth-century American politics were the closest thing, on the ground, to carriers of the high-modernist banner. Their gospel of efficiency, technical training, and engineering solutions implied a world directed by a trained, rational, and professional managerial elite.

How would this elite be created and selected? This is where high-modernist claims are, or were originally, a radical departure from a history of privilege and entitlement. The idea of a "meritocracy" is the natural traveling companion of high modernism. (Incidentally, the term "meritocracy" was coined in the late 1950s by the Englishman Michael Young in his dystopian fantasy: "The Rise of the Meritocracy," which mused on the disadvantages, for the working class, of a ruling elite chosen on the basis of IQ scores.) No longer would a ruling class be produced by the accident of noble birth, inherited wealth, or inherited status of any kind. Rulers would be selected, and hence legitimated, by virtue of their skills, intelligence, and demonstrated achievements. Meritocracy meant rule by the intelligent and knowledgeable. Here I pause to observe how many other qualities one might plausibly want in positions of power: compassion, wisdom, courage, and breadth of experience drop out of the meritocrats' account entirely. Intelligence, by the standards of the time, was assumed by most of the educated public to be a measurable quality. Most assumed, furthermore, that intelligence was distributed, if not randomly, then at least far more widely than either wealth or title. The very idea of distributing, for the first time, position and life-chances on the basis of measurable merit was a breath of democratic fresh air. It promised for society as a whole what Napoleon's promise of "careers open to talent" had promised the new professional middle class in France more than a century earlier. What was new was both the breadth of the promise and, at the same time, the industrial Taylorism at its core: the dream of an efficient society achieving maximum production and progress because every bit of human material is deployed to best utilize its capacity. This is the beginning of the vision that changes personnel departments into "Departments of Human Resources." The rationalization that Frederick Taylor had brought to the factory floor could now be applied to society as a whole.

Notions of a measurable meritocracy were democratic in still another sense. Not only did they supersede all claims to privilege by birth, they also severely curtailed the discretionary power previously claimed by professional classes. Historically, the professions operated as trade guilds, setting their own standards, jealously guarding their professional secrets, and brooking no external scrutiny that would overrule their judgment. Lawyers, doctors, chartered accountants, engineers, and professors were hired for their professional judgment — a judgment that was often ineffable and opaque.

How might claims to knowledge and expertise — claims that were not themselves transparent — be legitimated in a mass democracy? No longer was mere certification by the guild sufficient. Implying, as it necessarily does, that the citizen ought passively to defer to the mysterious decision of professionals and their guilds, the claim to expert knowledge is always suspect in a democracy. How, then, to justify the professional privilege of "knowledge elites" who, increasingly, were responsible for "social engineering," for decisions that determined the life-chances of millions of their fellow citizens? Who will have a university education? Where will irrigation works, dams, and regional development funds be located? Who is eligible for scarce medical services and welfare benefits? It is in the conjunction of measurement, meritocracy, and democracy, I believe, that we can understand the runaway success (and later the troubles) of assessment techniques such as the SAT and cost-benefit analysis.

Each technique is an attempt to substitute a transparent, mechanical, explicit, and usually numerical procedure of evaluation for the suspect practices of a professional elite. Each is a rich paradox from top to bottom. The technique is a response to political pressure — the desire of a clamorous public for procedures of decision and, in effect, rationing that are explicit, transparent and, hence, in principle accessible. Although each is a response to public political pressure — and here is one paradox — its success depends absolutely on appearing totally nonpolitical: objective, nonpartisan, evenhanded, and palpably scientific. Beneath this appearance, of course, the technique is deeply political. Its politics are buried deep in the techniques of calculation: in what to measure in the first place, in how to measure it, in conventions of "discounting" and "commensuration," in how observations are translated into numerical values, and in how these numerical values are used for decisions. While fending off charges of bias or favoritism, such techniques — and here is a second paradox — succeed brilliantly in entrenching a political agenda in procedures of calculation that are doubly opaque and inaccessible.

The growth of testing regimens and cost-benefit analysis is not, then, a result of scientific progress, although they use the rhetoric of measurement and neoclassical economics as protective cover. Objectivity and mechanical rationality are a set of liberal political strategies designed to deal with political demands for equal opportunity and political transparency. They are apparently nonpolitical ways of dealing with suspicion, distance, and volume. Thus, as Theodore Porter notes, "it is exactly wrong to assume that technocrats pursue objectivity except insofar as political pressures prevent them from doing so; instead, their mechanical objectivity arises as a response to political pressures to curb their discretionary power." When they are successful politically, the techniques of the SAT, cost-benefit analysis, and, for that matter, the SAT's predecessor, the IQ test, appear as solid, objective, and unquestionable as numbers for blood pressure, thermometer readings, cholesterol levels, and red-blood-cell counts. The readings are perfectly impersonal, and, so far as their interpretation is concerned, "the doctor knows best."

The nonpolitical, impersonal appearance of decisions made by quantitative indices is the key to their political success. The quantitative techniques seem to eliminate the capricious human element in decisions. Indeed, once the techniques with their deeply embedded and highly political assumptions are firmly in place, they do limit the discretion of officials. Charged with bias, the official can claim with some truth, that "I am just cranking the handle" of a nonpolitical decision-making machine. The vital protective cover such anti-politics machines provide helps explain why their validity is of less concern than their standardization, precision, and impartiality. Even if the Social Science Citation Index does not measure the quality of a scholar's work, even if the SAT doesn't really measure intelligence or predict success in college, each constitutes an impartial, precise, public standard, a transparent set of rules and targets. When they succeed, they achieve the necessary alchemy of taking contentious and high-stakes battles for resources, life-chances, mega-project benefits, and status and transmuting them into technical, apolitical decisions presided over by officials whose neutrality is beyond reproach. The criteria for decisions are explicit, standardized, and known in advance. Discretion and politics are made to disappear by techniques that are, at bottom, completely saturated with discretionary choices and political assumptions now shielded effectively from public view.

The Scholastic Aptitude Test

An example familiar to clients of the U.S. education system can be found in the SAT, which, from its inception in 1926, has been the obsession — whether stumbling block or ticket to success — of American teenagers aspiring to higher education. Much has been written attacking it and much in its defense: most recently Nicholas Lemann's fine volume *The Big Test: The Secret History of the American Meritocracy*. I will not repeat the story of the SAT's rise to pedagogical hegemony. Lemann, to whom I am indebted, tells it in great and convincing detail. Three aspects of that history, however, stand out for our purposes. First, the SAT is the lineal successor of various other tests: the Alfred Binet Intelligence Test (1905), Robert Yerkes's Army IQ Tests during World War I, the Iowa Every-Pupil Test, the Stanford Achievement Tests, among others. It has become *the* standard national test and spawned a highly profitable commercial empire: the Educational Testing Service (ETS). Second, its great breakthrough to prominence came in 1959 when Clark Kerr, then president of the University of California system, decided to mandate SAT tests for all in-state applicants. Finally, the problems of validity, "colonization" or "feedback" effects, and the stifling of political debate were all fully understood by at least two "inventors" of the test: Carl Bingham and Banesh Hoffman, later author of *The Tyranny of Testing*.

Whatever the reasons for the preeminence of the SAT in college admissions, the validity of the test as a measure of aptitude is not one of them. It is absolutely clear that aptitude or intelligence comes in many forms: aesthetic, combinatorial, mechanical, metaphoric, imaginative, syllogistic, emotional, to name but a few. Correlations between such aptitudes, assuming each could be measured, would probably be insignificant. The SAT, however, encourages us to think of aptitude or acquired intelligence as a single, testable quality. Well, double quality, actually: "Verbal and Quantitative," although for many purposes it is the combined score that counts. The two conceits behind the SAT are that a single, scalable metric can be devised to evaluate aptitude and that, for any individual, that metric provides a stable index of scholastic aptitude. Even in this last, restricted sense, the SAT fails its own test. Scholastic Aptitude Test scores explain only 18 percent of the variance in first-year college grades. Would we want to allocate one of life's great sweepstakes prizes on *this* basis without careful reflection and debate?

And yet, the SAT has become what Lemann calls a "National Personnel Department," allocating a principal means to prestige, wealth, challenging work, and comfort in a race that is substantially done by age eighteen. It is arguably the key mechanism for reward distribution in our society, and, as

Lemann notes, it has never been politically debated in a serious and public fashion.

Let us recall, as with high modernism and meritocracy generally, the democratic impulse at the origin of the SAT. Harvard president James Bryant Conant, patron of Henry Chauncey (who founded the Educational Testing Service, which administers the SAT), was an unabashed proponent of meritocracy against considerable opposition. He believed that higher education should be reserved for a small, intellectual aristocracy (his word, borrowed from Jefferson) selected openly and democratically on the basis of mental aptitude tests. Not only did he believe that standardized tests could measure intellectual talent; he believed that too many students then benefiting from higher education were undeserving. He was out to unseat what Lemann calls the "Episcopacy," or what one might call the WASPocracy. His plan would end the customary, cozy relationship whereby the Harvard or Yale admissions head would ask his friend at Andover or Groton or Saint Paul's to send a few of their "best boys." It would curtail the discretionary power of teachers' nonstandardized grades and recommendations as well as the tastes and prejudices of admissions officers.

That prejudices might prevail behind a cloak of vague general standards is a documented fact. Jerome Karabel's close study of admissions at Princeton, Yale, Harvard, and Columbia from 1840 to 1940 is a striking case. To recapitulate it briefly, all four schools had, until roughly 1920, admitted the sons of alumni (most especially of wealthy contributors) who, they thought, could do the work. The rest of the class was filled out largely on the basis of school grades and tests that each school administered separately. Beginning in 1918, this system roughly doubled the percentage of Jews in the entering freshman class. Alumni complained and threatened to withhold support, while anxious administrators, even the few who were not themselves anti-Semitic, began to run for cover. By 1921, Harvard, Yale, and Princeton collectively invented the concept of the "well-rounded applicant," the purpose of which I will leave to your imagination. Columbia, incidentally, being in New York City and having a somewhat different constituency, did not adopt the "well-rounded" policy and became more heavily Jewish. By 1922, the percentage of Jews in the freshman class at the other schools had returned to their pre-1918 levels.

By contrast, the ideal of relying almost entirely on a standardized, non-discriminatory, open, and transparent aptitude test seemed a nearly utopian step away from a dark past of prejudice, patronage, and intrigue. It is, despite its manifold shortcomings, still the only common standard by which students from various backgrounds and school environments can be compared. Valid or not, it is the only common coin of the educational realm. Moreover, it provides an identifiable, public target for achievement. Students, their parents, and teachers all know more or less what it takes to succeed and, as we shall see, they take great pains to beat the system. Plagued with pathologies though the system is, one would hesitate to abandon it altogether if the only alternative were the system it replaced.

Colonization

I've grasped for metaphors that would convey how one small measurement—one that has little validity or predictive value—could have come to have such a huge impact. Malevolent viruses, minute but murderous, come to mind. Let's just say that with respect to education, the SAT is not just the tail that wags the dog. It has reshaped the dog's breed, its appetite, its surroundings, and the lives of all those who care for it and feed it. Let's refer to this phenomenon as "colonization."

In emphasizing how deeply the SAT has transformed or colonized the world around it, I am telling a story that is both particular and generic. Were this not the United States, I could just as easily be telling a story about "exam hell" in Japan, France, Hong Kong, India, Brazil, and many other countries where a single national exam (often more substantive than our own) is decisive in allocating careers and life-chances. Confining ourselves to national tests misses just how generic and modern this story is. It could be applied, with minor modifications, to almost any quantitative audit system deployed by powerful institutions to measure, by a single metric, a quality that is decisive for the distribution of resources, status, and opportunity.

Let's begin with the obvious. In theory, SAT scores are (like their ancestor the IQ) assumed to be stable for each person and hence uncoachable. However, there's a man named Stanley Kaplan who has built a multimillion-dollar business on the proposition that if you go to school with him, he'll improve your score. Many studies (not to mention his bank balance) have shown he is right. His flyers on campus cry out: "Get a Higher Score, Anytime, Anywhere"; "Kaplan Gets You In"—not just to college but into law school, business school, medical school, graduate school, or dental school via all the tests that the Educational Testing Service has devised for these professional schools. He proclaims himself "The World Leader in Test Prep[aration]."

Kaplan is the tip of the iceberg. He saw his tutoring, from the 1930s on, as a "poor man's private school," giving outsiders, particularly Jews, a chance at advancement. Toward the base of the iceberg, there are thousands of cram courses and tutoring schemes working toward the same end. Stressing the generic quality of the feedback effect of the SAT, consider, for a moment, the larger effort in education to turn mere observations and decision criteria into targets. There are now thousands of educational consultants paid by anxious, wealthy families to secure their children's admission to anything from a quality kindergarten to an Ivy League college. They teach three-year-olds to make "eye contact" and to demonstrate both leadership and sharing in kindergarten interviews. They not only recommend SAT prep courses, they steer their charges into volunteer work, hobbies, and summer activities that will fit the "profile" desired by a good college, help craft application essays, and coach applicants for interviews. Thus, the perfectly reasonable expectations of college admissions officials have worked their way back to colonize the lives of aspiring teenagers in order to produce the simulacrum of what is required. I needn't remind you that money counts in this game; consultants and expensive prep courses are for the middle classes and higher. If this isn't the tail wagging the dog, I don't know what would be. Whole schools are now hiring firms like Achieva and the Princeton Review (aka ETS) to improve their records in college admissions.

Most demoralizing, perhaps, the SAT increasingly wags the curriculum dog in the schools themselves. In 2001, Richard Atkinson, former director of the National Science Foundation, an expert in testing, and president of the University of California System, recommended that the California universities drop the SAT I, which tests abstract reasoning, and substitute for it tests on specific subjects taught in high school. Why? Because he was shocked to see twelve-year-olds drilled week after week in test-taking skills and sample questions at the expense of coursework. The term "teaching to the test," now part of the language, expresses precisely that an observation with power behind it becomes a target and colonizes the very facts it is designed to record. To the degree that the SAT prevails, it encourages a more-or-less uniform national curriculum, thereby stifling educational diversity and experimentation. "Teaching to the test" occurs nearly everywhere, and we may expect it to flourish under President Bush's conception of school accountability via standardized tests. It thrived in Texas under Governor Bush's testing regimen, with students spending six weeks and more preparing for the dreaded TAAS (Texas Assessment of Academic Skills). Several districts (including that of Austin) have been caught cheating to improve scores — not surprisingly, since districts, principals, and teachers can be rewarded or punished based on the results they achieve. Nor is Texas a deviant case. In Nassau County, New York, on Long Island, fourth graders spend half their time for two months in the fall on "test prep" for a mandated reading exam and a like amount of time for two months in the spring preparing for the math and science exam. In New York City, ex–school chancellor Rudy Crew, who had removed five district supervisors for flat or declining test scores, cited thirty-two schools (two principals and forty-three teachers) for cheating by helping students with the answers or simply providing pre-prepared answer forms.

Accountability by standardized tests, born of anxiety, distrust, and quantitative management techniques, has, then, produced a kind of rote, technique-driven Frankenstein's monster in the classroom — often achieving the quantitative results sought, but without the substance. Having devised a currency of quantity to represent the gold of qualitative achievement, the educational "reformers" are repaid in fool's gold by an ironic alchemy. Much of the curriculum in elementary and high school has been "reverse-engineered" to raise scores on the SAT and other mandated tests. The Educational Testing Service promotes this retrofitting. It advertises curriculum programs tailored to the SAT: "Test Prep from the Test-Makers." First they sell the American educational system a yardstick, and then they sell the kit needed to measure up.

Happily, since I began this essay, a small but promising social movement of students and parents protesting "teaching to the test" has blossomed. In western Massachusetts several hundred tenth-grade students boycotted the first of eleven days of tests to call attention to the effects of testing on their education. Two hundred Illinois students boycotted the new State English and Math Exams. Rallies against the effects of mandatory testing, often with the encouragement of teachers and parents, have been held in Louisiana, Florida, Wisconsin, and Ohio.

The "colonization" or "feedback" effect, however, doesn't end there; it goes far deeper. At one level, it is the business of the test makers (and the ETS as a private company dominating college admissions testing is unique in the Western world) to push their tests aggressively. An encrusted set of interests develops: testing bureaucracies, test writers and publishers, curriculum developers, specialized teachers and counselors. Stanley Kaplan and all the other "test-beaters" are implicated too. They all feed the beast. The tests, though originally designed to assess individual abilities, have spawned a new world of statistics and comparison, heavily freighted with rewards and punishments. Teachers, principals, schools, and whole districts are judged by the average scores their students get — and woe to the administrator who cannot show improving scores. Little wonder that creative principals and supervisors have devised strategies to show apparent results, the same way a business can, by inventive accounting, produce a quarterly earnings statement that pleases investors, perhaps at the long-run expense of the enterprise itself. In Texas, a Mexican American group charged that schools were holding back minority ninth-graders who they feared would fail the tenth-grade exam. Many of those held back were discouraged and dropped out of school, thereby further improving the school's report card at the expense of the students. Since the schools are also downgraded for producing dropouts, those leaving were classified as "transfers." Some schools have artificially inflated the numbers of learning-disabled students, whose scores are treated separately, to improve their standing. Finally, and most abjectly, quite a few states, finding that many of their students were failing the state-standardized tests, simply lowered the passing grade.

Scholastic Aptitude Test scores have a flourishing life of their own outside the classroom. High average scores boost real-estate values; municipal bond rates are more advantageous in high SAT zones. Test scores combine with other indicators to form the all-important "scoreboard" ranking of colleges and universities by *US News and World Report*. In turn, this generates pressures to select only applicants with high scores, so as to raise the institution's standing and to encourage otherwise noncompetitive applications in order to appear more selective. The SAT has so reshaped education after its monochromatic image that what it observes are largely the effects of what it has itself conjured up.

The SAT system has, over the past half century, been opening and closing possible futures for millions of students. It has helped fashion an elite. Little wonder that the same elite looks favorably on the system that helped its members get to the front of the pack. It is just open enough, transparent enough, and impartial enough to allow elites and non-elites to regard it as a fair national competition for advancement. More than wealth or birth ever could, it allows the winners to see their reward as merited and deserved, although the correlations between SAT scores and socioeconomic status are enough to convince an impartial observer that this is no open door. The SAT has selected an elite that is more impartially chosen than its predecessor, more legitimate, and hence better situated to defend and reinforce the institution responsible for the "naturalization of its excellence."

In the meantime, our political life is impoverished. The hold of the SAT convinces many middle-class whites that affirmative action is a stark choice between objective merit on the one hand and rank favoritism on the other. We are deprived of a public dialogue about how educational opportunity ought to be allocated in a democratic and pluralistic society. We are deprived of a debate about what qualities we might want in our elites, individually and collectively. We are deprived of a debate about how different skills might be taught and evaluated in and out of schools, insofar as curriculums simply echo the tunnel vision of the SAT.

One might ask what, if anything, makes the SAT worse than other methods of selecting college students. Don't European- and Asian-style substantive tests also select one group of people to receive a university education and sentence the rest to less remunerative or interesting occupations? Don't they just reflect the values and interests of the political and social elite, in that a certain body of knowledge is declared canonical and made mandatory? And, insofar as performance in all education systems is enhanced by what a child learns at home, isn't there always some potential for the reinforcement of existing class divisions and the reproduction of an inherited elite?

Yes, all this may be true. Yet there is still a significant difference between the two systems: the degree of *depoliticization*. In the European case, the policy is overt: students who have mastered a certain officially prescribed body of knowledge are rewarded with admission to university. As a result, it is possible to argue about the content of the examinations, the criteria for admission to university, and, in fact, the purpose and fairness of the whole system. In the case of the United States, there is almost no acknowledgment that the SAT is, indeed, a policy that tests students' knowledge and produces winners and losers. Thus, a student's score is turned into an objective fact that confers (or ought to confer) an entitlement to receive a particular kind of education and ultimately social status, rather than being seen as the highly contingent outcome of a particular set of political decisions and social conditions.

As I suggested earlier, instances of this pathology are not limited to the education system. Indeed, the contemporary polity is pervaded by them. Here's an innocuous example. Customer-relations personnel at Amazon.com were rated, on a monthly basis, on their average "call-resolution-time": how long it took to serve the customer or answer his or her query or complaint. One employee, noting late in the month that his average was well below the standard, quickly improved that average by answering call after call with "Hello, Thank you for calling Amazon.com" and then immediately hanging up.

Here's a not-so-innocuous example. The desire for measures of performance that were quantitative, impersonal, and objective were, of course, integral to the management techniques brought from General Motors to the Pentagon by "whiz kid" Robert McNamara and applied to the war in Indochina. In a war without clearly demarcated battlefronts, how could one gauge progress? McNamara told General William Westmoreland, "General, show me a graph that will tell me whether we are winning or losing in Vietnam." The result was at least two graphs: one, the most notorious, was an index of attrition, in which the "body counts" of confirmed enemy personnel killed in action were aggregated. Officers were under enormous pressure to show progress and knew that the figures influenced promotions, decorations, and rest-and-recreation decisions. The body counts swelled. Any ambiguity between civilian and military casualties was elided; virtually all dead bodies became enemy military personnel. Soon, the total of enemy dead exceeded the known combined strength of the Viet Cong and the North Vietnamese forces. Yet in the field, the enemy was anything but exhausted.

The second index was an effort to take the measure of civilian sympathies in the campaign to Win Hearts and Minds (WHAM). At its core was the Hamlet Evaluation System: every one of southern Vietnam's 12,000 hamlets was classified, according to an elaborate scheme, as "pacified," "contested," or "hostile." Pressure to show progress was again unrelenting. Ways were found to show improvement: fudging figures, creating paper "self-defense militias" that would have made Czarina Catherine's Minister Potemkin proud, and ignoring incidents of insurgent activity. Outright fraud, though not rare, was less common than the understandable tendency to resolve all ambiguities in the direction that the incentives for evaluation and promotion invited. Gradually, the graphs suggested, the countryside was being pacified.

McNamara had created an infernal audit system that not only produced a mere simulacrum — a "command performance," as it were — of legible progress but also blocked a wider-ranging dialogue about what might, under these circumstances, represent progress. He might instead have heeded a real scientist's words: Einstein's "Not everything that counts can be counted and not everything that can be counted counts."

An example drawn from a different field of public policy illustrates a particularly striking feature of audits and quantitative indices: when taken to their logical extreme they actually *undermine* the power and authority of technocratic experts. A contrast is often drawn between the use of audit techniques by the U.S. Army Corps of Engineers and the emphasis on professional judgment by the French Ponts et Chaussées. Both institutions were created to supervise the planning and execution of large-scale public works projects such as the construction of roads, bridges, and dams. Yet their decision-making procedures were strikingly different. The staff of Ponts et Chaussées (the earlier institution and actually the model for the Corps of Engineers) were humanistically educated men who based their claim to authority on a sense of judgment developed by training and experience. They were expected to use that judgment to decide which projects would be in the national interest. In contrast, since 1926, the Corps of Engineers has been encumbered with an increasingly detailed set of decision rules based on the principles of cost-benefit analysis. The Corps of Engineers was supposed to evaluate proposed public works using a point system, in which the advantages and disadvantages of each proposal were assigned a fixed value. The project could proceed only if the benefits outweighed the costs, as expressed by the total points. Porter attributes these rules to an American "lack of trust in bureaucratic elites" and suggests that the United States "relies on rules to control the exercise of official judgment to a greater extent than any other industrialized democracy" (a point I shall return to at the end of my remarks). Thus, the audit, with its attempt to achieve total objectivity by suppressing all discretion, represents both the apotheosis of technocracy and its nemesis.

The point here is not that one system is really more democratic or more scientific than the other. As you can probably guess, the principles of cost-benefit analysis are not entirely determinate and are subject, shall we say, to a certain degree of manipulation. Rather, the distinction lies in the degree to which the political process underlying the decision is obfuscated. True, in both cases, an act with significant distributive consequences — a political act — is transformed into a technical procedure. In the Ponts et Chaussées, by contrast, the exercise of authority is at least not concealed: it resides with the bureaucrats. In the case of the Corps of Engineers, responsibility for the decision is completely evaded. In theory, the decision to build or not to build emerges logically and ineluctably out of a set of legislatively given rules. Thus, as in the contrast between the SAT and foreign examination systems, the real difference lies in the degree of depoliticization.

Finally, a more recent instance of this dynamic, with which many American investors have become sadly familiar, is furnished by the use of stock options as a form of executive compensation in major corporations such as Enron. This method of payment, ostensibly intended to reward executives for good management by linking their pay to business performance as measured by shareholder value, instead gave both executives themselves and the accounting firms they retained (i.e., their auditors!) an incentive to cook the books. In order to boost the value of their stock portfolios, they inflated profits and played down losses so that others would be conned into buying stock. In effect, executives were paid for "creating the illusion of success, never mind the reality," as economist Paul Krugman puts it. Thus, the attempt to make executive performance completely transparent by replacing salaries, given as a reward for labor and expertise, with stock option plans, backfired. This experience also illustrates the tendency in an "audit society" to replace the exercise of discretion and judgment with mechanistic, supposedly objective calculations. It also illustrates what we might call the political neutrality of audits. They are available for capture by just about any interest group that wants to make its own preferences look like objective truth. In the case of Enron and related business scandals, the mystique of numbers was used to lull investors and regulators into a misplaced confidence in the financial health of the corporations in question.

In closing, I would like to sketch what lessons the rise of audit and quantification holds for us as citizens. As we have seen, the drive for quantification often responds to legitimate or at least plausible critiques of an existing entrenched bureaucratic structure. The American higher education system *was* indeed extremely elitist before the 1940s; British research funding *was* tilted to a few privileged universities before the 1980s; French bureaucrats in the Ponts et Chaussées *did* wield enormous power over the placement of public works, possibly more than is compatible with a democratic polity. Nonetheless, our examples also suggest the dangers of overreliance on quantitative indices to represent huge complex realities such as success in war, a student's merit, or a scholar's productivity. So where do we draw the line between justified quantification, which seeks to achieve transparency, objectivity, democratic control, and egalitarian social outcomes, with metastasized quantification, which replaces and indeed stifles political discussions about the proper course of public policy?

We surely cannot conclude that all official uses of audit methods are wrong and foolish. Rather, we need to find ways to distinguish between sensible and dangerous uses of numbers. When confronted by audit or quantitative indices, we should ask ourselves a few questions. I would suggest asking questions that respond to the concerns I listed at the beginning of this essay and then explored: the presence or lack of construct validity, the possibility of "antipolitics," and the colonization or feedback danger. Thus, we as citizens should ask ourselves:

1. What is the relation between the proposed quantitative index and the thing in the world that it is supposed to measure? (For example, does the SAT accurately represent a student's aptitude or, more broadly, whether he or she deserves to go to college?)

2. Is a political question being hidden or evaded under the guise of quantification? (For example, did the "hamlet evaluation" point system and the "body count" method obfuscate the American debate about whether the Vietnam War was wise or indeed winnable?)

3. What are the possibilities for colonization or subversion of the index, such as misreporting, feedback effects, or the prejudicing of other substantive goals? (Does reliance on the SSCI in American universities lead to the publication of lousy articles or the phenomenon of "citation rings"?)

In short, I am not proposing an attack on quantitative methods, whether in the academy or in the polity. But we do need to demystify and desacralize numbers, to insist that they cannot always answer the question we are posing. And we do need to recognize debates about the allocation of scarce resources for what they are — politics — and what they are not — technical decisions. We must begin to ask ourselves whether the use of quantification in a particular context is likely to advance or hinder political debate, and whether it is likely to achieve or undermine our political goals.

7

Neither Capitalist nor American: The Democracy as Social Movement

MICHAEL DENNING

The *Democratic Vistas* project is a curious one: an undemocratic institution celebrating its tercentennial with a series of essays on democracy. After all, the dominant ethos at universities like Yale is neither a democratic one nor a market one (one is not allowed to buy and sell grades or degrees, or to hire people to write your papers and take your tests, and we regularly refuse to allow people to buy or invest in our goods if we think they are not "good" enough). Rather the Yale ethos is meritocratic: rule by those with merit, leadership by those with high SAT scores. Meritocratic vistas, perhaps. A merit system of promotion has many virtues — self-reliance, self-love, and self-invention, among them — but democratic it is not. This curious combination of an antidemocratic and antimarket ethos is what gives the Ivy League its paradoxical reputation of being a "liberal elite."

Moreover, during the past sixty years, the university has resisted at every turn the struggles on its campus to establish the basic democratic rights of employees to union organization. To this day, graduate teachers and hospital workers at the Yale–New Haven Hospital have yet to win the basic democratic rights — affirmed in a variety of international human rights instruments — to form a union, to bargain collectively, and to strike.

Perhaps, however, one should not be surprised at undemocratic institutions deciding to define democracy. After all, there is a long tradition of antidemocrats defining democracy, a tradition that goes back to the early American federalists like Madison and Hamilton and continues in the twentieth century with figures like Joseph Schumpeter and Samuel Huntington. What does it mean when antidemocrats like Huntington, who twenty-five years ago was warning against the excesses of democracy, was seen as the champion of a "third wave" of world democratization in the last quarter of the twentieth century? What do we make of the fact that the rise of political democracy around the world — celebrated in an enormous scholarly literature on the "transition to democracy" — has been accompanied by a global collapse of social democracy: the savaging of social safety nets, welfare systems, and price subsidies and the global privatization of public lands, public industries, and public services — a new round of enclosures?

The Yale celebration of democracy assumes that, as Dean Kronman puts it in his essay in this volume, we are all democrats now. In a sense, this has been true for half a century: in 1951, a United Nations Educational, Scientific, and Cultural Organization report noted that "for the first time in the history of the world, no doctrines are advanced as antidemocratic: practical politicians and political theorists agree in stressing the democratic element in the institutions they defend and the theories they advocate." And for Americans, this is hard to resist: the United States, we are regularly told, was the first democratic state. "The Revolution created American democracy," the historian Gordon S. Wood writes, and "made Americans . . . the first people in the modern world to possess a truly democratic government and society." A student could be forgiven for thinking that the title of Alexis de Tocqueville's famous book was "democracy is America," even though Tocqueville himself warned against confusing "what is democratic with what is only American": "We should therefore give up looking at all democratic peoples through American spectacles and try at last to see them as they actually are." It is worth recalling that for Tocqueville, with all his limitations as a democrat, democracy was not simply about elections: it was about "the equality of conditions." The United States was a democracy, he argued, because it had no proletarians and no tenant farmers; and he explicitly said that his account of democracy pertained only to "the parts of the country where there is no slavery." However, our latter-day democrats have dropped "equality of conditions" from their definitions. The "great" theoretical accomplishment of Schumpeter was simply to redefine democracy as the free market in votes: democracies are states not where the people rule, nor where there is equality of condition, but simply where ruling elites compete for votes in the marketplace of the election. It is not surprising that democracy and capitalism emerge as virtual synonyms and that "democratic capitalism" appears to be the global consensus.

For America, for free markets, and for Yale. It's almost enough to make you give up the term: if that's democracy, I want no part of it. But is that democracy? What do we mean by "democracy"? Is it the name of a type of political regime? Much of what counts as the debate over democracy pits "utopian" theorists who tell us what democracy should look like against "tough-minded" realists who use "minimal" definitions of democracy to describe what we might call "actually existing democracy." In this essay, I would like to cut across this debate by reflecting on the history of democracy, arguing that democracy is neither American nor capitalist but is, rather, the social movement that fought for and created the democratic institutions of the state and civil society that we have. Indeed one of the earliest names for that social movement was *the Democracy*. Moreover, since every democratic victory is threatened by powerful forces opposed to democracy, the democracy remains the social movements that fight to preserve and extend those democratic institutions. We are *not* all democrats.

The Democracy

In the years between the 1820s and the 1850s when the modern social movements—the labor movement, the women's movement, the abolitionist movement, and the anticolonial national movements—were invented, a new usage of the word "democracy" appeared, one that seems strange to our ears: "the democracy." "The portion of the people whose injury is the most manifest, have got or taken the title of the 'democracy,'" Thomas Perronet Thompson, one of the philosophical radicals who edited the *Westminster Review,* wrote in 1842. Tocqueville himself, writing in the 1830s, occasionally uses the term in this way: "Is it credible that the democracy which has annihilated the feudal system, and vanquished kings, will respect the citizen and the capitalist?" And John Stuart Mill, in his 1840 review of Tocqueville, writes that "the middle class in this country [that is, England] is as little in danger of being outstripped by the democracy below, as being kept down by the aristocracy above." The *Oxford English Dictionary* places the first use of this meaning of "the democracy" in 1828, and there are clear analogues in French and German. By the time of the Paris Commune, the *Times* of London was capitalizing the term, denouncing the "dangerous sentiment of the Democracy, this conspiracy against civilisation in its so-called capital."

How do we understand this meaning of the democracy? In the eighteenth century, the term "democracy" was rarely used in a positive sense: educated philosophers and political thinkers including the American constitutionalists disparaged it. An extensive study of the rhetoric of "democracy" in North

America concludes that, in the eighteenth century, democracy was a term of derogation: "There were very few men willing to call themselves democrats." Even Gordon Wood admits that "democracy was commonly used vituperatively"; to find a celebration of democracy, he leaps more than a generation to quote "a renegade Baptist" in 1809.

At the same time, among the sailors, the enslaved, indentured servants, and dispossessed peasants who lived through the enclosures, impressments, slave trades, and witch hunts of Atlantic capitalism's primitive accumulation, democracy was not a slogan. The "many-headed hydra" of food rioters, slave rebels, pirates, and heretics whose history has been recovered in the great book of that name by Peter Linebaugh and Marcus Rediker appealed to vernacular hopes and ideals: they spoke of leveling, of the commons, of jubilee, not of democracy. Though the struggles for independence in the North American colonies in the 1770s were a key moment in the development of democratic ideas and institutions, they were not unique: as Linebaugh and Rediker argue, the North American war of independence was itself part of two centuries of insurrection by that "motley crew," ranging from Masaniello's revolt in Naples and the struggles of the Levellers, Diggers, and Ranters in the English Revolution in the 1640s to the wave of eighteenth-century slave rebellions inaugurated by Tacky's Revolt in Jamaica in 1760.

It was into these struggles that "democracy" — one of those Greek and Latin words, like "proletarian," that Renaissance and Enlightenment political theorists with classical education reclaimed from antiquity — began to filter in the 1790s, as a few Jacobin radicals in France, England, and the United States invoked democracy positively. But after two decades of world war between Napoleon's revolutionary empire and Britain's counterrevolutionary empire, little of democracy — as theory, practice, or even as word — remained in the North Atlantic world. Modern democracy — "the democracy" — emerged in two extraordinary decades, the 1830s and 1840s, when the modern social movements — the labor movement, the women's movement, the abolitionist movement, the anti-imperial national movements, and the new ideologies of socialism and communism — were all born. The most comprehensive historian of the word "democracy" notes that its "broad application" does not occur until the 1830s and that 1848 "represents the zenith in the application of 'democracy.'" In England, it was in these years that the Chartists, the first mass working-class movement in the world, and perhaps the largest organization of mass political activity in any European country during the nineteenth century, came to speak of the Democracy as the movement of the people, often capitalizing the word in their press.

In the early 1840s, the young Germans Friedrich Engels and Karl Marx adopted this usage from the Chartists, as they joined "democrats of all nations" in founding the Society of Fraternal Democrats. In the midst of the German revolution of 1848, they subtitled their newspaper "Organ of the Democracy": "Through their personal connections with the heads of the Democratic party in England, France, Italy, Belgium and North America, the editors," they write, "are in a position to reflect the politico-social movement abroad. . . . In this respect, the *Neue Rheinische Zeitung* is the organ not simply of the German but of the European Democracy." The democracy becomes a synonym for the "social movement" — a phrase that also appears first in the 1830s and 1840s — uniting new forms of popular mobilization — marches, rallies, demonstrations, petitions, cheap pamphlets, and newspapers — with new ideologies of emancipation.

In the United States, there are many uses of "the democracy" in this sense in the 1830s and 1840s, although individual instances are tricky to interpret because Andrew Jackson's political alliance successfully appropriated the term for its party: what we in retrospect call the Democratic Party was usually referred to as "the Democracy." So an address to the democracy, a common subtitle of speeches of the era, sometimes means an address to the followers of Jackson and sometimes means simply an address to the people, to the social movement. Abolitionist critics of Jackson's Democracy called themselves the "True Democracy," and the working-class opposition to New York's Tammany Hall called itself the "shirtless" Democracy. Transatlantic connections between "the democrats of all nations" abounded: among the women's rights activists, among abolitionists — Frederick Douglass, like Friedrich Engels, met with Chartists when he was in England in the 1840s — and among radical artisans.

The revolutionary upheavals that broke out throughout the capitalist world-system in 1848 were seen as an act of the democracy: Thomas Carlyle spoke of "this universal revolt of the European populations, which calls itself Democracy" and François Guizot noted that "the chaos today hides itself under a word, Democracy . . . it is the sovereign, universal word." If the democracy was the name of the movement, emancipation was its aim. Emancipation was the great aspiration of the period: with its origins in the abolitionist movement's struggle for the emancipation of the enslaved and in the early-nineteenth-century battles for the political emancipation of Jews in Europe and for Catholic emancipation in Ireland, emancipation becomes the keyword among early women's rights activists and labor activists: "The emancipation of the working classes must be conquered by the working classes themselves," Marx wrote at the formation of the International Working Men's Association.

Within a year or two, however, the revolutionary republics were defeated, the Chartist leaders were imprisoned, the Fugitive Slave Act had been passed, and the democracy was in tatters. In the wake of the defeats, the democracy began to fragment. As a few elite political figures attempted to claim the banner of the democracy, one sees democrats of the social movement beginning to make a separation between political and social democracy, between bourgeois and popular democracy. As early as 1845, Mike Walsh, the tribune of New York's working-class "subterranean" or "shirtless" Democracy, wrote that "no man can be a good political democrat without he's a good social democrat." In 1851, Marx, now in exile in England, satirized Prime Minister Lord Russell's claim that "the Democracy of the country . . . has as fair a right to the enjoyment of its rights as monarchy or nobility," because Lord Russell had redefined the Democracy as "the Bourgeoisie, the industrious and commercial middle class," a "king-loving, lords-respecting, bishop-conserving 'Democracy.' "

If the "democrats of all nations" of 1848 were the founders of the modern democracy, none of them knew the universal-suffrage parliamentary state that we associate with democracy. The democratic state did not exist anywhere by the middle of the nineteenth century. Where did it come from? What is the relation between the democracy and the democratic state?

The Democratic State

Democratic states are youthful institutions, but most claim more ancient lineages. Sixteen eighty-eight, 1776, 1789: it is not only in the United States that we imagine that democracy sprang forth from the rhetoric of a founding bourgeois revolution. In reality, the democratic state — the universal-suffrage parliamentary state, with the freedoms of political opposition — is, as Robert Dahl notes at the beginning of his *On Democracy,* "a product of the twentieth century." Though historians and political scientists argue about the history of particular countries and the criteria of the democratic state — the extent of the franchise, of freedom of opposition, of peaceful alternation of regimes — there is general agreement that the universal-suffrage state first emerged in the late nineteenth century and early twentieth century and was well established only after the Second World War.

Nevertheless, democratic states are often called capitalist or bourgeois, as if they were created, fostered, and supported by capitalists. "No bourgeoisie, no democracy," Barrington Moore wrote in 1966, and few on the left or the right would have disagreed. It was precisely this analysis that had led one tradition of Marxism — that of Lenin — to reject "bourgeois democracy" completely. But a quarter century of scholarship — going back to a pioneering essay by

Göran Therborn — has fundamentally transformed our understanding of the roots of the democratic state. The democratic state may have emerged in capitalist societies, but not because capitalists created it. Rather, capitalism creates and strengthens large working classes, and, to quote the major comparative history of democratic states in Europe, North America, and South America, "the working class, not the middle class, was the driving force behind democracy."

The details of this history are beyond the scope of this essay. However, let me briefly make three points. First, the argument that working-class self-organization was central to democracy makes sense of the timing of the universal-suffrage parliamentary states: they were first decisively, though not irrevocably, won not in the age of Capital, the great boom years of the 1850s and 1860s, but a half century later, as a result of the organization of workers in the labor movements and socialist parties of the Second International and the revival of the women's movement in the militant new "feminism" of the suffrage campaigns. Bourgeois democracy, Therborn rightly notes, was the "principal historical accomplishment" of the Second International. Schumpeter himself recognizes this; his *Capitalism, Socialism, and Democracy* concludes with a historical sketch of the socialist parties.

Second, though the success of democratic reforms depended on the strength of working-class organizations — the weakness of Latin American democracy was in part due to its comparatively small working classes — it is clear that workers were not strong enough to win democratic states on their own in Europe, North America, or South America. Democratic victories depended on alliances with middle classes, either urban or rural, and the middle classes were always an ambivalent ally. They also depended on the weakness or defeat of the most consistent opponents of democracy, the large landlords who depended on cheap agricultural labor. Democracy failed where large landlords were strong enough to control the state. Capitalist development and democracy are therefore correlated because "capitalist development weakens the landed upper class and strengthens the working class."

The bourgeoisie, far from being a driving force behind democracy, was rarely even a positive force. Even the contemporary political scientists most impressed with "capitalist democracy" admit that capitalist elites are not supporters of democracy. Several even suggest that capitalists are so strongly opposed to democracy that political democracy can only exist and thrive if there is a strong party of the right to protect the interest of elites, and if large parts of social and economic life are not subject to political control — if, in other words, issues of social justice are not on the agenda. Without those restrictions, corporate elites support authoritarian attacks on democracy. As

Perry Anderson once noted, though we have yet to see a parliamentary transition to socialism, we have seen parliamentary transitions to fascism.

Third, the argument about the relation between working-class mobilization and democracy is not only a historical one; there is strong evidence that the working classes continue to be the driving force in the democratizations of the late twentieth century. Though little of the "transition to democracy" literature has seriously studied late-twentieth-century workers, the role of Poland's Solidarity, of the black unions of South Africa's Congress of South African Trade Unions, of Brazil's Workers' Party, and of the South Korean strikes of the mid-1990s would indicate that the organization and mobilization of working people continue to be fundamental to the establishment of universal-suffrage parliamentary states.

This account also helps us make some sense of the contradictory assessments of United States democracy: Samuel Huntington claims that the United States is the first democratic country, placing the date at 1828 with suffrage for a bare majority of white men; Therborn, among others, places the United States as the last of the core capitalist democracies, dating it from 1970 with the enfranchisement of black southerners. How do we make sense of this simultaneous "originality" and "belatedness"? The extension of the franchise in the early-nineteenth-century North did create a kind of "democracy" of smallholders, that historians have likened to those of Norway and Switzerland at the same time. But the continental United States was hardly akin to Norway and Switzerland, and what looks from one angle like remarkably early democratic institutions looks from another like a brief and regional exception. In most of Europe, after all, opposition to the extension of the franchise came from two sources: repressive landlords who opposed political rights for the peasantry and capitalists who opposed voting rights for workers. "The American peasantry, however, was," as Alexander Keyssar points out in his history of the right to vote, "peculiar: it was enslaved" and thus not "part of the calculus . . . of suffrage reform." The South was not a democracy but an authoritarian landlord regime. Similarly, as long as industrial workers remained far outnumbered by farmers in the North and West, they were a small part of the calculus of suffrage. In the only state where manufacturing workers outnumbered farmers in the 1840s — Rhode Island — those workers were excluded from political rights. The struggle of Rhode Island workers for the right to vote in 1841–42 resulted in the formation of a People's Convention and a separate, parallel constitution and government that challenged the legitimacy of the state government — a Providence Commune, if you like. An armed confrontation over control of the state arsenal led to the defeat and imprisonment of the suffrage advocates, a history that parallels the struggles of the Chartists across the Atlantic. The spokesman of the Dorr Rebellion, the carpenter Seth Luther, author of *Address on the Right of Free Suffrage,* stands as one of the great plebian theorists of democracy.

With the end of slavery and the growth of an immigrant working class, the United States witnessed a half century of disfranchisement, "a sustained nationwide contraction of suffrage rights." By the early twentieth century, the United States was not a democratic state; the present democratic state in the United States was the consequence of the self-organization of industrial workers in the Council of Industrial Organizations during the 1930s and 1940s and the self-organization of black Americans in the Civil Rights Movement of the 1950s and 1960s. From Seth Luther fighting for the suffrage in Providence to Robert Moses and Fannie Lou Hamer fighting for voting rights in Mississippi: that has been the line of the Democracy, not the antidemocratic meditations of Hamilton and Madison.

If we understand the close historical tie between the Democracy in the nineteenth-century sense—the social movements of working people—and democratic institutions of universal suffrage and freedom of assembly and speech, we see as well the mistake made by many contemporary scholars of democracy who would artificially separate "political democracy" from "social democracy." For just as there is a close correlation between the strength of democratic politics and that of working-class organization, so there is a close correlation between the strength of welfare states and that of working-class mobilization. As Alexander Hicks notes in his recent study of social democracy and welfare capitalism, "Even though democracy did not open the floodgate to demands for mass redistribution, it did function . . . as a sluice gate that permitted an ample flow of income security reforms." This is the case even outside the North Atlantic states: Patrick Heller's recent study of Kerala state in India notes that "under the impetus of a broad-based working-class movement organized by the Communist Party, successive governments in Kerala have pursued what is arguably the most successful strategy of redistributive development outside the socialist world. Direct redistributive measures have included the most far-reaching land reforms on the subcontinent and labor market interventions that, combined with extensive unionization, have pushed both rural and informal sector wages well above regional levels. . . . On all indicators of the physical quality of life Kerala far surpasses any Indian state and compares favorably with the more developed nations of Asia." If the universal suffrage state was the historical accomplishment of turn-of-the-century social democracy, the welfare state with its social rights to income security in the face of unemployment, injury, sickness, retirement, and parenting, as well as its right to universal public education, was the democratic work of social democracy after World War II. And the role of the social movement in the struggle for feminist democracy is equally clear: if women's suffrage was the historical accomplishment of the first wave of feminist movements, the reproductive rights of divorce, contraception, and abortion have been the democratic victories of the second wave. Democracy depends on "the democracy."

How then can the savaging of social democracy — the enclosure of the commons, the attack on social rights, and the privatization of public goods — that has taken place over the last two decades be seen as a "wave of democratization"? Why do democratic theorists wax lyrical about civil society, that most undemocratic sphere?

The Democratic Society

The irony of the democratic state has been that the extension of citizenship has been accomplished with a devaluation of the political and a restriction of the powers of the public. The Canadian political theorist Ellen Meiksins Wood has argued that this was the theoretical accomplishment of the American federalists: "It was the anti-democratic victors in the U.S.A. who gave the modern world their definition of democracy, a definition in which the dilution of popular power is an essential ingredient." The "freeing" of the market from the political realm — particularly the market in those two commodities that had rarely been considered alienable, labor and land — made victories in the political realm often hollow. As labor historian David Montgomery wrote of nineteenth-century America: "The more that active participation in government was opened to the propertyless strata of society, the less capacity elected officials seemed to have to shape the basic contours of social life . . . both the contraction of the domain of governmental activity and the strengthening of government's coercive power contributed to the hegemony of business and professional men."

This is now a fundamental part of the theories of "democracy" promoted by the "Washington consensus," which insist that economic or social democracy has nothing to do with political democracy. In fact, they argue that economic decision making must be carefully insulated from political power and from popular pressures for a more thoroughgoing democratization of society. As a result, over the last two decades many of the victories of new democratic states have been undermined by capitalist forces of privatization. Privatization, or what the Midnight Notes group have called the new enclosures, is the devolution of public lands, public industries, and public schooling and services from a realm that is potentially democratic to a realm where democracy rarely exists, a realm euphemistically called "civil society."

"Civil society," we are told by a chorus of its admirers, is the realm of freedom and democracy, the realm of voluntary associations and civic participation, outside the bureaucracies of the state. For Tocqueville, a fundamental part of democracy was freedom of association, and he argued that "Americans of all ages, all stations in life, and all types of disposition are forever forming associations." "If men are to remain civilized or to become civilized," he wrote, "the art of association must develop and improve among them." This was the closest Tocqueville came to the new socialisms of his era, for association was a common synonym for socialism in the 1830s and 1840s. Unfortunately, it was at this point that Tocqueville made a fateful conflation of what he called "intellectual and moral associations" and "manufacturing and trading companies." In Tocqueville and especially in his revivalists, capitalist enterprises are seen as simply one form of "civil association," whose free activity is necessary to the preservation of equality and liberty: this is one source of theories of "democratic capitalism." The same slippage can be seen in the German tradition that gave us the concept of "civil society": the German term *bürgerliche Gesellschaft* means both "civil society" and "bourgeois society."

However, if democracy has its limits even inside the universal-suffrage parliamentary state, rarely penetrating beyond the legislative branch through to the high courts or the bureaucratic apparatuses of the civil services, not to mention the national security state, it hardly exists outside the state. One finds little or no democracy in the institutions of "civil society," and particularly in those "manufacturing and trading companies." As the Italian political theorist Norberto Bobbio put it, "The present problem of democracy no longer concerns 'who' votes but 'where' we vote. Today, if you want an indication of the development of democracy in a country, you must consider not just the number of people with the right to vote, but also the number of different places besides the traditional area of politics in which the right to vote is exercised." There is a long tradition that has attempted to theorize socialism as a form of "economic democracy" or "industrial democracy," extending the procedures of representative democracy into the workplace. It goes back to John Stuart Mill and includes figures like Bertrand Russell, John Dewey, and Robert Dahl. But unlike extensions of the franchise, there has been little advance in the rights of what the Europeans called "co-determination." It was on the agenda of the European social democratic parties, particularly in Sweden, in the late 1970s, only to fall victim to the counterrevolution against social democracy mounted by Reagan and Thatcher. A quarter century later, those issues—the possibilities for the democratic control of the workplace and the labor process, for the democratic control of a firm's capital and investment, and for democratic elections of corporate and university boards, in short, the democratization of "civil society" — are hardly visible, though they will be on the agenda of the democracy of the twenty-first century.

Rather, at the present, the counterdemocracy has set the agenda. The centrality in people's lives of "civil society," including economic relations, has profoundly undemocratic effects. As a Human Rights Watch report released on Labor Day 2000 established, "Workers' freedom of association is under sustained attack in the United States, and the government is often failing its responsibility under international human rights standards to deter such attacks and protect workers' rights." The report continues: "Millions of workers are expressly barred from the law's protection of the right to organize. United States legal doctrine allowing employers to permanently replace workers who exercise the right to strike effectively nullifies the right. Mutual support among workers and unions recognized in most of the world as legitimate expressions of solidarity is harshly proscribed under United States law as illegal secondary boycotts. . . . [There are] millions of part-time, temporary, subcontracted, and otherwise 'atypical' or 'contingent' workers whose exercise of the right to freedom of association is frustrated by the law's inadequacy." The report goes on to say that "in general, workers who want to organize and bargain collectively should have the right to organize and bargain collectively, except where there are manifestly no employers to bargain with or where the essence of such workers' jobs is so truly managerial or supervisory that they effectively would be bargaining with themselves."

The Human Rights Watch report tells the story of the destruction of unions and lives with the permanent replacement of strikers in towns ranging from Pueblo, Colorado, to Jay, Maine, and Bisbee, Arizona: the "United States is almost alone in the world in allowing permanent replacement of workers who exercise the right to strike." It also gives many examples of the attack on the right to organize, drawn from all sectors of the economy: from primarily black workers in hog-processing plants in North Carolina to "perma-temps" working for Microsoft in the Northwest, from Mexican American and Mexican agricultural workers in the orchards of Washington and the fruit and vegetable fields of North Carolina to Asian and Latina immigrant women working in garment sweatshops in New York, from largely Haitian American nursing-home workers in Florida to shipyard workers in New Orleans.

This attack on the right to organize has also characterized the nonprofit institutions of "civil society," such as Yale University, over the last decade, as graduate teachers and hospital workers have attempted to form unions. As Rebecca Ruquist, a graduate teacher in the French Department and an organizer for the Graduate Employees and Students Organization (GESO), told a Yale audience,

I have taught two semesters of French 115, two semesters of French 130, both of which met five days a week, where I did the teaching, the grading, and all of the work for the course except for syllabus design. When I told the Director of Graduate Studies in my department a year ago that I was going to become GESO's next Chair, he fought with me for an hour about how I was wasting my time, and how ungrateful graduate students were to want a union. When in a meeting I suggested to the current DGS that she advocate for her graduate students with the administration, she pulled me into her office alone to lecture me about keeping graduate school issues out of department meetings. She promised me that she would include a mention of my GESO organizing in a future letter of recommendation. Both professors have refused to declare their neutrality towards GESO organizing in the department to the French Ph.D. students. This is wrong: it is our right to organize a union here, and faculty need to respect that. The Yale administration should not ask professors to bust their own teaching assistants' union. Yale needs more than to live up to the letter of the law, it needs to live up to the spirit of the law.

Similarly, Peg Tamulevich, a secretary in Medical Records who has worked at the Yale–New Haven Hospital for twenty-three years, said: "I have joined with many of my co-workers at the hospital to organize a union. We want better patient care, wages and benefits, but more importantly, we want respect. When I was handing out union leaflets outside the hospital, police officers with guns, who are employed by Yale–New Haven, told me that I would be arrested and forced me to stop. This is just one example of the intimidation tactics used by the hospital. I care deeply about our democracy in America. At Yale–New Haven Hospital, the fight for democracy is an everyday battle." Incidents like these are echoed throughout the case studies in the Human Rights Watch report: the one-on-one "meetings" with workers and the use of police and security services to harass organizers. Employers regularly walk just inside the law, and just as regularly break it, since there is no punishment for lawbreakers: under United States labor statutes, employers found guilty of violating a worker's rights only have to post a notice saying they won't do it again.

What does this have to do with democracy? When I was first approached about contributing to the DeVane lectures, I was asked to speak on democracy and the labor market. The "labor market": that peculiar term is the only guise in which work and workers appear in contemporary economics. Economists don't get up in the morning to go to work; they go off to truck and barter their human capital. For most of us, however, capitalism remains what Marx described: "anarchy in the social division of labor, despotism in that of the workshop." The labor market is an anarchic world we try to avoid as much as possible—by getting a job. We don't work in the never-never land of free market economics; we sell our weekdays in order to buy our weekends. The reality of capitalism is not the market but the working day, day after day. Even Tocqueville recognized that "between workman and master there are frequent relations but no true association." The workplace remains the fundamental *unfree* association of civil society, without civil liberties or rights, without freedom of speech and with little freedom of association, assembly, or opposition.

And yet, the difficult, exhausting, and often demoralizing struggle to organize and mobilize in the workplace has, as I have tried to suggest, been one of the fundamental driving forces of modern democracy. Unions, like other institutions, have their flaws, but they remain the most democratic institution of civil society, voluntary associations where leaders are elected in contested elections, where oppositions can organize, where ordinary people represent themselves. As a result, vital unions are central to a vital democracy; the decay and collapse of unions, as we have witnessed over the past decades, is a decay and collapse of democracy.

In his essay in this volume, Yale University president Richard Levin gives dramatic figures on the inequality of wealth and income in the United States and notes how the degree of inequality has fluctuated in the course of the twentieth century. He hazards a couple of explanations; I would suggest that degree of inequality is inversely related to the degree of working-class mobilization, measured by union density rates. The great drop in inequality was a result of the massive organization of American workers in the Council of Industrial Organizations between the 1930s and the 1950s, and the subsequent rise in inequality followed the concerted attack on and destruction of unions.

Similarly, much has been made in recent years about the decline in civic participation among Americans over the last three decades; we're all bowling alone, as Robert Putnam has famously phrased it. But though he notes the decline in union membership as an aspect of this decline in civic participation, he pays little attention to it, not even noting that that decline was involuntary. There was no organized campaign against people forming bowling leagues; there has been an organized campaign against people forming unions. Across the country, and at Yale University, we have seen repeated attacks—informal and formal—on the attempt to organize and associate. The market has efficiently allocated resources to a thriving industry of anti-union managerial consultants. If graduate teachers are not bowling alone, it is because they are striking together.

Moreover, unions are one of the few forms of civic engagement that are not skewed toward wealthier citizens. Critics of "civic engagement" platitudes have often noted that since those with more time and more money are more likely to participate in politics, civic engagement can have antidemocratic consequences. The historic tendency of the labor movement has been to empower the least powerful, to protect the rights of its members by the practice of what Walt Whitman called the "great word" of democracy: "Solidarity." It is true that unions have often been skewed to workers with more skills and more "market power," especially white and male workers. But the labor movement has struggled to reach across the divisions created by the labor market — divisions between "skilled" and "unskilled," "blue-collar" and "white-collar," the employed and the unemployed, "men's work" and "women's work," "white work" and "colored work" — to forge alliances where an injury to one is an injury to all. Anyone who reads the Human Rights Watch case studies of black, Latino, and women workers battling for their rights on the job can see why the right to organize is now a crucial civil rights issue.

The right to organize is the fundamental democratic issue of our time. One hundred million Americans working for a living do not have the democratic protections of a union. No democratization of civil society or revival of civic participation will be accomplished without their achieving the right to organize; no change in the inequality of wealth and income will come without that organization. Yale's tercentennial should have been a moment for the university to take a modest step toward the democracy and to assume at least a stance of neutrality as its employees decide whether and how to organize and associate. It was not. This may seem a local matter, hardly visible in the distant democratic vista, but the Democracy has always been about the struggles of ordinary people in the here and now.

But this is also a part of a wider struggle against the antidemocratic forces of "globalization," of what is called around the world "neoliberalism." The extraordinary proletarianization of millions of the world's peoples on a global assembly line — the world working class has doubled in the last thirty years — may well lead to a renewed Democracy. It has already generated a new social-movement unionism, pioneered in the 1980s by Brazilian, South African, and South Korean workers and now sparking new forms of organization and militancy by the young women in the world's *maquiladoras,* where toys, textiles, and electronics are processed for export. The 1999 protests against the World Trade Organization in Seattle by environmentalists and unionists, "turtles and Teamsters," was only the most visible part of the new century's Democracy. The spring of 2000 witnessed general strikes against government austerity programs in South Korea, South Africa, Argentina, Uruguay, Nigeria, and India: in India, where twenty million workers went out on May 11, 2000, a strike leader said that "the strike was aimed against the surrender of the country's economic sovereignty before the WTO and the IMF," the sur-render of political and social democracy to economic despotism. When we think of democracy, we must remember the Democracy, the social movements of working people that have been the driving force of the modern democracy around the world. It is working people who must, in the words of that old manifesto, "win the battle of democracy."

8

Democracy and the Market

RICHARD C. LEVIN

The robust condition of industry and commerce in the fledgling American democracy was not lost on its most perceptive visitor and ethnographer. Alexis de Tocqueville wrote: "The United States has only been emancipated for half a century from the state of colonial dependence in which it stood to Great Britain; the number of large fortunes there is small and capital is still scarce. Yet no people in the world have made such rapid progress in trade and manufactures as the Americans. . . . [T]hey have already changed the whole order of nature for their own advantage."[1]

For Tocqueville, the robust condition of private enterprise in America depended on the abundance of land, the absence of hereditary aristocracy, and, significantly, the presence of democratic institutions and egalitarian values. But Tocqueville foresaw the possibility that the growth of commerce and manufacturing might create a new aristocracy, which might in turn undermine the very democratic values that initially stimulated American economic development. Today, as if to prove that free expression survives, some believe that Tocqueville's prediction has come true, that the market has subverted our democracy, while others believe that the free market is an essential safeguard against the erosion of democratic values.

How should we understand the relationship of the market economy and American democracy? Does a developed market economy encourage or dis-

courage democratic values and institutions? And to the extent that an unfettered market economy creates forces inimical to democratic values, how
can these forces be most effectively — one might even say, economically —
countered?

These are the questions I address in this essay, which is divided into three
parts. First, I characterize the essential properties of the market economy.
Then I comment on how the market economy both supports in part and
undermines in part the central values of a democratic society. Finally, I describe how collective action through democratic government can, in principle,
temper the antidemocratic consequences of market forces. I note that, in practice, political intervention in the market often promotes one democratic value,
typically equality, over both economic efficiency and another democratic
value, individual freedom. I conclude by suggesting how public intervention in
markets might be structured to achieve greater equality of opportunity or
outcomes at minimal sacrifice of economic efficiency or freedom.

Although both market economies and democracies take varied forms around
the world, my principal subject is the relationship between the distinctively
American market economy and *American* democracy. Where I depart from the
abstract and general, it is the American example that I have in mind.

There is no better starting point than Adam Smith's enduring classic, *The
Wealth of Nations* (1776), especially his opening chapters and discussion of
international trade.[2] Nowhere else will you find the essential features of a
market economy so elegantly described.

Smith asserts that "the propensity to truck, barter, and exchange one thing
for another" is common to all humans possessed with the faculties of reason
and speech.[3] But we need not rely on Smith's anthropology to recognize that
voluntary exchange is at the center, both logically and historically, of the
development of the market economy. Voluntary exchange depends on the
decisions of autonomous individuals. Each party to a transaction decides: I
willingly surrender what I have for what you offer in exchange. Exchange
improves the position of both parties.

Smith develops the benign implications of this insight. We need not rely on
the altruism of our trading partner. Each of us can pursue our independent
self-interest and gain from trade. In Smith's famous formulation: "It is not
from the benevolence of the butcher, the brewer, or the baker that we expect
our dinner, but from their regard to their own interest. We address ourselves,
not to their humanity but to their self-love, and never talk to them of our own
necessities but of their advantage."[4]

The pursuit of self-interest has broader implications for the society as a
whole. Consider this argument of Smith's concerning the allocation of capital,

an argument that could be made equally well with regard to the allocation of labor: "Every individual is continually exerting himself to find out the most advantageous employment for whatever capital he can command. It is his own advantage, indeed, and not that of the society which he has in view. But the study of his own advantage naturally, or rather necessarily, leads him to prefer that employment which is most advantageous to society."[5] Smith continues: "It is only for the sake of profit that any man employs a capital in support of industry; and he will always, therefore, endeavor to employ it in the support of that industry of which the produce is likely to be of the greatest value."[6] By thus pursuing profit, in Smith's account: "Every individual necessarily labours to render the annual revenue of society as great as he can. . . . [H]e intends only his own gain, and he is in this, as in many other cases, led by an invisible hand to promote an end which was no part of his intention."[7]

Smith's conclusion that an individual will allocate capital, or indeed his own labor, to the use that he values most highly follows directly from the assumption that the individual rationally pursues his self-interest. But the conclusion that total social benefit (in Smith's words, "the annual revenue of society") will be thereby maximized requires more assumptions than are made explicit in the famous "invisible hand" passage.

Indeed, it was more than a century after the publication of *The Wealth of Nations* that neoclassical economists worked out the precise conditions required to show that decentralized decisions by self-interested individuals produce a socially beneficial result. Most important of these additional assumptions is that every individual, in calculating the best use of his resources, faces a common set of prices for goods or services; in other words, we need market prices that signal a common social valuation. No person or business enterprise can have the power to influence these prices, ruling out monopoly. And no good or service that creates utility for the individual or profit for the enterprise can be unpriced, ruling out the presence of externalities or missing markets. Finally, in the neoclassical analysis of Smith's "invisible hand" conjecture, the world is strictly static. That is, the resources available to each individual (labor, capital, and land) are fixed, as is the technology of transforming those resources into useful products.

These conditions, along with a couple of technical ones, assure that the market economy allocates resources efficiently, in the sense first defined by Vilfredo Pareto. That is to say, no individual can be made better off without making another worse off. This tendency to allocate a society's productive resources efficiently is one of the two most important advantages of a market economy.

Curiously, although the neoclassical economists focused almost exclusively on making rigorous this insight of Adam Smith, efficient resource allocation was not the central concern of his great treatise. Instead Smith focused on a larger question: What explains the differences in economic progress and material well-being among nations? The answer to this question is given in the first three chapters of book 1 of *The Wealth of Nations* and elaborated throughout the treatise. Progress in material well-being depends most significantly on the advantages derived from ever increasing specialization in production, which Smith calls "the division of labor."

Smith observes that specialization depends on the possibility of exchange, which frees the individual from self-sufficiency. He identifies three types of advantages from specialization: increased skill at a specific trade or subdivision of that trade, savings from eliminating movement from one activity to another, and the possibility of vast increases in productivity through mechanization. Smith recognizes that these potential benefits from the division of labor provide an incentive to innovate for both the worker on the job and the "philosopher," which is Smith's quaintly dignified way of describing what we today would call an inventor or entrepreneur. Workers and so-called philosophers alike thus have two powerful incentives arising from their self-interested pursuit of material well-being: first, to reallocate labor and capital from lower to higher valued uses (given the existing technology of production) and, second, to seek out new and improved technologies that increase society's productive capacity.

Differences in material well-being, according to Smith, depend on the extent to which nations have taken advantage of the potential benefits of the division of labor. And their capacity to do so depends on the extent of the market. The logic of this observation is simple: the benefit to be derived from a new piece of textile machinery, for example, depends on the size of the market for textiles. Some nations enjoy natural advantages from large populations and proximity to water transport, both of which create large potential markets.

Smith focuses much of his treatise on the policies of governments that inhibit the scope of exchange and the size of the market, and thereby limit the potential gains from new technology and the progress of material well-being. Over the past 225 years others have added refinements to his arguments against protective tariffs and inefficient forms of taxation, but Smith got the essential points right.

Among twentieth-century economists, who principally chose to work on problems of static resource allocation, Joseph Schumpeter stands out as the most spirited defender of the true Smithian tradition. He first articulates a view of capitalist development in his 1912 book, *The Theory of Economic Development*. But his most succinct argument for identifying dynamic rather than static efficiency as the central advantage of a market economy is given in part 7 of *Capitalism, Socialism, and Democracy,* written during the Second World War. Here he rails against those who denounce capitalism on the grounds that monopolistic and oligopolistic firms distort the allocation of resources away from the competitive, statically efficient, outcome. Instead he observes that the market economy is dynamic and evolutionary in its nature — that the technology and organization of production, as well as the nature of products themselves, are constantly changing. To evaluate an economy's performance simply with reference to static efficiency criteria is to miss the most important measure of economic performance — the rate at which material well-being is increasing.

To Schumpeter, the competition that matters is not competition to win customers within an existing market, but competition for "the new commodity, the new technology, the new source of supply, the new type of organization."[8] This process of "creative destruction" shapes the economy in far more profound ways than any competition within existing markets; it also produces advances in productivity and material well-being far in excess of the benefits attributable to the efficient allocation of existing resources. For example, most credible empirical estimates, crude as they are, of the economic losses from inefficient resource allocation range from less than 1 to about 2 percent of a fixed national product.[9] Yet the benefits from new technologies and new products might be conservatively reckoned to increase per capita national product by as much as 1 or 2 percent *per year*.

We have just described the two principal advantages of a market economy — its tendency toward efficient resource allocation and its tendency to foster innovation. We are now prepared to ask whether the workings of the market economy are favorable or inimical to the existence and survival of democracy. But first let us pause to consider briefly what the market requires from the political order in which it is embedded.

The answer to this preliminary question is pretty simple. The market rests on a foundation of voluntary exchange among self-interested individuals and the incentives that the possibility of voluntary exchange creates. For such a system to function, property rights must be well defined (I cannot trade what I do not own), and contracts, agreements among the parties to an exchange, must be enforceable. So the simple answer, as spelled out a century ago by Max Weber, is that markets require a rule of law — which entails both well-defined rules and a system to enforce those rules.[10] As a logical proposition, markets do not require democratic governments, only a stable and predictable rule of law, which, in theory, can exist in an authoritarian regime. France under Napoleon comes to mind. But, as an empirical proposition, markets have performed best in democratic regimes.

Accepting the view that political order is good for the market, let us now ask if the market is good for democracy. I want to address this question by focusing on the two central values of American democracy: freedom and equality. Because the connection is so manifestly self-evident, I pass quickly over the relationship between the market and one additional defining characteristic of American democracy noted by Tocqueville and favored by Emerson and Whitman: self-reliance. This characteristic American virtue is intrinsic in Smith's philosopher-entrepreneur — the rational actor who seizes every opportunity to maximize the value of his resources. There can be little doubt that the market, with the incentives it provides to the alert and reflective, promotes self-reliance. By the same logic, the market promotes self-invention, which Anthony Kronman describes as the quintessential aspiration of the democratic soul.

Less obviously, the relationship between the market economy and political freedom is entirely symbiotic; the health of one promotes the health of the other. In contrast, the relationship of the market economy and equality is much more problematic. On the one hand, the market provides for radical equality of opportunity, but on the other hand markets are indifferent to equality of outcomes. Depending on technology and other exogenous factors, markets can increase or decrease equality in the distribution of income and wealth.

I have already noted that voluntary exchange is logically and historically at the center of the market economy. In theory, individuals have complete freedom — to offer labor services where they choose, to employ capital in a preferred use, to invest in education and training, to purchase food, shelter, clothing, and other consumption goods as they wish. In practice, freedom of action is constrained by the resources available to the individual; it is in this sense that prosperity expands our freedom. Still, within the limits of their resources, individuals are free agents in the market economy. They alone choose where to live, where to work, and what to eat. One need only look at the experience of the Soviet Union from the 1920s through the mid-1980s — where residences and occupations were assigned and food was frequently rationed — to recognize that such freedom has not been universal, even in modern times.

The freedom of action inherent in market activity supports and reinforces freedom in other spheres of life. If we can choose our occupation by selling labor services in the market, should we not be free to choose, subject to appropriate entry standards, the course of study we pursue in publicly supported educational institutions? If we are free to purchase books, magazines, news-papers, and cable television programming as we wish, should sellers not be free to publish opinions of any kind? Indeed, should we not be free to express our own opinions? My point is simply this: our freedom in the marketplace accustoms us to expect freedom in the political and social realm.

Milton Friedman offers another reason why economic freedom is conducive to political freedom.[11] In the market economy, the decentralization of decision making tends to distribute power widely; there are more than two hundred billionaires, several million millionaires, and hundreds of very large, powerful corporations in America. In the political realm, however, power is more con-centrated. Potentially, the leader of the state, even if democratically elected, has immense coercive power that is unavailable to economic agents who must compete in the marketplace. Thus, Friedman claims that the dispersed sources of power created by the market economy act as a check and balance against excessive exercise of the state's power to coerce. No doubt Friedman exagger-ates the state's power to coerce by failing to acknowledge, on the one hand, that political power in our democracy is not in fact concentrated in a single leader and, on the other, that actions of the state can be enabling instead of coercive. Still, there is something to the argument that having a nonpolitical mechanism, the market, distribute power may help to preserve freedom better than a regime in which all power is created and distributed through political processes.

The relationship of the market to equality, the other principal democratic value, is less felicitous. It is true that just as the market promotes freedom, it creates a radical equality of opportunity. In principle, any individual with a good idea and access to capital can reap rewards in Schumpeterian competi-tion. Historically, access to capital may have been limited on grounds of race and gender, but capital (especially in the form of credit) has always been widely available to American farmers and small businesses, whether start-ups or family firms of long standing. Although in the aggregate there has been no systematic tendency toward income equality in the last century, individual mobility, from one income level to another, from one social class to another, has been persistently high throughout American history.[12] One interesting piece of evidence: of the four hundred wealthiest Americans identified an-nually by *Forbes* magazine, only one-third inherited their wealth or built their fortunes on a nucleus of inherited wealth.[13]

Now we come to the most disconcerting consequence of the market econ-omy. In the process of economic growth through "creative destruction," the market creates losers as well as winners. In dynamic competition, the race goes to the swift, and many are left behind.

The data yield three robust conclusions. First, there is significant inequality in income and wealth among Americans. Second, during the course of the twentieth century the extent of inequality has fluctuated; there has been no systematic tendency toward either increased or decreased inequality. Third, inequality has increased significantly since the early 1980s.

Let's begin with the current extent of inequality. In the mid-1990s, the top 5 percent of families received just over 20 percent of all pretax family income;[14] the top 0.5 percent of families received just under 10 percent of all such income.[15] To give these figures some life, consider a random sample of two hundred American families. On average, the ten highest income families (that is, the top 5 percent of the sample) would earn average incomes of $172,000, almost five times larger than that of the average income of the other 190 families (roughly $36,000). The top family alone, in any random sample of two hundred, would, on average, have an income of $860,000, nine times the average income of the next nine families ($96,000), or twenty-four times the $36,000 average income of the bottom 190 families. Household wealth — the value of stocks, bonds, real estate, and other assets — is even more unequally distributed. In 1995, the top 1 percent held 38 percent of all wealth; the top 5 percent held 60 percent.[16]

Over the course of the century, there has been no sustained trend in inequality, but rather fluctuations. Curiously, these fluctuations display no consistent correlation with the overall growth in incomes. Sometimes big boats get greater lift from a rising tide; sometimes the small boats rise the most.

To summarize, the share of family income going to the top 5 percent of families was 23 percent just after the First World War. It rose during the prosperity of the 1920s to a peak of 26 percent (1928–32) then fell during the depression years to reach 23 percent again on the eve of the Second World War (1939–40).[17] In contrast to the boom of the 1920s, the boom induced by the Second World War led to greater equality. By 1947, the top 5 percent of families had only 17.5 percent of family income. The share of the richest families fell gradually throughout the entire era of postwar growth, to about 15 percent, and it did not increase during the slump of the 1970s. As the stock market recovered in the 1980s preceding the acceleration of overall economic growth in the 1990s, income inequality began to rise again, with the share of the top 5 percent of families reaching 18 percent by 1989 and topping 20 percent by 1996.[18] It is particularly alarming that the share of income going to the very richest families has risen dramatically in recent years. The share going to the top 0.5 percent fluctuated between 5 and 6 percent of total family income from 1960 to 1982. Thereafter, it rose precipitously to between 9 and 10 percent in every year since 1988.[19]

Many factors have contributed to fluctuations in the extent of inequality. At the risk of oversimplification, I would suggest that the gradual reduction in inequality between 1945 and 1970 was probably most significantly influenced by the movement of lower income farmers and farmworkers to higher paying urban jobs. Underlying this change in the distribution of jobs, however, were steady increases in agricultural productivity and rapid growth in the production of automobiles, which created a derived demand for materials used in the production of automobiles, such as steel, as well as demand for complementary products such as gasoline. It is sometimes asserted that the Interstate Highway Act of 1956 was the most important piece of post–World War II social legislation, because it suburbanized our cities, altered the relationship of home and workplace, and restructured the use of leisure time. It may also have reduced inequality in the distribution of income.

By contrast to this somewhat speculative inference, the factors contributing to increasing inequality over the past two decades have been intensively studied. It is widely agreed that the most important source of rising inequality is technological change that has significantly increased the premium paid for highly educated, skilled workers. In fact, the wage premium earned by those with a college degree rose from 31 percent to 53 percent between 1979 and 1993, even as the proportion of workers with a college degree increased from 22 percent to 29 percent.[20] It should not be surprising that the rise in the relative pay of educated workers began just as the personal computer was introduced. Empirical investigation confirms that the premium paid for educated workers is highest in precisely those industries making the most intensive use of computers.

We have now examined, on the positive side, the market's reinforcement of democratic freedoms and its tendency to create opportunity for upward mobility. On the negative side, we find that market forces have caused increases in the inequality of income and wealth over the past two decades. Excessive inequality threatens the philosophical basis of democracy, which counts each individual as an autonomous agent, capable of self-invention.

Our American democracy appears willing to tolerate a substantial degree of inequality, but we have nonetheless used political means, acts of government, to temper the tendency to inequality that market forces produce. I will shortly discuss efforts to equalize incomes through progressive taxation and various welfare programs. But first we should note that inequality of income and wealth is only one of many consequences of market activity that might be viewed as adverse by a majority of citizens. Excessive air and water pollution, insufficient workplace and product safety, and the use of child labor come to mind as additional examples.

Therefore, I want to examine how politically undesirable aspects and outcomes of market activity are controlled. In practice, many adverse consequences of market activity are prevented or ameliorated by systems of industrial self-regulation. The financial and cost accounting standards used by corporations and even nonprofit organizations are a notable example of self-regulation, as are various codes of conduct adopted by industry associations. But I set this subject aside to focus instead on the action of government to ban, regulate, discourage, or otherwise constrain politically undesirable market processes and outcomes.

In our democracy, governmental intervention in markets is not rare; we do it all the time, with many different political objectives in mind. We intervene by prohibiting market activity in some cases, by taxing and subsidizing, and by promulgating and enforcing vast numbers of regulations regarding health, safety, environmental quality, information disclosure, employment conditions, and workers' rights — to give a very incomplete summary. Our interventions are not usually structured to ensure the best possible economic performance; efficiency is usually sacrificed in favor of political objectives. Our interventions are sometimes corrosive of important democratic values as well, such as personal freedom and self-reliance. Still, it is possible in principle to design, though not always possible in practice to achieve, interventions in the service of democratically determined political objectives that rely strongly on economic incentives to achieve their goals. Such interventions, if well conceived, can both minimize inefficiency and preserve a significant degree of freedom and self-reliance.

Consider the most drastic form of government intervention in the market — the prohibition of trade. We prohibit the sale of goods presumed to be harmful, such as narcotics, dangerous toys, and untested pharmaceuticals. We also prohibit the sale of universally distributed entitlements, such as the right to vote, the right to trial by jury, the right to marry one and only one spouse, and the right to public education as well as police and fire protection services.

Prohibiting the trading of rights inhibits the personal freedom of both buyer and seller, and it is economically inefficient. We do not allow an individual to sell her right to vote to another person, even if the second person's willingness to pay far exceeds the minimum price the seller would accept. Under such circumstances, both parties would be better off by trading. The seller presumably would not sell unless she valued the cash more highly than her right to vote, and the buyer would not buy unless she valued having a second vote more highly than the dollars paid for it.

Presumably, we bar the trading of votes because in the political domain we collectively assign absolute primacy to equality. Although we tolerate what many believe to be excessive expenditures to influence voting, we hold sacrosanct the principle that each citizen's right and responsibility to participate in collective decision making is inalienable. We insist on one person, one vote even at the cost of reduced freedom and economic inefficiency.

I digress briefly to note that most other prohibitions of trade are not so easily explained by reference to almost universally shared values. These prohibitions reflect instead the will of a political majority. We typically recognize that there are competing values involved, and we differ on how heavily we weigh the loss of personal freedom and economic efficiency that prohibition entails. Consider the current prohibitions on the sale of tobacco to minors, marijuana, pharmaceuticals approved and marketed in Europe but not yet cleared by the U.S. Food and Drug Administration, and alcoholic beverages to individuals between the ages of eighteen and twenty-one. In each of these cases prohibition has costs and benefits. I would conjecture that many Americans favor one or more of these prohibitions and oppose one or more. On the other hand, I would be surprised if many believed that we should permit the buying and selling of votes.

Declaring certain entitlements universal and banning market transactions in them is only one of the approaches available to a democratic government seeking to compensate for the market's disregard for equality. We can also reduce inequality by levying taxes and awarding subsidies at rates that depend on income. We call a tax "progressive" when the ratio of tax payments to before-tax income rises with income. A progressive tax tends to equalize the distribution of income. We likewise call a subsidy progressive when the ratio of benefits to before-tax income falls as income rises. This, too, tends to render the distribution of income more equal.

Were the U.S. tax code designed simply to reduce inequality while raising revenue for the government, it would be a relatively efficient instrument for the purpose. In theory, high marginal tax rates reduce the incentive to work and thus reduce national output. In practice, however, changes in marginal tax rates in the range of recent U.S. experience have not had a substantial impact on labor supply, except in the case of those on welfare — an issue to which I will return. The major inefficiencies in the tax code arise from provisions that serve political objectives other than reducing inequality — such as encouraging home ownership and favoring certain types of investments and holding periods over others.

How well, then, do federal taxes serve the objective of reducing inequality? The answer has two parts. First, the federal income tax is highly progressive, and taken alone its effects would have a significant effect on inequality. The average taxpayer with less than $20,000 pays no taxes and receives a net subsidy. Taxpayers in the $20,000 to $30,000 income range pay only 2 percent on average, while those with incomes between $75,000 and $100,000 pay 11 percent and those with incomes above $200,000 pay 24 percent. Second, however, several other federal taxes on individuals are less progressive than the income tax. These include payroll taxes for Social Security and Medicare paid by every wage earner and employer, unemployment insurance for the self-employed, and excise taxes on various consumption goods such as cigarettes and gasoline. The payroll tax that finances Social Security is actually regressive; there is no tax on income above $76,200. When all federal taxes are taken into account, the equalizing effects of the income tax are significantly attenuated. Average tax rates rise to 13 percent for incomes between $20,000 and $30,000, 23 percent for incomes between $75,000 and $100,000, and 28 percent for incomes above $200,000 — still progressive, but much less progressive than the income tax alone.[21] This modest degree of overall progressivity in federal taxes reduces inequality, but not dramatically.[22]

In recent years, efforts to reduce inequality have focused on subsidizing those at the lower end of the income distribution rather than on taxing the rich. These subsidies take many forms — Medicaid, food stamps, housing allowances, job training programs, and cash payments. The long and complicated evolution of the many federal and state programs to assist the poor has reflected shifting views of both the causes of and appropriate remedies for poverty. Some of the programs that were established or expanded in the 1960s, especially when taken in combination, created massive inefficiencies and horrendously perverse incentives for welfare recipients. Although recent legislation has been far from perfect, it has gone some distance toward providing constructive and efficiency-enhancing incentives for welfare recipients.

Setting aside the elderly who are in poverty, and whose Social Security benefits are augmented by cash grants from the Supplemental Security Income program, the majority of welfare recipients are female heads of households, many of whom have children. Prior to the numerous reforms instituted by individual states in the 1980s, many of these single mothers received food stamps, subsidized housing, and cash grants from the Aid to Families with Dependent Children (AFDC) program. Eligibility for each of these programs was means-tested, and each used separate and distinct formulas to phase out benefits as the earned income of recipients increased. In many situations, the combined benefits lost when recipients entered employment exceeded the after-tax income from earnings. In other words, welfare recipients often faced marginal tax rates in excess of 100 percent. In other circumstances, the tax rate was below 100 percent but still very high, in excess of the marginal tax rates facing the very highest income individuals in the nation. In fairness, not all welfare recipients faced such perverse incentives, but many did. And to the extent that those who did remained on welfare for protracted periods, their dependency might be more fairly represented as the pursuit of self-interest than as a moral failing. Intended to protect one democratic value, equality, our poorly designed welfare programs severely undermined another, self-reliance, while assessing an additional toll on economic efficiency.

The 1996 reform legislation sought to reduce dependency with both incentives and penalties.[23] Congress provided to the states two bloc grants to replace the AFDC cash grants to individuals and certain other child support programs. The first bloc of funds was for distribution to eligible recipients subject to two new requirements. First, to remain eligible for payments, able-bodied recipients must work at least part time after two years on welfare. Second, recipients lose eligibility for payments after five years, although states can exempt up to 20 percent of their caseload from this provision. The other bloc grant represented a substantial increase in funds to subsidize the child care expenses of low income working parents.

Enacted separately and often overlooked in the public discussion of welfare reform was a major improvement in the terms of the Earned Income Tax Credit, a feature of the tax code first enacted in 1975.[24] The Earned Income Tax Credit allows refunds against federal income taxes, calculated as a percentage of a taxpayer's first dollars of earned income. As income rises, the credit reaches a maximum at a certain threshold income. The credit then remains constant up to a second, higher income threshold. Then the credit is phased out, diminishing gradually to zero at a third, higher level of income. The size of the credit was very small in the early years, not nearly large enough to adequately counter the perverse incentives faced by welfare recipients who sought work. But successive improvements in 1987, 1990, 1993, and 1996 changed the incentives substantially.

To illustrate, by the year 2000, a single mother with two children was allowed a 40 percent credit against the first $9,540 she earns each year, roughly the equivalent of working at the minimum wage for thirty-five hours a week. In such a situation, the wage earner would receive not only the $9,540 she earned but an additional $3,816 for a total of $13,356. Needless to say, this provides a substantial incentive for welfare recipients to take employment when it is available. In 2000, over 18 million families received credits totaling $30 billion. Expenditures under this program now exceed cash payments under the AFDC and successor state programs, and they nearly equal the subsidy provided by food stamps.

The expansion of the Earned Income Tax Credit to its current level was an important step toward making welfare reform efficient rather than punitive.

But the program still has a major design flaw; the credit is phased out at a rate that is much too high. To continue with our hypothetical mother of two, for every dollar she earns in excess of $12,460, she would lose 21 cents of Earned Income Tax Credit, until no benefit remained. This phase-out provision, in combination with normal income and payroll taxes, creates an effective tax rate of 42.2 percent on earned income between $12,460 and $30,000. Eliminating the phase-out or spreading it over a much wider range of income would alter this perverse incentive.

Permit me a brief historical digression. If the Earned Income Tax Credit were reformed as I just suggested, the program would resemble even more closely the negative income tax proposals advanced in the 1960s by both James Tobin on the left and Milton Friedman on the right.[25] The idea, when earnestly put forward by George McGovern in his 1972 presidential campaign, was ridiculed by his opponents as a "$1,000 giveaway" and contributed to his crushing defeat. It is a lovely irony that the Earned Income Tax Credit was first enacted, below the radar screen of the national media, only three years later.

We have thus far explored two types of government intervention in the market economy. Prohibition of trading, we noted, is sometimes an expression of the absolute priority of one democratic value, such as equality in the case of voting rights, or public health in the case of cigarette sales to minors. In these cases, we deliberately subordinate both economic efficiency and conflicting democratic values, such as personal liberty. Taxes and subsidies, by contrast, often embody what Arthur Okun called "uneasy compromises"[26] between political objectives and economic efficiency. In fact, the compromises are often multi-sided, reflecting more than one political objective. The U.S. tax code, for example, displays, on the one hand, a desire of the Congress to reduce inequality through the progressive income tax, which is compromised, on the other hand, by a desire to ensure "fairness" in sharing the burden of payroll taxes. In the context of welfare reform, we have also seen that, without compromising the primary political objective of reducing poverty, it is possible in principle (though only imperfectly in practice) to improve economic efficiency and even achieve a secondary political objective — greater self-reliance.

A third type of government intervention holds great promise for correcting, at minimal cost, one of the major deficiencies of the market economy: its inability to economize on resources that are owned in common, such as the earth's atmosphere, oceans, and inland waters. I refer to the possibility of using the properties of markets to reduce pollution as efficiently as possible.

Most pollution control policies implemented since the enactment of the Clean Air Act in 1970 take one of two approaches. The first is to require the use of specific pollution control equipment, such as catalytic converters in automobiles in the early 1970s. The second is to set specific limits on the rate of emissions from a particular source, such as pollution per unit of fuel burned by an electric utility plant or an automobile. Both approaches have serious disadvantages. Requiring specific equipment can be a needlessly expensive way to achieve a desired result. For example, catalytic converters proved to be more expensive and less technically effective than making cars out of lighter materials and improving the efficiency of the combustion process itself. Setting limits on the rate of emissions from a particular source fails to take account of the wide disparities in the cost of reducing emissions from source to source. This is especially problematic for electric power plants, where pollution can be reduced by several means, including switching to cleaner fuels and adding filtering equipment (called "scrubbers") to the smokestack. For plants close to the source of low sulfur coal, for example, the cost of meeting emissions standards can be much lower than for others who must add a scrubber. In consequence, it has long been believed that the cost of complying with source-specific emissions limits is much higher than would be necessary to achieve any given regional or national target for aggregate reductions in emissions.

Economists solved these problems, conceptually, decades ago. By specifying a national limit on total annual emissions of a particular substance, let's say sulfur dioxide, and issuing tradable permits, a market will emerge that sets a price on the right to emit one ton of sulfur dioxide. Let's assume that the total amount of rights issued is less than the total amount of pollution that would be emitted without some remedial action. Every public utility can then ask itself the question: Am I better off using the rights I am issued or selling them at the market price?

The answer is that I will sell my right to emit one ton of SO_2 if its market price exceeds what I can earn by producing as much electricity as I can generate while emitting one more ton of SO_2. But notice this: the calculation changes if I can produce more electricity for every ton of SO_2 emitted. So I have an incentive to look for the lowest cost means of reducing my pollution per unit output. With tradable rights, the nation's utilities will minimize the total expenditure on reducing emissions to whatever level is established as the national target.

This is no mere theory: in 1990 Congress amended the Clean Air Act to establish just such a scheme for trading the rights to emit sulfur dioxide. The market for rights was established in 1993 and limits on aggregate emissions were established for every year beginning in 1995. The rights to pollute, called allowances, are dated by year. Unused rights can be banked for future use, but no borrowing from future allocations is permitted.

The operation and effects of this market have been thoroughly studied and documented in a study by Paul Joskow and other economists at MIT.[27] Suffice it to say that the market has worked smoothly. The annual emissions targets, which called for a one-third reduction from 1990 levels by 1997, were met in the aggregate, and every participating utility was in compliance. Nearly two-thirds of the reductions were achieved by switching fuels and just over one-third by installing control equipment. The MIT study estimates that, based on the evidence to date, the total cost of achieving the targeted reductions by the year 2007 will be approximately $16 billion. This is $20 billion less than it would have cost to achieve the same aggregate target by simply imposing quotas on each individual plant and not permitting the trading of rights.

One puzzle remains. How did such a rational and efficient means of achieving a political objective emerge from the legislative process? The MIT study suggests a serendipitous convergence of interests in 1989–90. The particular problem created by sulfur dioxide emissions was acid rain that threatened the destruction of lakes, forests, and associated species in the northeastern United States. Several attempts to impose stringent conventional regulations on SO_2 emissions had failed in Congress during the 1980s. But President Bush had campaigned on a platform of "looking to the market" for environmental solutions. He also had a summer residence in Maine, and his chief of staff, John Sununu, had been governor of New Hampshire. In the Senate, the majority leadership passed from Robert Byrd, from the coal-producing state of West Virginia, to George Mitchell of Maine. Presumably, the coalition of liberal Democrats with a regional interest in eliminating acid rain and Republicans predisposed to a market-oriented approach was sufficient to defeat legislators representing coal-producing regions and midwestern states with coal-burning power plants.

Perhaps I am guilty of excessive enthusiasm for rationalizing public policy. A partial welfare reform and one successful pollution-trading scheme do not necessarily foreshadow a revolution. Everyone knows, so the familiar argument goes, that public policy is not the product of rational design but the outcome of struggle between powerful interest groups. Those with interests to protect and money to spend will manage to subvert attempts at reform and use them to reinforce and strengthen their power.

I can only respond that skepticism about the efficacy of democratic governance has long had a place in American life. But so, too, has optimism about the power of ideas to improve human welfare. I refer not only to the optimism of the founders. I refer also to the optimism of the freedom riders — black and white — who rode buses and led marches to integrate the South forty years ago. I refer to the optimism of the small and dedicated band of writers, naturalists, and lawyers who put environmental quality on the national agenda thirty years ago. On a smaller and more local scale, I refer to the optimism that has impelled many of the nation's urban universities to reorient and reorganize themselves to contribute substantially to the betterment of the communities that surround them.

The market is the most powerful instrument for improving material well-being yet devised by humanity. But it is an imperfect instrument that rewards individuals unequally and fails to economize on unpriced goods such as clean air and water and the health of future generations. There is a role for democratic government to remedy the deficiencies of market outcomes, and there is also good reason to design remedies that achieve their objectives without compromising the incentives for socially productive activity that the market provides. That we have not done such a great job of this in the past should not deter us. There will be abundant opportunities for creative policy design as America confronts the challenges of the new century.

To reinforce this last point, I close with the words of Walt Whitman. I quote from the essay that we commemorate in the title of this volume, *Democratic Vistas:* "America, filling the present with greatest deeds and problems, cheerfully accepting the past, . . . counts . . . for her justification and success . . . almost entirely on the future. Nor is that hope unwarranted. . . . For our New World I consider far less important for what it has done, or what it is, than for results to come."

Notes

1. Alexis de Tocqueville, *Democracy in America,* trans. Henry Reeve, ed. Phillips Bradley (New York: Vintage, 1945), 2:165–66.

2. Adam Smith, *An Inquiry into the Nature and Causes of the Wealth of Nations* (Chicago: University of Chicago Press, 1976), book 1, chaps. 1–3, and book 4, chap. 2.

3. Ibid., 17.

4. Ibid., 18.

5. Ibid., 475.

6. Ibid., 477.

7. Ibid.

8. Joseph A. Schumpeter, *Capitalism, Socialism, and Democracy,* 3d ed. (New York: Harper, 1950), 84.

9. For a review of these estimates, see F. M. Scherer and David Ross, *Industrial Market Structure and Economic Performance,* 3d ed. (Boston: Houghton Mifflin, 1990), 661–67.

10. See especially Max Weber, *Economy and Society,* trans. Ephraim Fischoff et al., ed. Guenther Roth and Claus Wittich (New York: Bedminster, 1968), 1:311–38.

11. Milton Friedman, *Capitalism and Freedom,* 2d ed. (Chicago: University of Chicago Press, 1982), 15–19.

12. Peter Gottschalk and Sheldon Danzinger, "Family Income Mobility — How Much Is There and Has It Changed?" Boston College, Department of Economics Working Paper #398, December 1997. Much empirical work on the subject of mobility is, in my view, conceptually flawed. The typical studies of mobility look at an individual's movement from one income class to another. But it is well known that income tends to rise and then fall over the life cycle of most individuals. We need studies that control for these life cycle effects or, better still, finesse them entirely by looking at intergenerational mobility, rather than an individual's progress from year to year or decade to decade.

13. *Forbes,* October 9, 2000, 362.

14. The calculation is based on pretax income, excluding capital gains. Nonmonetary income — such as employer-provided health benefits, Medicare, Medicaid, and food stamps — is also excluded. Frank Levy, *The New Dollars and Dreams* (New York: Russell Sage Foundation, 1998), 199, 203.

15. This calculation is based on standardized pretax adjusted gross income, excluding capital gains. See Daniel R. Feenberg and James M. Poterba, "The Income and Tax Share of Very-High Income Households, 1960–1995," *American Economic Review* 90(2) (May 2000): 264–70.

16. Edward N. Wolff, "Recent Trends in the Distribution of Household Wealth," *Journal of Economic Perspectives* 12(3) (summer 1998): 136.

17. Simon Kuznets, *Shares of Upper Income Groups in Income and Savings* (New York: National Bureau of Economic Research, 1953), 585.

18. The data covering 1947 through 1995 are drawn from Levy, *New Dollars,* 199. Levy and Kuznets use different methods for calculating and ranking family incomes. Thus, the direction of movement in the prewar and postwar data is accurately portrayed, but the prewar income shares of the top 5 percent should not be directly compared to the postwar shares. Where the data overlap, however, in 1947, the share calculated by Kuznets is only 0.1 percent lower than Levy's.

19. Feenberg and Poterba, "Income and Tax Share."

20. Peter Gottschalk, "Inequality, Income Growth, and Mobility: The Basic Facts," *Journal of Economic Perspectives* 11(2) (spring 1997): 29–31.

21. Joint Committee on Taxation, U.S. Congress, *Distribution of Certain Federal Tax Liabilities by Income Class for Calendar Year 2000* (JCX-45-00), April 11, 2000.

22. See Levy, *New Dollars,* 205–8. Changes in the tax code in the 1980s and early 1990s contained both progressive and regressive elements and neither mitigated nor accentuated the trend toward greater inequality over the period. See Peter Gottschalk and Timothy Smeeding, "Cross-National Comparisons of Earnings and Income Inequality," *Journal of Economic Literature* 35(2) (June 1997): 670.

23. For details on the recent reforms, see Committee on Ways and Means, U.S. House of Representatives, *Summary of Welfare Reforms Made by Public Law 104-193: The Personal Responsibility and Work Opportunity Reconciliation Act and Associated Legislation* (Washington: U.S. Government Printing Office, November 6, 1996).

24. For details, see Committee on Ways and Means, U.S. House of Representatives, *Green Book, 2000* (Washington: U.S. Government Printing Office, 2000), 808–13.

25. James Tobin, "The Case for an Income Guarantee," *Public Interest,* no. 4 (summer 1966): 31–41, and Milton Friedman, *Capitalism and Freedom,* 190–95. The proposal was given serious consideration by the first Nixon administration. The difference

between the Earned Income Tax Credit and the negative income tax is that the former provides a stronger incentive to work at the very lowest levels of income, while the latter gives a lump-sum credit to all and imposes a flat tax on all earned income.

26. Arthur M. Okun, *Equality and Efficiency: The Big Tradeoff* (Washington: Brookings Institution, 1975), 1.

27. A. Denny Ellerman, Paul L. Joskow, Richard Schmalensee, Juan-Pablo Montero, and Elizabeth M. Bailey, *Markets for Clean Air: The U.S. Acid Rain Program* (New York: Cambridge University Press, 2000).

9

Democracy and Distribution

IAN SHAPIRO

We have become accustomed to the coexistence of democracy with substantial economic inequality, but this is surprising when considered in a larger historical and theoretical perspective. Nineteenth-century elites who resisted expansion of the franchise and socialists who endorsed the "parliamentary road to socialism" agreed that if majority rule were imposed on a massively unequal status quo, then most voters would favor taxing the rich and transferring the proceeds downward. This was formalized in political science as the "median-voter theorem," which predicts majority support for downward redistribution, given startling inequality like that in the advanced capitalist democracies.

In fact, no relationship has emerged between an expanding democratic franchise and downward redistribution. Indeed, even with a universal franchise, democracy has sometimes coexisted with regressive redistribution. The United States saw a sharp rise in inequality between the early 1970s and the mid-1990s, despite the 1965 Voting Rights Act and a 1971 constitutional amendment lowering the voting age to eighteen. The real incomes of many lower-income workers declined during this period, and the gap between the poor and the wealthy widened significantly.[1] Similar patterns arose in other advanced industrial democracies. Although democracies spend somewhat more than non-democracies on the poor, this spending has no systematic impact on inequality and leaves significant proportions of the populations in poverty.[2]

The purpose of this essay is to ask why, despite so many forecasts of downward democratic redistribution, history has demurred and even produced the opposite. Allow me two prefatory observations. First, because the dearth of redistribution to the poor in democracies results from numerous factors, analyzing it is unlikely to produce any single diagnosis. My approach here is to break the causes down to the "demand side," asking why there is not more popular pressure for redistribution to the poor; and the "supply side," asking why politicians and other elites do not put more redistributive policies on the table. Of course these dimensions interact: the absence of elite proposals to benefit the poor compounds their political alienation, which in turn strengthens politicians' incentives to ignore them. The split into supply-side and demand-side causes nonetheless provides a useful heuristic for focusing discussion.

A second observation: in thinking about which factors deserve attention, we should distinguish two senses in which a factor is important. On the one hand, we want to know which factors cause the relative lack of downward redistribution. On the other, we want to know which factors are more and less likely to be alterable, so that we gain some idea of how increased redistribution to the poor might come about. It is unlikely that these factors will be the same. The most important creative challenge for those interested in redistribution is to devise ways to alter factors that would otherwise be unchangeable, and overcome the tendency of inequality to be self-reinforcing.

The Supply Side

Let us begin with the supply side. If we assume that there would be demand (that is, a potentially winning electoral coalition) for more downwardly redistributive policies than we see, the question is: why are those policies not on offer?

On the supply side we should distinguish taxing from spending. There are several barriers that make it difficult for the government to tax anyone, and especially the wealthy. Since Marx and Engels coined the phrase "the executive committee of the bourgeoisie" to describe elected government, some have argued that democracies bow before the power of capital. Contemporary scholarship[3] does indeed show that politicians are reluctant to tax because they anticipate capital strikes — the withholding of money by those who already have it. We should expect this to get worse with globalization and the expansion of free trade, as capital strikes become capital flight. Both internationally and within federal and other decentralized systems, money flees to where tax rates are lower, accelerating the so-called race to the bottom.[4]

Then there is the influence of campaign contributions on political agendas. It seems obvious that campaign contributions will have a big effect on campaign platforms, because politicians must first compete for campaign dollars, and only then for votes. Perhaps there would be majority support for confiscatory taxes on estates worth over $10 million, but no party proposes this. Indeed, in 2001 the U.S. Congress abolished the existing estate tax — paid by only the wealthiest 2 percent of Americans.[5] It seems likely that politicians avoid taxing the wealthy for fear of the funds that would be channeled to their electoral opponents if they sought to do so. Empirical study of such claims is inherently difficult, because politicians may be influenced by the fear of potential contributions to their opponents rather than by any actual contributions, but it seems reasonable to suppose that the proposals politicians offer are heavily shaped by the agendas of campaign contributors; why else would the wealthy contribute? Particularly if the wealthy give to both parties, we should anticipate bipartisan support for distributive policies to the right of the median voter (such as abolishing the estate tax). Add to this the fact that with a handful of major parties this means that what we really get is oligopolistic competition, and it becomes clear that political parties are not as attentive to voters as firms in competitive markets are to consumers.

Various proposals for campaign-finance reform are on offer, and the Congress passed the McCain-Feingold ban on soft money in 2001. It is not clear that such reform promises much difference to how well the poorest fifth or so of the population fares. The reforms mostly aim to promote deliberation, understood in one way or another, and it is far from clear that more deliberation would lead to more downward redistribution.

What about the structure of American political institutions? There is good reason to believe that this matters. The American system of checks and balances is full of "veto points" where strategically well-placed groups can stop a proposal from becoming law. Generally, the greater the number of veto points, the more difficult it is to pass a new policy. This means that if the status quo is highly inegalitarian, or the economy is continuously manufacturing new inequalities, the political system will be less able to ameliorate the inequality. The United States is hamstrung by federalism, which contains more veto points than unitary systems; bicameralism, which contains more veto points than unicameral systems; and separation of powers, which contains more veto points than parliamentary systems.[6] Separation of powers is especially significant in American politics because of the interventionist attitude of the federal courts, most notably in the *Lochner* era but also in our own, in limiting attempts at downward redistribution by state and federal governments. Increasingly it seems that the Warren era was an outlier that gave the left imprudent faith in the courts as engines of progressive reform.[7]

The recent trend in democracy toward ceding authority for monetary policy to independent banks may create another institutional limitation on downward redistribution. Bankers are likely to perceive fiscal policies designed to achieve it to be inflationary and will counteract them with the monetary instruments they control. There is some evidence that democratic governments increasingly tie their own hands by ceding such authority to such veto players, and to other veto players such as international financial institutions, to insulate themselves from populist demands.[8]

A significant implication of highlighting the role of veto players in limiting institutional capacity to redistribute concerns claims for political decentralization, strong civil society, transferring government functions to civic groups, and so on. These come from the left[9], center[10], and right (as in George Bush senior's appeal to "a thousand points of light," framed as policy in George W. Bush's "faith-based initiatives"), but they may be classified together as deleterious from this point of view — whatever their other advantages.

Another facet of this problem concerns institutional arrangements in the legislature. For instance, party leaderships are comparatively weak in the U.S. Congress. Senators and representatives are often unresponsive to party leaders and much more attuned to geographic constituencies (hence Speaker Tip O'Neill's famous dictum that "all politics is local"), campaign contributors, lobbyists, and interest groups.[11] The greater the "herding cats" problem that legislative leaders face, the less likely they are to be able to line legislators up behind redistributive agendas that cut across constituency boundaries and are at odds with the interests of these other players.

I have already referred to the oligopolistic competition of a two-party system. There is some evidence to suggest that two-party systems are less likely to produce downward redistribution than systems of proportional representation (PR), in which each party has a share in the legislature proportionate to its percentage of the national vote. Because PR systems produce policies that are closer to the preferences of the median voter than two-party systems, if we credit the median-voter theorem at all we would expect PR systems to be relatively redistributive.[12]

It is rare that countries change their electoral systems, and highly unlikely that PR will be adopted in the United States. Nonetheless, the topic might receive more attention than it does, especially in a country so rhetorically committed to protecting competition in private enterprise. The idiom of competition needs to be taken more seriously in politics, perhaps on analogy with the antitrust laws that were designed to prevent private companies from blocking competition by controlling markets. If competition for power is the lifeblood of democracy, then the search for bipartisan consensus (and the ideal of deliberative agreement that lies behind it) is really anticompetitive collusion in restraint of democracy. Why is it that people do not challenge legislation that has bipartisan backing, or other forms of bipartisan agreement, on *these* grounds? It is far from clear that there are fewer meritorious reasons to break up the Democratic and Republican Parties than there are to break up AT&T and Microsoft.[13]

The constitutional obstacles to applying antitrust principles to politics are rooted in the right of petition and the "ability of the people to make their wishes known to their representatives."[14] But these reasons for protecting political parties from regulation do not justify forms of collusion that undermine free political expression itself. Political parties keep out potential competitors by maintaining prohibitive costs of entry, agreeing to exclude minor parties from political debates and related practices. Because the Sherman Antitrust Act has been held to apply only to business combinations,[15] and to organizations that have commercial objectives,[16] antitrust regulation of such behavior would require new laws. It is hard, for obvious reasons, to envision legislators enacting such laws, but it is less difficult to think of political antitrust measures being adopted as a result of ballot initiatives to limit the "market share" of any particular party's votes. In an analogous spirit, one could imagine campaign-finance reforms limiting the amounts that could be given to particular parties or the number of parties that the same contributors could support.

Certain periods are more propitious than others for revenue-raising, particularly on the rich. In the United States at any rate, it appears only to be possible to increase taxes on the rich during wars and other times of great crisis. Otherwise there is little change in the structure of progressivity over time.[17] Perhaps counterintuitively, it appears to be more difficult to raise taxes in times of expansion than in recessions and when there are budget surpluses than when there are deficits.[18] When times are good and budgets are in surplus, the pressure is to cut taxes.

So much for revenue-raising issues. What about the spending side of redistributive policies? One possible conclusion from what has been said thus far is that those who would like to see more downward redistribution should forget about increasing progressivity in tax-raising. Given the difficulty of making the system more progressive than it is, perhaps it would be better just to worry about distributive agendas on the expenditure side — particularly if one's interest is in increasing what those at the bottom get, rather than decreasing what those at the top get, this may be the way to go. This argument tends to be made in third world contexts, where the limits of the state's power to tax are more dramatically evident; but arguably they make sense more generally.

Some types of spending policies are harder to pass than others. Outlays, which show up in the budget as spending, are more difficult to enact than tax expenditures, such as deductions and exemptions, which have to go through fewer institutional veto points and often are not perceived as government spending (think of deductions for charitable contributions and mortgage payments).[19] This is presumably why it is so difficult to have discussion of a social wage or universal basic income in the United States. Even when elements of it exist, it seems it must be euphemistically named a "refundable tax credit" or a "negative income tax." This seems likely a significant cultural difference between the United States, on the one hand, and Europe and Japan, on the other.

The moral of the story for redistributionists is, arguably, Get your foot in the door in the dark, given that most tax expenditures begin as obscure loopholes, growing over time into vast programs. Yet if incrementalism and camouflaged policies are better bets than bold innovations to improve the condition of the poor, what are the costs of these policies? Such approaches seem to run counter to arguments for publicity and transparency that often go with defenses of democracy.[20] This is an under-attended subject in debates about deliberation, which tend to make optimistic assumptions that informed discussion will lead to enlightened policies. Perhaps it won't. If we leave normative considerations to one side, however, the danger of politics by stealth is presumably that those with regressive agendas and more resources are likely to be better at it, so that, on balance, pragmatic considerations favor openness and attempting to expose the hypocrisies attending the hidden welfare state rather than trying to emulate it. In any case, the very poor, who don't pay taxes, could not benefit from tax expenditures.[21]

Are there fixed components of the budget such as interest payments and certain types of military expenditures that limit the possibilities for transfer programs? Some literature suggests there is a "crowding out" effect on redistributive policies when deficits are large. Theda Skocpol argued in *Boomerang* (1996) that the failure of President Bill Clinton's health-care reform proposal was made more or less inevitable by the deficits President Ronald Reagan left behind (though this is in some tension with the argument that it is actually easier to raise taxes in a period of deficits). Perhaps there are upper ceilings on the tax levels that voters will tolerate in non-crisis times, and the *Boomerang* logic prevails once this threshold has been passed. Some of the literature suggests that there are limits to the proportion of the budget available for transfer payments, so that increasing the numbers who benefit from transfer payments leads to reductions in the size of the payments themselves.[22] If this is so, it may be a reason for redistributionists to go the tax-expenditure rather than the transfer route.

Some of the literature suggests that transfer payments are more palatable to voters when they require recipients to work. It stands to reason that transfer payments are more likely to survive when they command support from interest groups of the left and the right for which work seems to be important.[23] Think of Aid to Families with Dependent Children, containing no work requirement, which was wiped out by President Clinton's welfare reform bill and replaced by Temporary Assistance to Needy Families, which has a lifetime five-year cap. By contrast, the work-dependent Earned Income Tax Credit, which was sharply expanded in 1990 and again in 1993, survived welfare reform.[24]

Given the difficulties on the expenditure side, an important challenge for those who want to see more downward redistribution is to think about policies that do not operate through the fisc, or only minimally in the sway that tax expenditures do. This suggests the wisdom of trying to structure things with tax incentives to encourage redistribution of the kind one wants to see. This could mean, among other things, tax write-offs for specified transfers (a more specific version of deductions for charitable contributions) or incentives for hiring unemployed workers. In this approach to redistribution, the role of government would be effectively shrunk to the operations of the Internal Revenue Service.

One could go even further and work for redistributive policies that do not operate through the fisc at all, such as Bill Bradley's proposal to index the minimum wage to the median income. This might be described as a kind of unfunded mandate on the economy. There are some advantages to this, though economists will say it will "distort" labor markets. A disadvantage is that it will not get to those who are completely outside the labor market — at least not directly. Since levels of welfare payments seem to track changes in the minimum wage, however, there may be an indirect benefit even to them. And to the degree that those not employed in the labor market are dependents of minimum wage workers, they will benefit as well.

The Demand Side

Having held the demand side constant, it is now time to recognize that it is not. For many reasons, demand does not exist for the type of redistribution predicted by classical theorists and the median-voter theorem. These reasons have less to do with strategic action and rational self-interest — which often seem to govern the supply side — than with the concerns of psychology and sociology.

A major theme here is "logics of distributive reference" — or to put it more simply, equality with whom? In 1984 Ronald Reagan ran for reelection trumpeting the brutally effective slogan: "Are you better off than you were four years ago?" It directed people to think about a bundle of goods represented by their disposable income and ask whether their stock of it had increased. This is self-referential comparison: it requires no attention to what others have. In the world of self-referential comparisons everyone is seen as trying to get more desirable things, and the well-being of others is purely incidental. Equality and inequality do not come into the picture.

Now consider this: you are department chair and your colleague Brown walks in declaring, "I don't care what my raise is, so long as it's larger than Jones's." Brown's well-being depends on what Jones gets; that is, it rests on an other-referential standard. Other-referential comparisons need not be selfish. An egalitarian colleague might insist on a raise that is no larger than anyone else's, and a parent's well-being might be improved by securing opportunities for her child that she does not have herself. The point is that how well we think we are doing depends on a comparison with others.

A more extreme type of other-referential comparison trades on internal relationships among people's experiences. Economists call these interdependent utilities.[25] The rapist or sadist gets his jollies from the suffering of another, as does the divorcing spouse when we transfer a dollar from the other spouse's pocket to that of a lawyer. Interdependent comparisons can also be altruistic rather than malevolent, as when a parent's happiness is critically reliant on the happiness of his child. Hatred and love involve internal relationships of this kind almost by definition; they anchor one polar extreme on the continuum from self- to other-referential comparisons. Chronic autism stands at its opposite end.[26]

Classifying motivation as self- or other-referential leaves many questions unanswered. It tells us nothing about whether people are selfish or altruistic, their views about redistribution and government's appropriate role in it, or to what extent people are alike in the comparisons they make. Nonetheless, we learn some things about distributive politics by finding out more about whether and to what extent people are self- or other-referential in thinking about distribution and, if other-referential, who the relevant others are.

A simple example will drive this home. The market wage for a certain type of production line worker is $40,000 per year. There are ten such workers in a corporation owned by one individual, paid the going rate. The owner discovers that by renting five machines for $40,000 apiece per year and laying off half the workforce, he can increase the productivity of the remaining five workers by 400 percent. These workers are able to negotiate a 25 percent raise, due to the higher market wage for the skills they develop to operate the new machinery. Are they better off than before? By self-referential comparisons, certainly. By other-referential comparisons, it depends on who the relevant other is. If they compare themselves to the owner (as Marx hoped they would), they will conclude that his relative share of the surplus has increased more than theirs, and they will regard themselves as worse off — hence more exploited. If, however, their comparative point of reference is the five fired employees they will see themselves as better off. Likewise if the reference group is workers in similar firms where there has been no technological innovation and wages are still $40,000.

Egalitarian redistribution does not require that people's judgments be other-referential. Economics conventionally assumes not just that people want more than they have, but that they want as much as they can get. So, notwithstanding the judgment that their circumstances have improved, at the margin they would always want to be better off still. To explain why self-referentially motivated people might not demand redistribution — as the redistributive thesis predicts they should — we must consider other factors.

In its Marxist variants the redistributive thesis depends exclusively on other-referential comparisons. The capitalist employer's increasing share of the surplus value produced by the worker is the source of the worker's escalating alienation, galvanizing him eventually to revolutionary action.[27] In reality, although other-referential comparisons motivate people a good deal of the time, they are not made with the comparators Marx had in mind. People make more local comparisons, based on class, status, and physical proximity. All the research shows that workers do not compare themselves to their employers in assessing their circumstances. They do not even compare themselves to the wealthy classes, but rather to similarly situated workers. This is true up and down the occupational scale. A professor will be much more troubled to learn that her salary is $10,000 less than that of a peer down the corridor than that it is $200,000 less than that of the cardiologist down the street.[28]

The reasons for this are much debated, and no doubt more than one dynamic is often at play. Cognitive limitations, the need for recognition from peers, "availability heuristics," and physical proximity all influence perceptions of relative well-being.[29] All these factors may help to explain why in contemporary Western countries the overwhelming majority conceives of itself as middle class. People tend to see the world as an enlarged version of their — comparatively homogeneous — local reference groups, pushing those very different from themselves into the background.[30]

This leads to the matter of people's knowledge and beliefs. People's perceptions that they are better off than they actually are are buttressed by their beliefs about how income is distributed and where they fit in the distribution. Long ago Max Weber observed that inequalities in some societies are more visible than in others.[31] In 1971 Frank Parkin developed this into the "transparency thesis" to explain why people are generally less well informed about the distribution of income and wealth in market systems (believing them more egalitarian than they are) and about their place in them (believing themselves better paid than they are) than in non-market systems.[32] Parkin contended that market systems are comparatively opaque because the allocation of economic rewards is not in the hands of a visible social group. On the Weber-Parkin account, part of why people look to local reference groups in market systems is that others are shrouded in fog. We need visible benchmarks to perceive inequality. The formal egalitarianism of market systems obscures it.

No less consequential than people's beliefs about the nature of inequality are their beliefs about its causal dynamics and what these mean for them. Most obviously, there are trickle-down arguments, invariably contentious but never vanquished. Don't squabble over the cake; let's get a bigger one for all. The rich will burn their crops before giving them to the poor. South Africa needs the white man. In this spirit people might embrace a version of Jeremy Bentham's distinction between actual or practical equality, which led him to advocate redistribution only to the (concededly elusive) point at which it began to reduce the overall stock of wealth.[33] To the extent that people believe versions of this claim (setting its veracity to one side), they might temper their redistributive demands. On this view governments do not need to resist redistributive pressure from below. Rather, voters—whether rational or ideological dupes—would never create the pressure that the redistributive thesis predicts.

One reason not to demand redistribution is the expectation that one will benefit from others' wealth. Another, standard in some economic models, is the belief that one will become those fortunate others.[34] Here, formal egalitarianism seems to be essential. Formally closed systems, such as apartheid, galvanize collective opposition, but formal openness, like that of American capitalism, forestalls it. Hence Parkin's observation that with systems of racial exclusion "the social visibility of the dominant group is especially marked and the dividing line between exploiters and exploited can be represented in a fairly unambiguous way." Inequalities that stem purely from the market, however, "rarely have this degree of transparency, so that perceptions and identities of a class character are less easily formed" than those of a racial character.[35] This suggests an explanation for why American blacks in the civil rights era could be mobilized against legal racial exclusion from full civic participation, whereas comparably effective mobilization against economic exclusion has failed to materialize. Likewise with the recent South African experience: apartheid's transparent racial exclusions bred massive — eventually irresistible — organized opposition; yet since 1994 many commentators have been surprised at the dearth of significant pressure on the African National Congress government for downward redistribution. Like Parkin, Alexis de Tocqueville might have predicted it. Of the rich in democratic societies he said: "They have no conspicuous privileges, and even their wealth, being no longer incorporated and bound up with the soil, is impalpable and, as it were, invisible." They no longer form "a distinct class, easily identified and plundered."[36]

This result is less surprising in light of empirical research in social psychology that supports the notion that in formally egalitarian systems people opt for individual advancement rather than collective action to improve their circumstances.[37] In one study, participants took rigged tests, which they failed, to enter a more "elite" group. However, the relative "openness" of the elite group was varied over the course of the experiment. The result: subjects opted overwhelmingly to pursue individual action when faced with rejection by an elite group that was said to be open to all who were qualified. In contrast, individuals opted for socially disruptive collective action when faced with rejection by a closed elite group.[38] Perhaps more interesting, it seems that very little openness is needed to forestall collective action. Even when faced with a strict restriction (such as a 2 percent quota of admission), most subjects still opted for individual action.[39] This underscores how powerful the preference for individual advancement is, at least in the United States. These results are in line with a 1993 study in which subjects were asked how they would respond to unambiguous discrimination in housing or employment. The overwhelming preference was for individual rather than collective redress. Only in circumstances of total exclusion, as when people lose fundamental rights such as the right to vote, do they consider collective action.[40]

Modest tokenism may thus be sufficient to defuse demands for collective redistribution, even when the status quo is seen as unjust.[41] No doubt some of the reasons for this have to do with the same irrational optimism that leads people in the millions to buy lottery tickets every day. And some of these reasons have to do with the well-documented human reluctance to identify with disadvantaged groups.[42] Whatever the causes, it seems that people opt for individual mobility over collective action unless individual advancement is undeniably impossible.

This research might well explain why we will never see junior faculty unions at Harvard or Yale, but the redistribution predicted by the redistributive thesis does not require that kind of collective action. With the advent of a universal franchise, all that is required for change is a majority of votes; there is no longer a collective action problem to be overcome. It is this fact, after all, that motivates the redistributive thesis. It is testimony to how powerful beliefs in individual efficacy are if tokenism and minimal opportunity for advancement can forestall support for collective redistribution even in the democratic context.

This suggests that more is at work than people's beliefs about how the world works. Ideological beliefs about what is just and fair are also at work here. James Tobin notes that people often oppose increases in the estate tax even when it is pointed out to them that they will not be subject to this tax.[43] That they take this stand may be due to the way the issue is dealt with (or not) in the media, but it may also be rooted in normative beliefs. An inquiry into the veracity of the redistributive thesis must come to grips with what people believe is just, since this is likely to influence their propensity to press for redistribution through collective institutions. Unsurprisingly, disadvantaged people who believe they live in a just world show less propensity for group discontent than those who believe their world is just.[44] The question arises, therefore, how widespread the belief is that the inequalities generated by market systems are just.

In the United States, at least, although people might be egalitarian in many facets of social life, they accept the market's economic differentiation.[45] Distributive outcomes are accepted as legitimate unless they are seen to be both procedurally and substantively unfair, and this seldom happens because the market is widely believed to be a fair distributive instrument.[46] Jennifer Hochschild's 1995 study of American beliefs reveals remarkably widespread endorsement of the ideology of the American Dream, understood to include the ideas "that skill rather than need should determine wages" and that "America should promote equal opportunity for all" rather than "equal outcomes."[47] Overwhelming majorities from different occupational, racial, and political groups endorse this view. Eight out of ten whites and nine out of ten blacks agree that "the American Dream is alive today"; and although blacks tend to believe there is more racial discrimination in the system than do whites, as a group they are actually more confident than whites of their own prospects.[48]

To be sure, not everyone believes in the justness of capitalism or the American Dream. Hochschild herself notes that a subset of the population is estranged from it. Other scholarship displays a different side of poverty, which involves notably less optimism about upward mobility. Jonathan Kozol's *Amazing Grace* (1995) portrays the South Bronx as a center of hopeless despair, where many of the poor are going nowhere and don't seem to care.

William Julius Wilson records a sense of desolation and inefficacy in inner-city neighborhoods in *When Work Disappears* (1997), and Elijah Anderson's ethnographic study *Streetwise* (1990) documents a similar lack of concern for upward mobility among inner-city teenagers.

Because desolation and apathy are unlikely to coexist with ambition and determination for success, it seems clear that differently situated poor people have different beliefs and aspirations. It also seems clear that any distinction between a despairing "underclass" and the rest of the poor who believe in upward mobility and the American Dream is untenable. For instance, in an ethnographic study of two groups of teenagers in the same housing project, one white, one black, most of the blacks thought of themselves as upwardly mobile and were working to advance themselves, while the white teenagers simply wasted their time smoking pot and skipping school.[49] Another ethnographic study found high degrees of aimlessness and apathy among the working poor in Buffalo.[50] This suggests that aspirations for advancement are not limited to the working poor and that apathy is not monopolized by those who are often stigmatized as the "underclass."

A more promising candidate for distinguishing the alienated from those who buy into the American Dream may be experience of, and prospects for, rewarding employment. In the study of blacks and whites in the same housing project, the parents of the alienated white teenagers were predominantly not high school graduates; they had other children who were dropping out of school; they had lived in the projects for up to three generations; and, if employed, they worked in temporary menial jobs. By contrast, parents of the ambitious black teenagers were new residents in the projects and had steady employment.[51] In the study of Buffalo's working poor, too, it seems to have been the disappearance of heavy industry jobs that had paid a "family wage" and their replacement by low-paying fast-food and other service jobs that explained the apathy and disillusionment.[52] Other ethnographic studies describe a sharp distinction between the older generation with traditional Protestant work-ethic values and younger generations who reject those values.[53] What is the main difference between the generations? As William Julius Wilson emphasizes, steady employment in manufacturing jobs that the older generation enjoyed is unavailable to the younger inner-city generation. They subsist either on welfare or in dead-end service-sector minimum wage jobs. This, he speculates, erodes their sense of efficacy and ambition.[54]

If experience of, and prospects for, rewarding employment account for the distinction between the apathetic and the upwardly mobile, what are the implications for the redistributive thesis? Jay Macleod contends that the disaffected are mobilizable for redistributive politics on the grounds that those "who see their chances for upward mobility as remote are more likely to involve themselves in collective political action than will their counterparts who see considerable opportunity for significant individual mobility."[55] But those who do not seek individual advancement may not be mobilizable for collective action either. It is well known that participation increases with both education and income. There are additional reasons for thinking that those most disaffected from the system may also be those who are least inclined to try to change it. Robert Lane argues that low status and a sense of deprivation tend to be associated with the belief that one is ineffective. Unlike anger, unhappiness (which is negatively associated with anger) is immobilizing; depressed people do not engage in politics.[56] This is intuitively plausible. It is difficult to imagine the South Bronx communities described by Kozol as suddenly galvanized into petition drives and town hall meetings to demand better services, housing, and police protection. There is too much despair and not enough anger.[57] Political disengagement, perhaps interspersed with occasional riots of the kind we saw in Los Angeles in 1992, seems like a more plausible prognosis. Perhaps those who could organize for redistributive politics are insufficiently disaffected to embrace the role, while those who are sufficiently disaffected are incapable of organizing.

Closely related to knowledge, beliefs, and ideologies concerning redistribution, but distinct from them, are the framing effects that shape what people see as pertinent alternatives.[58] Here the concern is not with what people might in principle, or on reflection, believe or know, but rather with what they actually focus on when making a particular decision. Economic models that suppose that people act on complete information, and even general surveys of what people believe about the distributive consequences of different policies, might not get us close to how they will behave in concrete situations. Consider some possibilities.

One reason people might not make demand after demand, ceasing only at death, stems from the reactive and backward-looking character of much human behavior. The question "Are you better off than you were four years ago?" directs attention to a worse status quo ante — with the implication that the alternative to the present is not further advance, but backsliding into the old world. Once a marginal advance has occurred, there is always the possibility of losing it. Reagan's 1984 slogan sought to trade on that fear, suggesting that a Mondale victory would mean a return to 1970s stagflation and erosion of the gains made since. People who are surprised that there are not more demands for downward redistribution tend to work on the assumption that those near the bottom of the economic distribution think they have nothing to lose but their chains. This is true of a handful of the population only—certainly not of the median voter. In many circumstances voters might indeed make the judgment that things could get worse—particularly if they have been worse in the recent past.[59]

Then there are inward-looking framing effects—the tendency to focus on oneself or one's own community in explaining deprivation. Rallying grass-roots supporters for the Million Man March in October 1995, Louis Farrakhan insisted that the time had come for the dispossessed in the black community to draw on their own resources and bootstrap themselves out of poverty. "Clean up, black man, and the world will respect and honor you. But you have fallen down like the prodigal son and you're husking corn and feeding swine. . . . Black man, you don't have to bash white people. All we've got to do is go back home and turn our communities into productive places."[60] The message is unequivocal: forget the inequality out there and focus on yourself. When people internalize ideologies of this kind, they will not demand redistribution through public institutions. Instead they will blame themselves for their distributive circumstances, and accept that they should look inward when trying to improve them.

Inward-looking framing effects are likely significant in accounting for the dearth of redistributive demands in the United States, given the power of bootstrapping ideologies there. Whether the inward-looking focus is on the self or on a comparatively dispossessed identity group, it is significantly *not* on the distribution of goods and opportunities in the larger society—hence arguments questioning the wisdom of identity politics from a progressively redistributive point of view.[61]

Moreover, people have multiple priorities. People who are aware of the full dimensions of economic inequality might nonetheless deem other things more important than trying to redress it, such as the redistribution of status and dignity. This seems particularly likely in new democracies. In South Africa, for instance, abolition of second-class citizenship, acquiring the dignity that comes with the act of voting, and the right to speak one's own language in court are all tangible gains. Those who have never been subject to second-class citizenship may discount them. Those who have might value them, however, and perceive tangible noneconomic gains from democracy.

Perhaps new democracies are not so distinctive in this regard. Presumably part of the appeal of ethnic and other forms of identity politics in countries like the United States comes from the persistence of status inequalities. The rage Farrakhan articulates reflects this.[62] Much of the women's movement over the past four decades has been about the reduction of status inequality. Some of it has also been distributive, as in the demand for equal pay for equal work (though this may have no effect on the reduction of class inequality in the society).[63] But much of it has to do with matters that are not distributive in the conventional sense at all, such as abolition of the marital rape exception and intra-spousal tort immunity. To the degree that the redistribution of status and dignity motivates people, the propensity to press for reductions in economic inequality may take a back seat.

Commentators on capitalism from the left and the right may have underestimated various dynamics that focus working- and middle-class attention on the people below them in the social order. These people can seem threatening in at least three ways: they will rise up and kill us; they will bankrupt us with their welfare benefits; or we will fall down into their ranks.

Fear of the marauding rabble of dispossessed poor long predates democratic capitalism. Christopher Hill points out that a recurrent theme in early Stuart literature was a strong upper-class mixture of fear and contempt for the "many-headed monster" (Sir Philip Sidney's phrase in *Arcadia*) of dispossessed poor. The same sentiment is repeated in many of the political tracts of the propertied classes, as summed up in Thomas Deloney's quip in 1597 that "the poor hate the rich because they will not set them on work; and the rich hate the poor because they seem burdensome."[64] Ruling-class fear of the masses seems to have intensified in response to the visible social consequences of economic and demographic changes that got under way in the mid-seventeenth century: urbanization and the growth of a wage-laboring class.[65] The propertied classes often expressed similar fears in the eighteenth century, not least in their enactment of vast numbers of capital crimes for minor offenses against property.[66] And Adam Smith is famous for the steely-eyed declaration that it is only the power of the civil magistrate that prevents the poor from expropriating the rich.[67]

Rather than disappear under democratic capitalism, however, fear of and contempt for the poor seems to take on distinctive forms. For one thing, it has a petty bourgeois flavor, since it revolves importantly around middle-class, especially lower-middle-class, antipathy for those below them. For another, there is the tendency of elite strata within disadvantaged groups in formally egalitarian systems to distance themselves from the larger disadvantaged group, identifying instead with the dominant culture.[68] This may partly reflect a need to have some group to look down on, and partly the softening effect of even minimal mobility and opportunity on social discontent. Perhaps more significant is that a good deal of democratic electoral politics seems to revolve around stoking middle-class fears of the underclass in ways that reinforce downward-looking framing effects. Much of the trench warfare around affirmative action, for instance, is about promotions in the police department, the post office, and the fire department; it has little impact on people who live in Scarsdale. It also has little impact on the structure of the income distribution, moving people around within it instead. This is why Michael Lind can write of a white overclass, whose members support racial preferences and multiculturalism from which they are largely immune, that they "live right and think left." They look askance at lower-middle-class opposition to these policies, seeing them as "not so much immoral as simply *vulgar*."[69] Whether one would want to go as far as he does in portraying affirmative action as the result of a divide-and-rule conspiracy to keep the lower orders squabbling among themselves, it may often have that effect: feeding racism and fracturing what would otherwise be natural constituencies for redistributive change.[70]

Downward-looking framing effects are sustained by demonizing those toward the bottom of the social order. In *Why Americans Hate Welfare,* Martin Gilens shows that hostility to welfare in the United States is not the result of opposition to the welfare state, or even to targeted welfare programs when they are seen as "helping the deserving poor help themselves."[71] Rather, hatred of welfare stems from the perception that most recipients are the undeserving poor. Media portrayals of welfare recipients as disproportionately black and blacks as disproportionately lazy reinforce this hostility, if they do not produce it, sustaining the picture of an extractive underclass that must be contained or otherwise warded off.[72]

This is to say nothing of crime. No account of downward-looking framing effects in the United States can be complete without attending to this issue. The vast numbers of people we now incarcerate constitute a demonized threatening group — even if, despite public perceptions to the contrary — most of them have not committed violent crimes.[73] Criminalizing the poor provides a convenient target — even a magnet — for downward-looking framing effects.

Another important part of the ideology of fairness is what we might call anecdotal distractions. In *Albion's Fatal Tree* Douglas Hay tells the story of an eighteenth-century criminal law that operated in the almost exclusive interests of propertied elites, but in which the occasional member of the nobility was publicly subjected to an extreme form of punishment, even the death penalty, for relatively minor offenses against property.[74] Part of the explanation for this has, no doubt, to do with the need for strong deterrence when enforcement institutions are weak.[75] Hay argues powerfully, however, that much of it had to do with instilling awe for the legal order that protected the propertied classes. What better way to get the poor to think that the law is not the instrument of the rich than to have it so visibly enforced against a member of the nobility? Comparable stories could perhaps be told about Michael Milken and Leona Helmsley today: that they were endlessly portrayed in the media as getting their comeuppance provides anecdotal legitimation for the system, regardless of how unrepresentative they actually might be.

Anecdotal distractions need not be directed at the rich only: lurid stories about "welfare queens" driving Cadillacs focus attention away from the behavior of most recipients to corruption of welfare by freeloaders. Stories about the venal behavior of public officials can serve a similar purpose, reinforcing the perception that redistributive taxation is less of a Robin Hood enterprise than rent-seeking by bureaucrats — less "from the rich to the poor" and more "from us to the government." Horatio Alger stories are also effective anecdotal distractions, as Reagan understood all too well when he declared in 1983 that "what I want to see above all is that this country remains a country where someone can always get rich."[76] When politicians visibly single out individuals who have moved from welfare to work or otherwise triumphed over adversity — standard fare in State of the Union presidential addresses since Reagan — they exhibit their understanding of the power of anecdotal distractions. The man or woman in the street does not ask questions about random sampling or selecting on the dependent variable.

The expectation that democracies will redistribute downward is often motivated by the spectacle of poverty amid opulence. It seems reasonable to anticipate that the greater the manifest opulence of the few, the stronger will be the redistributive pressure from below. Paradoxically, however, something closer to the opposite might often be the case.

Another challenge to redistributive ambition is the limits of the imagination — specifically, what might be described as "empathy gulfs." Aspirations do not form in vacuums. People must be able to conjure up in imagination the objects and lifestyles for which they will strive. For this, psychic distance matters. You can imagine yourself stepping unaided over a puddle, perhaps swimming a lake, but not paddling across the Atlantic. At some point the gap between where you are and where you might hope to get will seem so huge that certain goals will be excluded from your field of aspirations. Hence the notion of an empathy gulf, intended to suggest that exceedingly high levels of inequality might actually dampen redistributive demands from the very poor. An extreme example will make this point. In Cape Town it is common for domestic cleaners who live in squatters' camps to work for ten dollars a day cleaning half-million-dollar houses, where the cars in the garages cost many multiples of the domestics' expected lifetime earnings. It may just be impossible for them to imagine themselves in their employers' shoes.[77]

Empathy gulfs can operate in the opposite direction as well. To the degree that willingness to tolerate downward redistribution is part of a prudential calculation — "there but for fortune go I . . ." — it has to be believable. If the gap between you and the poor you see around you is so massive that no calamity you can imagine befalling you will put you into their circumstances, then any prudential reasons you might have for improving their lot disappear.

Presumably this is one reason why most people can tune out panhandlers and street people and acquiesce in the demonization of the underclass. The mighty might tumble in Zola's novels, but those who read Zola don't really expect to experience the tumble themselves.

The more extreme is income inequality, then, the greater is the psychic distance between the have-nots and the haves. Beyond certain thresholds (which would have to be determined empirically) inequality spawns empathy gulfs that reduce demands from below and harden attitudes above. Vast empathy gulfs may breed resentment, crime, and, in the limiting case, revolution. But if the resources for that are lacking, or the political order is not seen as fundamentally illegitimate, then empathy gulfs will reinforce the inegalitarian status quo. This may fuel characteristic types of conflict among different groups and classes toward the lower end of the socioeconomic spectrum, but it is unlikely to have much effect on the overall distribution of income and wealth.[78]

Geography produces other kinds of distance that attenuate redistributive demands. One might think of this as another kind of framing effect: out of sight, out of mind. But it is both more and less than this. It is more than a framing effect in that segregation of the have-nots from the haves in capitalist democracies is real and increasing. The starkest illustration of this in the United States is the middle-class dash from cities to suburbs that took off a generation ago and is now culminating in enclave living. As recently as 1960 "gated communities" numbered in the hundreds and were for the elderly and the super-rich. By 1997 there were as many as 20,000 gated communities in the country, consisting of more than three million housing units, at least a third of which were middle class and a growing number even working class.[79] These numbers greatly understate the real extent of enclave living, since many country towns (often functional suburbs) can for all practical purposes be inaccessible to inner-city residents.[80]

The net effect is the development of what Douglas Rae has described as "segmented democracy" in which the only public spaces (that is, having no charge for admission) are the inner cities.[81] Formal freedom of movement lives cheek by jowl with effective segregation by race and class that is in many respects as extreme as it was in apartheid South Africa.[82] Movement by poor black and brown people from the inner cities into middle- and upper-class neighborhoods is not a practical option, given the realities of transportation and local policing practices. This was underscored with poignancy in the 1992 Los Angeles riots following the acquittal of four white police officers in the beating of a black man, Rodney King, which had been filmed on videotape and was shown endlessly on television for months before the trial. Although inner-city blacks rioted, they turned the vast bulk of their aggression on other local ethnic groups, notably Koreans. None of them headed for Beverly Hills.

Spatial segregation also means that the middle and upper classes restrict their urban life to business districts and daylight hours, a trend that is greatly enhanced by the flexibility to work from home afforded by the Internet. And those who live in refurbished parts of inner cities have enclaves of their own. Their daily paths from guarded apartment buildings, to work, to gyms and yuppie restaurants enable them to keep contact with people disturbingly different from themselves to a minimum. In this way the physical gulfs of Rae's segmented democracy reinforce the empathy gulfs already discussed.

Yet physical gulfs amount to less than a framing effect, in the television age, in that out of sight is not — strictly speaking — out of mind. The paradox is that despite the geographic reality of physical segmentation, the have-nots are not ignorant of what the haves have. Tocqueville said that the poor knuckle under in aristocracies because they are ignorant of comfort: "They despair of getting it and they do not know enough about it to want it."[83] The implied suggestion is that, were it available, such knowledge would become the engine of redistributive demands. Yet, despite the fact that people are bombarded with images of how the other half (or, more accurately, the other 2 percent) lives, the demand does not arise. Knowledge by acquaintance is more important, it seems, than knowledge by television.[84] This is consistent with research suggesting that what people learn through the media is not a substitute for everyday proximity in shaping their aspirations.[85] It also suggests that, once again, formal equality and a minimum of mobility may be enough to defuse discontent. On this view, official segregation, such as the Group Areas Act that launched South Africa's residential segregation in 1950, should be expected to breed collective resistance, but removing the legal prohibitions will take the wind out of its sails. People will respond, rather, by aspiring toward individual physical mobility — even if the odds of success are negligible. The contemporary United States provides anecdotal evidence in support of this contention, and post-apartheid South Africa offers a natural experiment to test it. Nine years into the new regime there is negligible erosion of residential segregation (though there is an even more explosive growth of gated communities than in the United States in response to the proliferation of squatters' camps that encircle the enclave suburbs). Time will tell whether the demand for collective policies to produce integration will remain as muted as it has been to date.

A different set of factors has to do with the structure of inequality itself. Nineteenth-century formulations of the redistributive thesis depended on a crude Marxian picture of capitalism evolving into a two-class system: a tiny bloated ruling class and a vast working class whose members were scraping by at subsistence. A small subset of the bourgeoisie might make it into the ruling class, but most would fall down into the proletariat—all the more easily mobilized because of the seething resentments they would bring with them.

Part of Marx's failure here was conceptual. His theory of exploitation moves illicitly between the claim that the relative immiseration of the proletariat will increase (which follows analytically from his theory of exploitation) to the claim that their absolute immiseration will (which does not). As the earlier example of the newly mechanized factory showed, the rate of Marxian exploitation can increase while wages remain constant or even rise. Part of Marx's failure was empirical: in all capitalist democracies an enduring middle class includes many people Marx would have classified as workers: they must sell their labor-power to others in order to survive. Yet they live nowhere near subsistence (even defined to include a "historical and moral" component, such as that a car may be a subsistence necessity in much of the United States), nor are they going to do so. They do not confront the proverbial state of affairs in which they have nothing to lose but their chains.

Marxian political economists have sometimes claimed that this is a transient state of affairs: working-class discontent is bought off through welfare states that will eventually succumb to fiscal crises, after which inexorable contradictions will surface and lead to two-class polarization.[86] In fact a three-class dynamic might be quite stable for reasons that are distinct from the considerations about reference groups, knowledge, beliefs, framing effects, and empathy and physical gulfs already discussed. Even in a world of full-information self-referential maximizers (an economically "rational" world) it is far from clear that the median voter will always vote to redistribute downward. An illustration is suggestive of the possibilities. One reason there is not significant pressure for downward redistribution from the grass roots of the African National Congress in South Africa flows from the extreme character of the maldistribution of income and wealth there. An increase in taxes on even the top 20 percent of the population would be an increase on much of the black working class, so they have self-interested reasons to oppose it. And, if they did support redistribution, it would scarcely be to those at the bottom of the economic order in a country where 40 percent of the black population is unemployed.[87] This suggests the importance of looking seriously into the counterintuitive possibility that the more unequal the distribution, the harder it may be to mobilize lower-middle- and working-class support for redistribution downward—certainly for redistribution to those at the bottom.[88]

In conclusion, then, the nineteenth-century expectations and the median-voter theorem were wrong. There is no systematic relationship between democracy and downward redistribution, and quite likely no relationship at all.

No single explanation of why not will do; it is a host of interacting factors on the supply side and the demand side: some structural, some embedded in the logic of democratic decision rules, some contextual, some psychological, some geographic.

If one thinks that achieving improvements in the relative and absolute well-being of the bottom quintile is important for minimal justice, as I believe that we should, two types of research are needed: We need a better understanding of which factors are most important in a causal sense, and how they interact with the others. And we need more creative attention to the types of feasible democratic reforms, on both the supply side and the demand side, that are most likely to push redistributive politics in the desired directions.

Notes

A more elaborate version of this essay appears as chapter 5 of the author's book *The State of Democratic Theory* (Princeton: Princeton University Press, 2003).

1. Winnick 1989; Wolff 1994; Shammas 1993.

2. For data on the changing absolute and relative shares of income and wealth for the bottom quintile of the population in the United States over the past half century, see Mishel, Bernstein, and Schmitt (2000: 48–51, 261–64). See also Nickerson (2000).

3. Przeworski and Wallerstein 1988.

4. Globally, the distributive results of trade openness may be more complex than one might expect. Garrett (2001) finds, for example, that while there are mild distributive costs to trade openness for the poor in first world economies, most of the benefits accrue to populations in middle-income economies and the wealthy elites in poor countries, with no benefits to the poor there. This casts in a dubious light the claim that protectionist workers in the first world are in fact contributing to starvation wages in Malaysia. It is also unclear how much the growth of wage inequality in the first world is due to trade rather than technology; cf. Adrian Wood and his critics as discussed in Shapiro (1999a: 191–95). In the United States there is some evidence of a race-to-the-bottom phenomenon, though also some stickiness. See Peterson and Rom (1989); Tweedie (1994); Figlio, Koplin, and Reid (1999).

5. The Death Tax Elimination Act of 2000 was passed by Congress in the summer of 2000 and vetoed by President Clinton. President Bush signed a similar provision into law as part of the tax cut that was passed with considerable bipartisan support in the summer of 2001.

6. Tsebelis 1995; Treisman 2000.

7. Comparative evidence seems to corroborate this claim (Hirschl 1999; Hirschl 2000).

8. Stokes 1996; Vreeland 1999.

9. Cohen and Rogers 1995; Bardhan 1999.

10. Putnam 2000.

11. Steinmo 1993.

12. Powell 2000.

13. The Progressives did advance a version of this critique; see Epstein (1986: 17–71). The lone voice in the contemporary literature seems to be Wittman (1973).

14. *Noerr*, 356 U.S. 137, 138 (1961). Thus the court rejected a claim by the State of Missouri that the National Organization of Women had violated the Sherman Act by organizing a conference boycott in states that had not ratified the Equal Rights Amendment, holding that the participants were engaging in legitimate forms of political organizing rather than undermining commercial competitors. *Missouri v. National Organization of Women, Inc.*, 467 F. Supp. 289, 304 (1979), cert. denied 449 U.S. 842 (1980).

15. *Parker v. Brown*, 317 U.S. 341, 351 (1943).

16. *Klor's, Inc. v. Broadway-Hale Stores, Inc.*, 359 U.S. 207, 213 n. 7 (1959), and *Apex Hosiery Co. v. Leader*, 310 U.S. 469, 493 n. 5 (1940).

17. Witte 1985; Steinmo 1993.

18. Witte 1985.

19. These are among the findings of Howard's *Hidden Welfare State* (1997).

20. See, e.g., Fishkin (1995); Gutmann and Thompson (1996).

21. Some of the literature suggests that it is easier to enact universal programs such as Social Security rather than one targeted at groups, such as AFDC—the theory being that the targeting brings demonization with it. However, there is some contrary evidence too. There are intermediate possibilities; see Skocpol (1991) on "targeting within universalism." This is better tackled under the demand side (below) since the logic is about the amounts and kinds of opposition different policies should be expected to provoke.

22. Peterson and Rom 1989.

23. Ribar and Wilhelm 1996; Ribar and Wilhelm 1999; Moffitt, Ribar, and Wilhelm 1998.

24. Pierson 1996.

25. As in the claim that income inequality makes the poor unhappy because they envy the rich, or the rich unhappy because they pity or fear the poor. See Yunker (1983: 132–55).

26. Some types of motivation will be difficult to classify by reference to this distinction. If I want a better computer than I now have, that is self-referential; and if I want a better one than you have, that is other-referential. But there is a difference between my wanting at least as good a computer as you own and my wanting the fastest possible computer purely from the perspective of budgeting my time, and I see that your computer meets that test better than mine. By the same token, if, on becoming aware of a new limited edition car, I want it because it performs better than my present car, then I remain in the world of self-referential comparisons. If, however, my reason for wanting it is that it is a limited edition, then (like all status-based desires) it is inherently other-referential.

27. For elucidation of various ways in which this is unpersuasive, see Roemer (1995).

28. Frank 1985: 39–107. Generally, see Kelley and Evans (1995).

29. On availability heuristics, see Tversky and Kahneman (1981) and Kahneman, Stovic, and Tversky (1982). In different ways all these explanations lend credence to W. G. Runciman's (1996) view that deprivation relative to a salient group of comparatively local others is more important than global economic position in influencing the demands people are likely to make—though there is more than one way of being local. Although Runciman's relative deprivation thesis has a mixed empirical record in predict-

ing collective mobilization for political change, it does better than objective class position; and in any case its failures may have more to do with lack of organizational resources, or to the requirements of spatial proximity, than with the thesis itself (Kelley and Evans 1995: 174–75). As an account of how people see their entitlements in relation to others, it seems to do reasonably well a good deal of the time.

30. Evans, Kelley, and Kolosi 1996: 461–82; Hodge and Trieman 1968: 535–47. See also Canache's (1996: 556–66) argument that poor people are more prone to violence if they find themselves in comparatively homogeneous rich neighborhoods where "the contextual evidence of deprivation is most explicit" than in more diverse neighborhoods, even if they are equally wealthy overall.

31. Weber 1997: 183–84.

32. Parkin 1971: 160–64.

33. Bentham 1954: 442.

34. See Bénabou and Ok (1998), who argue that it is possible for a majority of the population simultaneously to be poorer than average in terms of current income yet rationally oppose downward redistribution, provided future income is anticipated to be increasing and is a concave function of present income. For an account that links views about redistributive taxation to beliefs about social mobility, see Piketty (1995).

35. Parkin, 1971: 161. For an account of the origins of the Solidarity movement in Poland in the high levels of economic awareness of Polish workers, see Laba (1986: 47–67).

36. As he elaborates: "I am not suggesting that they [the middle class] are themselves satisfied with their actual position or that they would feel any natural abhorrence toward a revolution if they could share the plunder without suffering the calamities; on the contrary, their eagerness to get rich is unparalleled, but their trouble is to know whom to despoil." Tocqueville 1969 [1835–40]: 635–36.

37. Here, bearing the South African reality in mind, we should perhaps include crime in the category of individual advancement.

38. Wright, Taylor, and Moghaddam 1990: 994–1003.

39. Wright, Taylor, and Moghaddam 1990: 1001. In a subsequent study Lalonde and Silverman also found a greater preference for collective action when groups are closed than when they are open, and that even when groups are closed the preference is no stronger than for individual action (Lalonde and Silverman 1994: 78–85).

40. Lalonde and Cameron 1993: 257–88. This individual response may make a degree of pragmatic sense. For instance, Martin proposes a "sequential contingent model," according to which people consider a sequence of behaviors to alleviate perceived injustice, starting with those that involve the least personal effort. Thus someone who feels relatively deprived will seek first to improve his or her individual economic situation before sparking a class rebellion out of practical considerations of time, energy, and risk-tradeoffs. Martin 1986: 217–40.

41. As Wright (1997: 1286) sums up another experimental study: "The success of a very small number of disadvantaged group members can undermine endorsement of collective action by focusing attention on personal rather than collective injustice and by reducing confidence about the illegitimacy and instability of the intergroup context."

42. There is considerable evidence, for instance, that even when people perceive discrimination as directed toward the group with which they identify, they perceive less

discrimination being directed at themselves as individuals. See Crosby (1984: 371–86); Taylor, Wright, Moghaddam, and Lalonde (1990: 254–62).

43. Tobin 1988: 161.

44. Hafer and Olson 1993: 30–38.

45. Hochschild 1981: chap. 3.

46. See Martin (1986); Taylor, Moghaddam, Gamble, and Zeller (1987: 259–72); îSmith and Tyler (1996: 171–200).

47. Hochschild 1995: 55–60. See also Olson (1986: 57–78), who finds that having appropriate qualifications is perceived as part of procedural fairness that legitimates inegalitarian outcomes.

48. Hochschild 1995: 55–69, 184–213. See also Elster (1995: 305–8).

49. Macleod 1987.

50. Fine and Weis 1998.

51. Macleod 1987: 55.

52. Fine and Weis 1998: 29–39.

53. Anderson 1990: 69–73; Duneier 1992.

54. Wilson 1996: 76.

55. Macleod 1987: 158–59.

56. Lane 1991.

57. In response to the question of why the poor in the South Bronx don't rise up in organized political resistance, one of Kozol's interviewees replies, "No. People protest specific actions of the city. They protested the waste burner. But there's a sense of powerlessness that makes it hard to keep up momentum." Another: "Everything breaks down in a place like this. The pipes break down. The phone breaks down. The electricity and heat break down. The spirit breaks down." Kozol 1995: 81, 181.

58. Tversky and Kahneman 1981.

59. Presumably there would be links here to the literature on retrospective voting. See Fiorina (1981).

60. *Time,* October 16, 1995, http://cgi.pathfinder.com/time/special/million/minister2 .html.

61. Fraser 1997: 11–39; Barry 2001.

62. "Some of us are here because it's a march through which we can express anger and rage with America for what she has and is doing to us." *Time,* October 16, 1995.

63. Rae et al. 1981: chaps. 5–6.

64. Hill 1965: 300–02.

65. Hill 1961; Hill 1965: 306–14; Hill 1972: 39–56.

66. Hay 1975: 17–63.

67. "The affluence of the rich excites the indignation of the poor, who are often both driven by want, and prompted by envy, to invade his possessions. It is only under the shelter of the civil magistrate that the owner of that valuable property, which is acquired by the labour of many years, or perhaps many successive generations, can sleep a single night in security. He is at all times surrounded by unknown enemies, whom, though he never provoked, he can never appease, and from whose injustice he can be protected only by the powerful arm of the civil magistrate continually held up to chastise it." A. Smith 1937 [1776]: 670.

68. See C. Cohen (1999: chap. 2) on the phenomenon of middle-class blacks internalizing the norms of the dominant culture and distancing themselves from members of dispossessed black communities.

69. Lind 1995: 150.

70. Lind 1995: 139–80. For a general treatment of the undernoticed importance of race in American politics, see R. Smith (1997). On the tensions between racism and progressive redistributive politics, see Leiman (1993) and McMath (1993: 171–75); the latter contends that the culturally ingrained racism of southern and midwestern Populists was largely responsible for their failure to achieve class solidarity and significant redistributive reform. McMath notes in particular how initial attempts at black-white solidarity among the Populists eventually crumbled in the face of relentless race-baiting by the Democratic Party in the South.

71. This stands in contrast to the conventional wisdom, which holds that Americans generally support universalist programs but are hostile to targeted ones. See Skocpol (1991: 414). Consistent with Gilens (1999) and in opposition to this conventional orthodoxy is a study by Bobo (1998: 996), which finds, perhaps surprisingly, that "the more whites are committed to notions of reward for hard work, the less likely they are to hold negative beliefs about the effects of affirmative action for blacks."

72. Gilens 1999: 3, 6–7.

73. For data on the explosive growth of incarceration in the United States (which has transformed the United States from a country that incarcerated around 100 per 100,000 between World War II and 1970 to one that was incarcerating over 400 per 100,000 by the mid-1990s), see Irwin and Austin (1997: 1–61), who note that almost three-quarters of those incarcerated have not committed violent offenses of any kind, convictions for drug possession or trafficking accounting for the great majority of the increase.

74. Hay 1975: 32–39.

75. In particular with the inverse relationship between the severity of punishment and the probability of apprehension. See Posner (1985).

76. Quoted in Hochschild (1988: 168).

77. Note that this can be true whether people are self- or other-referential.

78. Lind 1995: 139–80.

79. Blakely and Snyder 1997: 6–7.

80. It is thus possible to live in Branford, Connecticut, a fifteen-minute drive from New Haven, and not own a key to one's house.

81. Rae 1999: 165–92; Sugrue 1993.

82. Blakely and Snyder 1997: 152–56.

83. Tocqueville 1969 [1835–40]: 531.

84. Hence the research suggesting that poor young men who live in middle- or high-status communities are more likely to be delinquent than those living in poor communities. See Johnstone (1978: 49–72).

85. Frank 1985: 8–9; Canache 1996.

86. See, for instance, Miliband (1969) and O'Connor (1973).

87. Nattrass and Seekings 2001.

88. In one attempt to model this type of logic, Breyer and Ursprung show formally that economically powerful (i.e., above-average) income earners are indeed in a position to

bribe the small segment of voters with incomes between the median and the mean to resist the temptation of confiscatory taxation (Breyer and Ursprung 1998: 197–230). In a comparable model Snyder and Kramer note that a majority of middle- and upper-income taxpayers might support a relatively progressive income tax to reduce their tax burden at the expense of the poor (Snyder and Kramer 1988: 197–230). Breyer and Ursprung note that such equilibria are likely unstable, for the well-known reason that all taxation schemes are vulnerable to being overturned by some majority coalition. My observation on this is that the logic of divide-a-dollar games does not do well empirically in the taxation area, given the manifest stability of taxation arrangements in most democracies over time. Perhaps, therefore, results like theirs can be shown to be retentive in practice, and more strongly retentive the more inegalitarian the status quo is. Intuitively: the more the wealthy minority has, the more affordable it will be for them to continue bribing the voters between the median and the mean, as Breyer and Ursprung suggest, whether through marginal tax cuts, middle-class tax benefits such as home-mortgage interest deductions, or subsidies for their children's higher education. And this middle group's members may well be more concerned about what they stand to lose from an aggressive system of progressive taxation than attracted to the uncertain benefits of allying with those below them in order to soak the rich.

Works Cited

Ackerman, Bruce. 1993. "Crediting the voters: A new beginning for campaign finance." *American Prospect.* No. 13: 71–80.

Anderson, Elijah. 1990. *Streetwise: Race, Class, and Change in an Urban Community.* Chicago: University of Chicago Press.

Ayres, Ian. 2000. "Disclosure versus anonymity in campaign finance." *Designing Democratic Institutions,* ed. Ian Shapiro and Stephen Macedo. New York University Press.

Bardhan, Pranab. 1999. "Democracy and development: A complex relationship." In *Democracy's Value,* ed. Ian Shapiro and Casiano Hacker-Cordón. Cambridge: Cambridge University Press.

Barry, Brian. 2001. *Culture and Equality: An Egalitarian Critique of Multiculturalism.* Cambridge: Harvard University Press.

Bénabou, Roland, and Efe A. Ok. 1998. "Social mobility and the demand for redistribution: The POUM hypothesis," C. V. Starr Center Working Paper. June.

Bentham, Jeremy. 1954. "The psychology of economic man." In *Jeremy Bentham's Economic Writings,* ed. W. Stark, vol. 3. London: George Allen and Unwin.

Blakely, Edward, and Mary Snyder. 1997. *Fortress America: Gated Communities in the United States.* Washington, D.C.: Brookings.

Bobo, Lawrence. 1998. "Race, interests, and beliefs about affirmative action." *American Behavioral Scientist.* 41(7) (April): 985–1003.

Breyer, Friedrich, and Heinrich W. Ursprung. 1998. "Are the rich too rich to be expropriated? Economic power and feasibility of constitutional limits to redistribution." *Public Choice.* 94: 135–56.

Canache, Damarys. 1996. "Looking out my back door: The neighborhood context and the perceptions of relative deprivation." *Political Research Quarterly.* 493 (September): 547–71.

Cohen, Cathy J. 1999. *The Boundaries of Blackness: AIDS and the Breakdown of Black Politics.* Chicago: University of Chicago Press.

Cohen, G. A. 1995. *Self-Ownership, Freedom, and Equality.* Cambridge: Cambridge University Press.

Cohen, Joshua, and Joel Rogers, eds. 1995. *Associations and Democracy.* London: Verso.

Crosby, Faye. 1984. "The denial of personal discrimination." *American Behavioral Scientist.* 27: 371–86.

Di Palma, Guiseppe. 1990. *To Craft Democracies: An Essay on Democratic Transitions.* Berkeley: University of California Press.

Duneier, Mitchell. *Slim's Table.* Chicago: University of Chicago Press, 1992.

Elster, Jon. 1995. "Local justice and American value." *Local Justice in America,* ed. Jon Elster. New York: Russell Sage.

Epstein, Leon D. 1986. *Political Parties in the American Mold.* Madison: University of Wisconsin Press.

Evans, M. D. R., Jonathan Kelley, and Tamas Kolosi. 1996. "Images of class: Public perceptions in Hungary and Australia," *American Sociological Review.* 61: 461–82.

Figlio, Koplin, and William E. Reid. 1999. "Do states play welfare games?" *Journal of Urban Economics.* 46(3): 437–54.

Fine, Michelle, and Lois Weis. 1998. *The Unknown City.* Boston: Beacon.

Fiorina, Morris P. 1981. *Voting in American National Elections.* New Haven: Yale University Press.

Fishkin, James S. 1995. *The Voice of the People: Public Opinion and Democracy.* New Haven. Yale University Press.

Frank, Robert. 1985. *Choosing the Right Pond: Human Behavior and the Quest for Status.* Oxford: Oxford University Press.

Fraser, Nancy. 1997. *Justice Interruptus: Critical Reflections on the "Postsocialist" Condition.* New York: Routledge.

Garrett, Geoffrey. 2001. "The distributive consequences of globalization." Mimeo. Yale University.

Gilens, Martin. 1999. *Why Americans Hate Welfare.* Chicago: University of Chicago Press.

Green, Donald, and Ian Shapiro. 1994. *Pathologies of Rational Choice Theory: A Critique of Applications in Political Science.* New Haven: Yale University Press.

———. 1996. "Pathologies revisited: Reflections on our critics." In *The Rational Choice Controversy: Economic Models of Politics Reconsidered,* ed. Jeffrey Friedman. New Haven: Yale University Press.

Gutmann, Amy, and Dennis Thompson. 1996. *Democracy and Disagreement.* Cambridge, Mass.: Belknap Press.

Hafer, Carolyn, and James Olson. 1993. "Beliefs in a just world, discontent and assertive actions by working women." *Personality and Social Psychology Bulletin.* 19(1):30–38.

Hay, Douglas. 1975. "Property, authority and the criminal law." In *Albion's Fatal Tree: Crime and Society in Eighteenth-Century England,* by Douglas Hay, Peter Linebaugh, John Rule, E. P. Thompson, and Cal Winslow. New York: Pantheon.

Hill, Christopher. 1961. *The Century of Revolution, 1603–1714*. New York: Norton.

———. 1965. "The many-headed monster in later Tudor and early Stuart political think-ing." In *From the Renaissance to the Counter-Reformation: Essays in Honor of Gar-rett Mattingly*, ed. Charles H. Carter. New York: Random House.

———. 1972. *The World Turned Upside Down*. New York: Pelican.

Hirschl, Ran. 1999. "Towards Juristocracy: A Comparative Inquiry into the Origins and Consequences of the New Constitutionalism." Ph.D. diss., Yale University.

———. 2000. "The political origins of judicial empowerment through constitutionaliza-tion: Lessons from four constitutional revolutions." *Law and Social Inquiry*. 25(1): 91–147.

Hochschild, Jennifer. 1981. *What's Fair? American Beliefs about Distributive Justice*. Cambridge: Harvard University Press.

———. 1988. "The double-edged sword of equal opportunity." In *Power, Inequality, and Democratic Politics*, ed. Ian Shapiro and Grant Reeher. Boulder: Westview.

———. 1995. *Facing Up to the American Dream: Race, Class, and the Soul of the Nation*. Princeton: Princeton University Press.

Hodge, Robert, and Donald Trieman. 1968. "Class identification in the United States." *American Journal of Sociology*. 73: 535–47.

Howard, Christopher. 1997. *The Hidden Welfare State*. Princeton: Princeton University Press.

Huntington, Samuel P. 1991. *The Third Wave: Democratization in the Late Twentieth Century*. Norman: University of Oklahoma Press.

Irwin, John, and James Austin. 1997. *It's About Time: America's Imprisonment Binge*. Belmont, Calif.: Wadsworth.

Johnstone, John. 1978. "Social class, social areas, and delinquency." *Sociology and Social Research*. 63(1): 49–72.

Kahneman, Daniel, Paul Stovic, and Amos Tversky. 1982. *Judgment under Uncertainty*. Cambridge: Cambridge University Press.

Kelley, Jonathan, and M. D. R. Evans. 1995. "Class and class conflict in six western nations." *American Sociological Review*. 60 (April): 157–78.

Kozol, Jonathan. 1995. *Amazing Grace: The Lives of Children and the Conscience of a Nation*. New York: Crown.

Laba, Roman. 1986. "Worker Roots of Solidarity." *Problems of Communism*. July–August: 47–67.

Lalonde, Richard, and J. E. Cameron. 1993. "Behavioral responses to discrimination: A focus on action." In *The Psychology of Prejudice: The Ontario Symposium*, ed. M. P. Zanna and J. M. Olson, vol. 7. Hillsdale, N.J.: Lawrence Erlbaum Associates.

Lalonde, Richard, and Randy Silverman. 1994. "Behavioral preferences in response to social injustice: The effects of group permeability and social identity salience." *Journal of Personality and Social Psychology*. 66(1): 78–85.

Lane, Robert. 1991. *The Market Experience*. Cambridge: Cambridge University Press.

Leiman, Melvin M. 1993. *Political Economy of Racism*. London: Pluto.

Lind, Michael. 1995. *The Next American Nation*. New York: Free Press.

Macleod, Jay. 1987. *Ain't No Makin' It: Leveled Aspirations in a Low-Income Neighbor-hood*. Boulder: Westview.

Martin, Joanne. 1986. "Tolerance of injustice." In *Relative Deprivation and Social*

Comparison, ed. James Olson, C. Peter Herman, and Mark Zanna. Hillsdale, N.J.: Lawrence Erlbaum Associates.

McMath, Robert C. 1993. *American Populism.* New York: Hill and Wang.

Miliband, Ralph. 1969. *The State in Capitalist Society.* New York: Basic.

Mishel, Lawrence, Jared Bernstein, and John Schmitt. 2000. *The State of Working America, 1998–1999.* Washington, D.C.: Economic Policy Institute.

Moffitt, Robert, David Ribar, and Mark Wilhelm. 1998. "The decline of welfare benefits in the US: The role of wage inequality." *Journal of Public Economics.* 68(3): 421–52.

Nattrass, Nicoli, and Jeremy Seekings. 2001. "A Divided Nation: Distribution in Post-Apartheid South Africa." *Daedalus.* 130(1): 45–70.

Nickerson, David. 2000. "Do autocracies obey Wagner's law?" Mimeo, Yale University.

O'Connor, James R. 1973. *Fiscal Crisis of the State.* New York: St. Martin's.

Olson, James. 1986. "Resentment about deprivation." In *Relative Deprivation and Social Comparison,* ed. by James Olson, C. Peter Herman, and Mark Zanna. Hillsdale, N.J.: Lawrence Erlbaum Associates.

Parkin, Frank. 1971. *Class, Inequality, and Political Order.* New York: Praeger.

Peterson, Paul E. and Mark Rom. 1989. "American federalism, welfare policy, and residential choices." *American Political Science Review.* 83(3): 711–28.

Pierson, Paul. 1996. *Dismantling the Welfare State? Reagan, Thatcher, and the Politics of Retrenchment.* Cambridge: Cambridge University Press.

Piketty, Thomas. 1995. "Social mobility and redistributive politics." *Quarterly Journal of Economics.* 110(3): 551–84.

Posner, Richard. 1985. "An economic theory of the criminal law." *Columbia Law Review.* 85(6): 1193–1231.

Powell, G. Bingham. 2000. *Elections as Instruments of Democracy: Majoritarian and Proportional Visions.* New Haven: Yale University Press.

Przeworski, Adam. 1999. "Minimalist Conception of Democracy: A Defense." In *Democracy's Value,* ed. Ian Shapiro and Casiano Hacker-Cordón. Cambridge: Cambridge University Press.

Przeworski, Adam, and Michael Wallerstein. 1988. "Structural dependence of the state on capital." *American Political Science Review.* 82(1): 11–29.

Putnam, Robert. 2000. *Bowling Alone: The Collapse and Revival of American Community.* New York: Simon and Schuster.

Rae, Douglas. 1999. "Democratic liberty and tyrannies of place." In *Democracy's Edges,* ed. Ian Shapiro and Casiano Hacker-Cordón. Cambridge: Cambridge University Press.

Rae, Douglas, et al. 1981. *Equalities.* Cambridge: Harvard University Press.

Ribar, David C., and Mark O. Wilhelm. 1996. "Welfare generosity: The importance of administrative efficiency, community values, and genuine benevolence." *Applied Economics* 28(8): 1045–54.

———. 1999. "The demand for welfare generosity." *Review of Economics and Statistics.* 81(1): 96–108.

Roemer, John. 1995. "Should Marxists be interested in exploitation?" *Philosophy and Public Affairs.* 14 (Winter): 30–65.

———. 1998. "Why the poor do not expropriate the rich: An old argument in new garb." *Journal of Public Economics.* 70(3): 399–424.

———. 1999. "Does democracy engender justice?" In *Democracy's Value*, ed. Ian Shapiro and Casiano Hacker-Cordón. Cambridge: Cambridge University Press.

Runciman, W. G. 1966. *Relative Deprivation and Social Justice*. London: Routledge and Kegan Paul.

Schumpeter, Joseph. 1942. *Capitalism, Socialism, and Democracy*. New York: Harper.

Shammas Carol. 1993. "A new look at long-term trends in wealth inequality in the United States." *American Historical Review* 98(2): 412–31.

Shapiro, Ian. 1996. *Democracy's Place*. Ithaca: Cornell University Press.

———. 1999a. "Group aspirations and democratic politics." In *Democracy's Edges*, ed. Ian Shapiro and Casiano Hacker-Cordón. Cambridge: Cambridge University Press.

———. 1999b. *Democratic Justice*. New Haven: Yale University Press.

———. 2002. "The state of democratic theory." In *Political Science: The State of the Discipline*, ed. Ira Katznelson and Helen Milner. New York: Norton.

Skocpol, Theda. 1991. "Targeting within universalism." In *The Urban Underclass*, ed. Christopher Jencks and Paul E. Peterson. Washington, D.C.: Brookings.

———. 1996. *Boomerang: Clinton's Health Security Effort and the Turn against Government in U.S. Politics*. New York: Norton.

Smith, Adam. 1937 [1776]. *An Inquiry into the Nature and Causes of the Wealth of Nations*. New York: Modern Library.

Smith, Heather, and Tom Tyler. 1996. "Justice and power: When will justice concerns encourage the disadvantaged to support policies which redistribute economic resources and the disadvantaged willingly to obey the law?" *European Journal of Social Psychology*. 26: 171–200.

Smith, Rogers. 1997. *Civic Ideals: Conflicting Visions of Citizenship in U.S. History*. New Haven: Yale University Press.

Snyder, James M., and Gerald H. Kramer. 1988. "Fairness, self-interest, and the politics of the progressive income tax." *Journal of Public Economics*. 36: 197–230.

Steinmo, Sven. 1993. *Taxation and Democracy*. New Haven: Yale University Press.

Stokes, Susan C. 1996. "Accountability and policy switch in Latin America's democracies." Paper prepared for the New York–Chicago Seminar on Democracy conference "Democracy and accountability," New York University.

Sugrue, Thomas J. 1993. "The structures of urban poverty: The reorganization of space and work in three periods of American history." In *The Underclass Debate*, ed. Michael Katz. Princeton: Princeton University Press.

Taylor, D. M., Stephen Wright, F. M. Moghaddam, and Richard Lalonde. 1990. "The personal/group discrimination discrepancy: Perceiving my group, but not myself, as a target for discrimination." *Personality and Social Psychology Bulletin*. 58(6): 994–1003.

Taylor, Donald M., Fathali Moghaddam, Ian Gamble, and Evelyn Zeller. 1987. "Disadvantaged group responses to perceived inequality." *Journal of Social Psychology*. 127(3): 259–72.

Tobin, James. 1988. "Roundtable discussion: Politics, economic and welfare." In *Power, Inequality, and Democratic Politics: Essays in Honor of Robert Dahl*, ed. Ian Shapiro and Grant Reeher. Boulder: Westview.

Tocqueville, Alexis de. 1969 [1835–40]. *Democracy in America*. Trans. George Lawrence. Ed. J. P. Mayer. New York: Anchor Books.

Treisman, Daniel. 2000. "Decentralization and inflation: Commitment, collective action, or continuity?" *American Political Science Review*. 94(4) 837–57.

Tsebelis, George. 1995. "Decision-making in political systems: Veto-players in multicameralism, presidentialism, and multipartyism." *British Journal of Political Science*. 25 (July): 289–325.

Tversky, Amos, and Daniel Kahneman. 1981. "The framing of decisions and the rationality of choice." *Science*. 211: 543–58.

Tweedie, Jack. 1994. "Resources rather than needs: A state-centered model of welfare policy making." *American Journal of Political Science*. 38(3): 651–71.

Van Parijs, Philippe. 1995. *Real Freedom for All: What (If Anything) Can Justify Capitalism?* Oxford University Press.

Verba, Sidney, Kay Schlozman, and Henry Brady. 1995. *Voice and Equality: Civic Voluntarism in American Politics*. Cambridge: Harvard University Press.

Vreeland, James. 1999. "The determinants and consequences of IMF programs." Ph.D. diss. New York University.

Weber, Max. 1997. *From Max Weber: Essays in Sociology*. Trans. and ed. H. H. Gerth and C. Wright Mills. New York: Routledge.

Wilson, William Julius. 1996. *When Work Disappears: The World of the New Urban Poor*. New York: Knopf.

Winnick, Andrew J. 1989. *Toward Two Societies: The Changing Distribution of Income and Wealth in the United States since 1960*. New York: Praeger.

Witte, John. 1985. *The Politics and Development of the Federal Income Tax*. Madison: University of Wisconsin Press.

Wittman, Donald A. 1973. "Parties as utility maximizers." *American Political Science Review*. 67(3): 490–98.

Wolff Edward N. 1994. "Trends in household wealth in the United States." *Review of Income and Wealth*. 40(2): 143–74.

Wright, Stephen. 1997. "Ambiguity, social influence, and collective action: Generating collective protest in response to tokenism." *Personality and Social Psychology Bulletin*. 23(12): 1277–90.

Wright, Stephen, Donald Taylor, and Fathali Moghaddam. 1990. "Responding to membership in a disadvantaged group: From acceptance to collective protest." *Journal of Personality and Social Psychology*. 58(6): 994–1003.

Yunker, James A. 1983. "Optimal redistribution with interdependent utility functions." *Public Finance*. 28(1): 132–55.

IO

Democracy and Foreign Policy

JOHN LEWIS GADDIS

One of the most significant things historians of future centuries will remember about the one through which we've just lived is that the world, during the course of it, became predominantly democratic. In 1900 there were no democracies if we can define that term, as the human rights organization Freedom House does, to mean states in which universal suffrage produced competitive multiparty elections. Not even the United States or Great Britain qualified, since both at that time denied the vote to women and, in the case of the United States, to African Americans and other minorities as well. Half a century later in 1950, after two world wars, twenty-two states met the Freedom House standard, comprising some 31 percent of the world's population. But by the year 2000, after a dangerous and protracted cold war, there were 120 democracies, which meant that 63 percent of the earth's people lived under democratic rule.[1]

The history of states goes back about five hundred years, and the history of empires goes back about ten times further. Democracies in the modern sense, therefore, have existed for only something like one-fiftieth of the history of human governance. For democracy to have spread so far and so fast is, by any standard of historical judgment, a remarkable development. It's all the more remarkable that it did so in a century filled with so much violence, for at no other time had people perfected the techniques of killing one another with so much efficiency and on such a scale.

How was it, then, that the predominantly democratic world that exists today arose from such unpromising circumstances? What has been the role of the United States, if any, in bringing all of this about?

The traditional American explanation for the spread of democracy goes something like this. The founding fathers, drawing on their admiration for ancient Greek precedents while fearing the loss of their liberties within an all too contemporary British Empire, imported long-dormant seeds of democracy into a new world, where they immediately took root and flourished. The resulting democratic ideology then exported itself back to Europe, where it quickly undermined the most powerful continental empire — that of France — and set in motion a more gradual but no less significant political evolution within Great Britain itself. So when Woodrow Wilson brought the United States into World War I in 1917 with his call to "make the world safe for democracy," he was only continuing on a wider scale the process of democratic transplantation that Thomas Jefferson began in 1776 when he had proclaimed that "all men are created equal." The American Revolution was, thus, the most potent of all revolutions, which explains why so much of the world today follows its example.

There are, however, several problems with this explanation. First, the founding fathers were far more republican than democratic in their thinking: to the extent that ancient precedents shaped it, they came as much from Rome as from Greece.[2] Second, the idea of a competitive multiparty system badly frightened these leaders, and the prospect of universal suffrage would have astounded them.[3] Third, the history of the United States during its first century would hardly have inspired democratization elsewhere. One of its central features, after all, was the persistence of slavery long past the time it had ceased to exist in most other advanced societies, together with the fact that one of the bloodiest wars of the nineteenth century had been required to eradicate it. For decades afterward, the American practice of democracy retained glaring inconsistencies: Wilson himself, who spoke so grandly of extending democracy throughout the world, had not the slightest intention of extending that same right to the former victims of slavery at home.

So let us scrap this traditional explanation of democratic diffusion and consider another one. It falls within the category of what we might call historical tectonics: those great underlying forces in history that are set in motion by no person and no state, but that nonetheless move all persons and states, rather as the great continental plates move all of us about on the face of the earth. Two in particular might plausibly have paved the way for the expansion of democracy in the twentieth century.

The first of these was the emergence, in the aftermath of the Industrial Revolution, of an open market system that broke down the old patterns of mercantilism by which states had sought, however ineffectually, to control the economic lives of their citizens. The free exchange of commodities, according to this argument, cannot help but promote the free exchange of ideas: politics follows economics. The second tectonic shift was the communications revolution of the late nineteenth century—I mean here the expansion of literacy together with the development of mass-circulation newspapers and, in the telegraph and telephone, the first primitive forms of instant electronic communication—all of which made it harder than it had been for states to conceal information, or to keep people from sharing it among themselves.

But there's a problem with this explanation as well, for it's possible to argue that it was precisely these two tectonic forces—market capitalism and mass communications—that paved the way for the most appalling authoritarian excesses of the twentieth century. Karl Marx anticipated the mechanism with his claim that because capitalism distributes wealth unequally, it also encourages social alienation; and most historians would see in such alienation, as it manifested itself during the late nineteenth and early twentieth centuries, the roots of both communism and fascism. The success of these movements, in turn, owes much to the skill with which their leaders—Lenin, Trotsky, Stalin, and especially Hitler—exploited the new means of mass communication. The tectonic explanation gets us little further than Jeffersonian transplantation in helping us to understand the spread of democracy, therefore, since it also helps to explain the spread of authoritarianism.

Let us switch, then, to an explanation that, while it does not neglect the impact of either the American example or the underlying tectonics, does not depend on them either: it has to do with the role of contingency in history. Because great events determine so much that happens afterward, we tend too easily to assume that they could only have happened in the way that they did. A prime example is World War I, or the Great War as it was known until an even greater one came along. Without this catastrophe, we can safely surmise, the remaining history of the twentieth century would have been very different. But because we cannot know the nature of those differences, we too often rely on the dubious doctrine of inevitability in seeking to explain the origins of the war and its subsequent evolution.

That makes one of its most important consequences—the emergence of Woodrow Wilson as the first world leader with a global democratic vision— seem far more predetermined than it actually was. No one had expected a major European war to break out in the summer of 1914. Once it had, hardly anyone anticipated that it would still be stalemated three years later, or that the United States would then enter it and help to bring about an allied victory. Certainly Wilson had not foreseen, when he entered the White House in 1913, that he would be shaping a European peace settlement in 1918–19: "It would be the irony of fate," he commented, "if my administration had to deal chiefly with foreign affairs."[4]

Wilson's commitment to "make the world safe for democracy," therefore, grew more out of circumstances than destiny. He seized an unexpected opportunity to project national power onto the international scene, but he had no plan in place to implement his lofty vision. His reasons for invoking it, indeed, were less than lofty: he was trying to win the support of a still isolationist country for a war aimed at restoring the balance of power in Europe. The easiest way to do that seemed to be to portray adversaries as autocrats and allies as democrats, despite the fact that among these allies, had he not been overthrown only a few weeks earlier, would have been the greatest autocrat of them all at the time, the Russian czar. What Wilson was doing, in short, was enlisting idealism in the defense of realism, a technique Jefferson would fully have understood.

It took another unexpected event — the triumph of Bolshevism in Russia several months later — to transform Wilson's tactics into a highly effective grand strategy. For although Wilson had welcomed the czar's collapse, he had been horrified when the resulting chaos allowed a tiny band of revolutionaries to seize control of that country, withdraw it from the war, and then challenge the legitimacy of the existing social order everywhere else. Wilson and other allied leaders took the Bolshevik Revolution sufficiently seriously that, during the final year of the fighting, they gave almost as much attention to containing its effects as to defeating Germany.[5]

That was the context, then, in which Wilson made his Fourteen Points speech of January 1918, arguably the most influential public pronouncement by any leader at any point in the twentieth century. For in seeking to counter the attraction of Bolshevism, Wilson pushed himself into proclaiming two great interlocking principles that would shape the American approach to the world for decades to come: political self-determination and economic integration. People should have the right, he insisted, not only to choose their own forms of government but also to benefit from the open markets that would ensure their own prosperity. The world was now to be made safe for *both* democracy and capitalism.

In making this connection, Wilson was grounding his idealism in a more compelling realism than even those consummate realists, Marx and Lenin, were able to achieve. It's true that they, like Wilson, saw themselves as seeking democracy — what else would a classless society be? — but they did so by relying on dictatorships, whether in the management of politics or in the control of economics, to bring that condition about. They believed, almost as a matter of religious conviction, that coercion in the short run would produce liberation in the long run; that means disconnected from ends would not corrupt ends. It proved to be one of the costliest leaps of faith in all of history.

Wilson was far more practical. He sensed the need for *simultaneous* advance toward social and material well-being. He saw the danger of seeking one while postponing the other. He understood that economics sustains politics even as politics disciplines economics, that the relationship is symbiotic, not separate. There was, to be sure, nothing new about such thinking: it had been the basis for British liberalism throughout much of the nineteenth century and for American progressivism in the early twentieth century. But it was one thing to have it said by John Bright or Herbert Croly in a book or from a lecture platform. It was quite another to have it proclaimed by the most influential man in the world, as by the final year of the war Wilson had become. Or by the man of the century, a distinction future historians may well regard Wilson as having merited.

But would Wilson have looked, to his contemporaries, like the man of the century? I very much doubt it, for not only did he fail to get the settlement he wanted at the Paris peace conference; he could not even sell membership in the League of Nations — the institution critical to sustaining his global vision — to his own people. He left office broken in health and embittered in spirit, with the events that would ultimately vindicate him nowhere in sight on the horizon.

Given the American withdrawal back into political isolationism in the 1920s and then into economic isolationism in the 1930s; given the demoralizing failures of both capitalism and democracy in Europe during those years; given the rise of authoritarian alternatives in the consolidation of communist rule in Russia, the emergence of fascism in Italy and Germany, and the rise of militarism in Japan: given all of these things, it was possible on the eve of World War II for many people to say and for more to believe that authoritarianism, not democracy, was the wave of the future. The organization America First, which attracted such widespread support after the fighting broke out in Europe in 1939, had as its goal insulating the United States from the rest of the world, not inspiring or leading it.[6]

We tend to remember World War II today as a good war, in the sense that it so thoroughly crushed the challenges to democracy that the Axis states had mounted, and so decisively propelled the United States into the position of global hegemon. As a consequence, it's easy to forget two things: that the outcome of the war, until at least half of the way through it, was by no means assured; and that victory, when it finally did come, guaranteed little about the future safety of either democracy or capitalism.

Recent scholarship has tended to confirm, for World War II, what the Duke of Wellington said about the Battle of Waterloo: that it was "the nearest run thing you ever saw."[7] The reasons for this reside not just in the improbable coincidence of the democracies having leaders like Winston Churchill and Franklin D. Roosevelt, who rose magnificently to occasions neither of them could have anticipated; nor in the amazing shortsightedness of Adolf Hitler in declaring war on *both* the Soviet Union and the United States within a six-month period; nor in the unexpected tenacity of the British, the remarkable fortitude of the Russians, the awesome technological prowess of the Americans, and the increasingly frequent military incompetence, as the war wore on, of the Germans and the Japanese. All of these things had to come together to produce victory, along with the incalculable *moral* effect of fighting enemies that had come to be seen as truly evil.[8]

Even so, the end of the war was no clear triumph for democracy or capitalism. For despite the fact that Roosevelt, in the Atlantic Charter, had sought to revive Wilson's vision, victory had come only through collaboration with an ally who in no way shared it. Stalin's Soviet Union had not engaged, as had Hitler's Germany, in purposeful genocide; but its record was bad enough. During the decade from 1929 to 1939 it had managed, through the brutalities associated with the collectivization of agriculture, the resulting famine, and the purges that followed, to kill at least twice the number of people who died in the Nazi Holocaust.[9] And yet the war's outcome left this regime controlling half of Europe. The famous pictures of Roosevelt, Churchill, and Stalin posing amicably together reflected no vanquishing of autocracy by democracy, therefore, but rather the desperation with which democracy had hung on by the skin of its teeth.

The vision of the future most people would have had at the time, I suspect, would not have been that of Wilson, but rather the one laid out in George Orwell's novel *1984,* published in 1949. Big Brother was Stalin transparently disguised. The very indispensability of his role in defeating fascism now made communism seem close to invincible: with Mao Zedong's recent victory in China, that ideology dominated a huge stretch of territory extending from the Baltic to the Pacific. There were, to be sure, some twenty-two democracies in the world in 1950, but there were twice as many regimes that would have qualified, by the Freedom House standards, as either authoritarian or totalitarian.[10] The world was hardly safe for democracy yet.

So did the Cold War make it so? That's an intriguing question, because promoting democracy is not exactly what the Cold War was noted for while it was going on. And yet the Freedom House statistics — the jump from twenty-two democracies in 1950 to 120 by the year 2000 — suggest some connection between the Cold War and the expansion of democratic governance: this did not all happen after that conflict ended. So did democracy spread because of the Cold War, or in spite of it? Correlations, it's worth remembering, aren't always causes.

The "in spite of" arguments would emphasize the following: the division of most of the postwar world into Soviet and American spheres of influence; the extent to which that influence constrained the autonomy of those who fell within it; and especially the means by which Washington and Moscow chose to conduct so much of their competition — the nuclear balance of terror. This seemed the ultimate affront to democracy, because it risked the denial of life itself in the pursuit of geopolitical stability. The United States would win, one air force general is said to have commented, if after a nuclear war there were only two Americans left. "You'd better make damn sure, general," a civilian aide replied, "that one is a man and the other a woman."[11]

Critical to the "in spite of" argument is the assumption of moral equivalency: the claim that the two Cold War systems were equally repressive. It's easy to forget now what a popular position this once was. It grew out of the anti–Vietnam War and anti–nuclear weapons protests of the 1960s and 1970s. It informed much of the revisionist historiography on the origins of the Cold War that blamed the United States exclusively for that conflict and was being produced during those years. It was why Ronald Reagan felt obliged so pointedly to characterize the Soviet Union, in 1983, as an "evil empire." And as late as 1984 — Orwell's year — it was still possible for that exquisite barometer of academic self-indulgence, the Oxford Union, to debate the proposition: "Resolved, there is no moral difference between the foreign policies of the U.S. and the USSR."[12]

Such arguments began to lose their credibility, though, as people like Andrei Sakharov, Vaclav Havel, Lech Walesa, Pope John Paul II, and ultimately Mikhail Gorbachev made it clear that *they* saw a considerable moral difference between the democratic governments that were flourishing on one side of the Cold War divide and the autocratic regimes that were hanging on, increasingly desperately, on the other side of it. It became far more difficult to charge the Americans and their allies with maintaining an antidemocratic system when their erstwhile adversaries were so eloquently condemning — and effectively dismantling — their own. Even before the Cold War ended, then, moral equivalency arguments had lost much of their appeal: today hardly anyone makes them.

A more serious objection to the claim that the Cold War fostered the growth of democracy has to do with the underlying tectonics I mentioned earlier. If late-nineteenth-century improvements in marketization and mass communication continued throughout the twentieth — as they surely did — would they not have incubated democracies quite effectively whether there had been a cold war going on or not? Is not what happens beneath the surface of events ultimately more significant than the events themselves?

The problem here, though, is the evidence from the first half of the twentieth century that marketization and mass communication could as easily incubate authoritarianism. Using them to explain democratization during the Cold War requires showing that these processes had somehow changed: that at some point they began to reward only lateral but no longer hierarchical forms of political organization. I think it's possible to make that case, but only by bringing in what my political science colleagues would call exogenous variables. Did markets themselves generate safeguards against their own excesses, or did states learn, from the painful experience of the 1930s, that they had better impose these? Did the means of communication shift all that dramatically in the 1940s, or was it the war that sensitized people to their possible abuses? Tectonic determinism is always difficult to confirm, because the tectonics tend to manifest themselves in particular contexts, the effects of which can't always easily be distinguished.

There has been one attempt to link democratization to technological advance by way of the Cold War, though: it's what we might call the Teflon argument. The National Aeronautics and Space Administration used to remind the Congress, when budgets for the space program looked likely to be cut, that without it housewives would never have had Teflon, since this better method of frying bacon had evolved from the need to avoid frying astronauts as their space capsules reentered the atmosphere. The Teflon explanation has been expanded in various ways: without the inducements the Cold War provided to develop the necessary technology, it's often said, we would never have had such innovations as jet-powered airliners, interstate highways, 500-channel satellite receiving dishes, mobile phones, and of course the Internet, which began as a supplementary command and control network for the Pentagon in the event of nuclear war. And without these things, we could never have had globalization, which in turn has promoted democratization. Or so the argument runs.

I don't think much of it, though, for a couple of reasons. First, it reverses chronology: the movement toward democratization was well under way before most of these innovations were. Second, it assumes that what people have is more important than what they think. The perils of this approach became clear in 1999 when the *New York Times* columnist Tom Friedman published his "Golden Arches Theory of Conflict Resolution," which noted that no state with a McDonald's franchise had ever gone to war with another one. Unfortunately the United States and its NATO allies chose just that inauspicious moment to begin bombing Belgrade, where there were an embarrassing number of golden arches.[13]

All of these "in spite of" arguments — and, in their own way, the Teflon and golden arches explanations as well — disconnect democratization from the mainstream of Cold War history. They build a *wall* between domestic politics and geopolitics that seems unlikely to have existed in the minds of people at the time. They strike me, for that reason, as less than plausible. So what if we were to take seriously the alternative position, however unlikely it might seem, which is that the Soviet-American superpower rivalry actually *promoted* democratization? That the diffusion of democracy is at least in part an offspring, even if an unexpected one, of the Cold War itself?

The case in favor of this argument would focus on the role of the United States, and especially on the differences in the way it handled its responsibilities in the two postwar eras. Go back to Wilson's insight that economic and political progress had to proceed simultaneously; that just as one could not expect prosperity without open markets and unconstrained politics, so one could not postpone prosperity — as Marxism, Leninism, and ultimately Maoism also attempted to do — and still expect to get democracy. Wilson's countrymen had not embraced this logic, though, after World War I, and as a consequence the United States made no sustained effort to implement his vision. It did after World War II. What made the difference?

Part of the answer, I'm sure, was simply guilt: despite their power the Americans had done so little to prevent the coming of the second war that they were determined after it was over not to repeat their behavior after the first war. But part of the reason also was that the world of the early 1920s had seemed relatively benign: there were no obvious threats to American security. The world of the late 1940s, in contrast, seemed anything but benign. We can of course debate the accuracy of the view that Stalin posed as great a threat to the European balance of power as Hitler had: the few Soviet documents we have are inconclusive on that point, and even if we had all the documents my fellow historians would still find ways to disagree as to what they showed.[14] For our purposes here, though, what's important is not what Stalin's intentions really were, but what American leaders *believed* them to be. About that there's little doubt, and as a consequence the Truman administration had resolved, by 1947, to act very differently from the way in which its predecessors had acted a quarter century earlier.

What it did was to transform Wilson's idea of a world safe for democracy and capitalism into a strategy of containment, and then to sell it — as Wilson had never managed to do — to the American people. Stalin certainly helped, for although planning for the United Nations and the Bretton Woods system preceded the onset of the Cold War, it's not at all clear that the United States would have sustained these commitments to internationalism had there been no Soviet threat. There certainly would have been no Truman Doctrine, no Marshall Plan, and no North Atlantic Treaty Organization. And I suspect there would not have been, as well, what now looks to have been the single most important contribution the Americans made toward global democratization: that was a new and remarkably ambitious effort at democratic transplantation, aimed this time at two of the most persistently authoritarian cultures on the face of the earth, those of Germany and Japan.

Only Americans would have attempted something as rash as this. Only an innocence bordering on ignorance of the countries involved could have led them to consider it. Only authoritarian proconsuls like General Lucius Clay in Germany and General Douglas MacArthur in Japan would have bypassed a Washington bureaucracy more attuned to the punishment of defeated enemies than to their rehabilitation. Only the willingness to make distasteful compromises — to cooperate with recently hated adversaries — could have made the new policy work. And only the realization that a greater adversary was arising out of the Eurasian heartland, and that the Germans and the Japanese, if not quickly integrated into the system of Western democratic states, could wind up as allies of the new enemy — only this, I think, could have provided a basis for justifying this new policy to the American people and to those other American allies who had themselves suffered at the hands of the Germans and the Japanese.[15]

Each of these improbabilities had to intersect with and reinforce the other in order to produce an effect we today take for granted: that these two formerly authoritarian states are now, and have long been, safe for democracy and capitalism. It was, however, another of Wellington's "nearest run" things. The course of events could easily have proceeded otherwise. To see how, try a historical thought experiment: rerun the sequence, changing only the variable of German and Japanese democratization to see what difference this might make.

Begin with the death of Franklin D. Roosevelt in April 1945, but let the new president, Harry S. Truman, stick with and apply to both Germany and Japan the harshly punitive occupation policies laid out by the late president's influential treasury secretary, Henry Morgenthau Jr., which FDR had at one point himself endorsed. The scenario then proceeds as follows. After the sacking of Generals Clay and MacArthur, the American occupation authorities in Germany and Japan dutifully follow Washington's orders. The Germans and the Japanese quickly come to resent the resulting repression, combined with starvation, and communists in both countries begin to gain support for their view that the right to eat is more important than the right to vote. The resistance they generate makes the occupation so difficult to administer that the new Republican majority in Congress resolves early in 1947 to "bring the boys home" and to "stop pouring money down foreign rat holes."[16]

Truman and his advisers belatedly try to save the situation by devising various plans that they name for themselves, but when the Soviet blockade forces the Western powers out of Berlin early in 1948, American authority crumbles throughout West Germany and the spillover effects are felt in Japan as well. Coordinated coups bring both countries into the communist camp that summer, just on the eve of a Democratic National Convention that feels it has no choice but to replace Truman with the only American who seems to have a chance of cutting a deal with Stalin, the former vice president Henry A. Wallace.

Having run successfully on the platform "He'll keep us out of the Cold War," President Wallace follows the example of Neville Chamberlain ten years earlier and negotiates "peace in our time" with a Soviet Union that, now that its ally Mao Zedong has triumphed in China as well, dominates the entire Eurasian continent. George Orwell's book is of course suppressed, but still it's his vision, not Wilson's, that turns out to have been the wave of the future.

Outrageous, you say? Off the wall? Well, no more so, I think, than what any American would have said at the beginning of the 1940s, if told what the Americans would actually have accomplished by the end of the 1940s. *That* scenario would have seemed not just counterfactual but fantastical.

Anyone interested in chaos theory — or in Tom Stoppard's theatrical renderings of it — will know something about "butterfly effects": those tiny perturbations at the beginning of a process that can make an enormous difference at the end of it.[17] The term originated in meteorology with the suggestion that a butterfly fluttering its wings over Beijing can, in theory at least, set off a hurricane over Bermuda: that's why weather forecasting is so difficult. It's since extended into the realms of physics, mathematics, paleontology, economics, and now even politics with the recently discovered Florida butterfly ballot.

What's implied in all of this is something historians have known all along but haven't always explained well: that under certain circumstances small events can set in motion much larger ones; that the relationship between causes and consequences isn't always proportionate; that there are great turning points in the past, and that the points on which they turn can be exceedingly small. The 1945–47 period was just such a turning point, I think, for Wilson's vision of a world safe for democracy and capitalism. Until that moment, the cards had seemed stacked against it. Even victory in World War II had not reversed a trend that seemed more likely to lead to authoritarianism than to democracy. But after 1947, the authoritarian tide—if you will pardon this profusion of metaphors—began to recede. What it left behind was a slowly emerging democratic world.

For if two of the most authoritarian states in history were on the way to becoming democracies—and if they were recovering their economic strength as they did so—then that was as powerful a demonstration as can be imagined of the *practicality* as well as the principled character of Wilson's vision. The Soviet Union had nothing with which to counter it: all it could offer was an ideologically based promise that seemed increasingly at odds with practicality. It would take years—indeed decades—for the contrast to become so clear that it began to shape the Cold War's outcome; but in the end it did just that. The nuclear weapons and other instruments of war the superpowers piled up during that conflict did little to determine how it actually came out. But the distinction between a Wilsonian vision realized on one side and denied on the other turned out to be decisive.

Would it all have happened without the Cold War? I rather doubt it, for, in the classic tradition of what free enterprise is supposed to do, it was the *competition* that forced the United States, in this critical instance, to do the right thing.

What's the right thing to do today, though, in a very different world in which there's so little competition—in which democracy is no longer the exception but the norm? How can the United States use its influence to help ensure that the twenty-first century remains at least as hospitable to democratic institutions as the twentieth century turned out to be? Several things occur to me, which I should like to list in ascending order of their importance.

First, *admit our shortcomings*. The Cold War was a brutal time, and the United States committed its share of brutalities in trying to win it. Paradoxically, the further we got from Europe, which was always the main arena of

Cold War competition, the less scrupulous we were about supporting democracy: too many people in Latin America, Africa, the Middle East, and Southeast Asia suffered as a result. Even in Europe we did not always prefer the democratic alternative, as our record in Spain, Portugal, and Greece clearly demonstrates. Our enthusiasm for capitalism was always more consistent than our enthusiasm for democracy, despite our ideological commitment to the principle that the two went hand in hand.

The historian's equivalent of truth in advertising demands that we acknowledge this, even as we should try to understand the reasons for it. They involved chiefly a lingering pessimism about the climate for democratic transplants — a fear that these might not survive in places where the resentments generated by poverty or injustice were too great. Some of this pessimism grew out of guilt over the extent to which the United States and its Western European allies had contributed to these conditions, whether through formal or informal imperialism. Some of it reflected a tendency to attribute to the Soviet Union and its allies a far greater capacity than they actually had to win friends and influence people in the third world. Some of it resulted from a widespread habit within the U.S. government — understandable in a generation of leaders that had survived depression and war — of assuming the worst, even as one hoped for the best.

Three Americans, I think, should get particular credit for having reversed this long history of official pessimism about democratic prospects, although only one of them normally does. Jimmy Carter's achievement in making human rights the centerpiece of his foreign policy and mostly meaning it is justifiably well known. But I would also give credit to Henry Kissinger, who as he neared the end of his years in government, repudiated his own earlier policy of supporting white minority regimes in southern Africa; and to Ronald Reagan, who despite a dubious record in Central America had the imagination, with the Reagan Doctrine, to turn the table on the Soviets and begin demonstrating that it was they, not the Americans, who were more often the imperialists in a postcolonial world.[18] What Carter, Kissinger, and Reagan were all moving toward — even if at different rates and under differing circumstances — was the view that the United States need not fear the choices the third world, if freed from imperialism, would now make.

My second recommendation, after acknowledging our history, is that we *reacquire our humility*. Even Americans do not normally associate that quality with themselves, but if you go back and study carefully what everyone now acknowledges to have been the most creative period in our foreign policy — the one in which we were transplanting democracy to Germany and Japan, while seeking to revive it elsewhere in Europe — you'll find that we showed a remarkable sensitivity to the interests and advice of others. There was no effort to transform the countries we occupied or supported into clients or even clones of ourselves. MacArthur presided, in Japan, over one of the few successful land redistribution projects in modern history. The Marshall Plan wound up reinforcing the European social welfare state. The movement for European economic integration, which we consistently supported, was intended to create competitors to ourselves. From the start NATO was a European initiative, and despite the disproportionate power we've always wielded within the alliance, it was the Europeans who largely shaped its evolution during the Cold War.

We exhibited this openness to the views of others, I think, for several reasons. One was that we often weren't sure what to do ourselves, and so needed all the help we could get. But there was also the sense, at least in Europe, that if we appeared too domineering, the Russians would only benefit from this. Their own arrogance and brutality in Eastern Europe, it was clear from the earliest days of the Cold War, was a liability for them. That made us all the more determined to treat our own allies with respect, to give them reasons for wanting to be within the American sphere of influence, and not to feel that they'd had it forced on them. We allowed their interests to shape the disposition of our power. In short, we listened.[19]

After the Cold War ended, though, we fell into a different habit, which was that of instructing. This was one of Woodrow Wilson's less attractive personal characteristics — perhaps growing out of his previous career as a professor — and it seemed for a while that, in its otherwise quite justifiable rediscovery of Wilson, our foreign policy was embracing it too. The Clinton administration expected the world to be impressed by its repeated claims of American "indispensability," even as it failed to define coherently the purposes for which we were indeed indispensable. The Bush administration's unilateralism has suggested a disregard for the opinions of others that's quite at odds with how we waged — and won — the Cold War.

That brings me to my third suggestion, which is that we *acknowledge contingency*. If the history of democratization during the twentieth century suggests anything at all, it is that this was a contingent, not a determined, process: there was nothing inevitable about it. An improbable combination of circumstances allowed what in the long sweep of history will seem like a relatively small push by the Americans — the democratization of Germany and Japan — to have very big effects. No theory of which I am aware could have predicted this sequence of events, and that ought to caution us as we assess the prospects for democratization in the future.

It would be a great mistake, it seems to me, to assume that democracy grows automatically out of any one thing. To say that it depends solely on support from the United States ignores the uniqueness of the situation in which that support was indeed critical during the early Cold War. To say that it results from economic integration is to ignore the fact that the world was about as integrated at the beginning of the twentieth century, when there were no democracies at all, as it is now.[20] To say that it grows out of capitalism ignores the role capitalists have played — and not just in Nazi Germany — in supporting authoritarianism. To say that it grows out of allowing people the right to determine their own future neglects the fact that some people are determined to deny other people any future at all: does anyone really believe that democracy, if fully practiced by all sides in the Balkan crises of the 1990s, or by the Israelis and the Palestinians today, would fully benefit all sides? And to say that because democracy turned out to be the wave of the future during the twentieth century doesn't necessarily make it so for the twenty-first.

It's also the case that combinations of causes can have contradictory as well as complementary effects. We tend to assume the complementarity of Wilson's great principles, economic integration and political self-determination, because they mostly were during the Cold War. But has not the post–Cold War era already exposed fault lines suggesting that these two tectonic processes are not in fact moving in the same direction? The backlash against globalization that has surfaced so conspicuously over the past several years in places like Seattle, Washington, Prague, and Davos only reflects a basic reality that we should long ago have anticipated: it is that people do not always vote in the way that economists think. And now we know something else about globalization, which is that it has not changed human nature. Evil still lurks in the hearts of men, and the events of September 11 show how easily the instruments of globalization — the unrestricted movement of people, commodities, and cultures — can be turned against it.[21]

My final suggestion, as we consider what we might do to sustain democracy in the face of these contradictions, is to *remember Isaiah Berlin.* It was my privilege to know the great man slightly, and to witness at first hand his congeniality and conversational brilliance, his interest in everything and everybody, and his emphatic impatience with any effort to look at the world from any single point of view. He was, more than anyone else I've ever met or read about, a true *philosopher of democracy.* As befits a man who loved the distinction between foxes and hedgehogs, Sir Isaiah taught us many different things but also one big thing, and yet he avoided the contradiction this might seem to imply.

I have in mind his concept of the *incommensurability of values:* the idea that while we can and should pursue multiple goods, they are not all mutually compatible. Some will complement one another; some will contradict one another: we cannot, to the same extent and in all situations, have them all. The art of politics—certainly of democratic politics—is the art of balancing incommensurate goods, of making tough choices, of keeping the whole picture and not just part of it in mind, of taking an *ecological* view of our own existence.

The word *ecology*, in this sense, implies the balance it takes to keep an organism healthy. We understand it well enough when it comes to our plants, our pets, our children, and ourselves: we know how easily there can be too much of any good thing, and how harmful the consequences can be. I'm not sure we know that yet, though, in a political world—to say nothing of an academic world—that so often encourages investments in single causes, even if in the name of democratic principles. For this is, as Berlin reminds us, fundamentally an antidemocratic procedure: "The search for perfection," he writes, "does seem to me a recipe for bloodshed, no better even if it is demanded by the sincerest of idealists, the purest of heart."[22]

This is, then, democracy's Achilles' heel: it's a disconnection of means from ends not all that different from the one at the top of the slippery slope that produced, at its bottom, the great antidemocratic movements of the century that recently ended. It's what ought to haunt us as we think about the century that's now beginning.

Notes

1. Freedom House, *Democracy's Century: A Survey of Global Political Change in the 20th Century* (New York: Freedom House, 1999), available at http://www.freedomhouse.org/reports/century.html. I have used revised statistics from the Web site, which show 120 democracies in the year 2000, rather than the 199 cited in the original published report.

2. H. Trevor Colbourn, *The Lamp of Experience: Whig History and the Intellectual Origins of the American Revolution* (New York: Norton, 1974), discusses this preoccupation with precedents.

3. Joanne B. Freeman, *Affairs of Honor: National Politics in the New Republic* (New Haven: Yale University Press, 2001), brilliantly reconstructs this (to us) unfamiliar political environment.

4. Quoted in Arthur Link, *Woodrow Wilson and the Progressive Era, 1910–1917* (New York: Harper and Row, 1954), 81.

5. The best analysis is still N. Gordon Levin, *Woodrow Wilson and World Politics: America's Response to War and Revolution* (New York: Oxford University Press, 1968).

6. Manfred Jonas, *Isolationism in America, 1935–1941* (Ithaca: Cornell University Press, 1966), provides a succinct introduction to this subject.

7. Elizabeth Longford, *Wellington* (London: Weidenfeld and Nicolson, 1992), 333.

8. For an account that stresses how easily the war could have gone the other way, see Richard Overy, *Why the Allies Won* (New York: Norton, 1996).

9. For the figures, see John Lewis Gaddis, "The Tragedy of Cold War History," *Diplomatic History* 17 (Winter, 1993): 10–11.

10. See note 1 for the source of these statistics.

11. William Kauffman relates this story in an interview for the CNN television series *Cold War*.

12. John Lewis Gaddis, "On Moral Equivalency and Cold War History," *Ethics and International Affairs* 10 (1996): 131–48.

13. Friedman made this claim in *The Lexus and the Olive Tree* (New York: Farrar, Straus and Giroux, 1999), 195–217.

14. See Ralph B. Levering, Vladimir O. Pechatnov, Verena Botzenhart-Viehe, and C. Earl Edmondson, eds., *Debating the Origins of the Cold War: American and Russian Perspectives* (New York: Rowman and Littlefield, 2002).

15. I have relied heavily here on Tony Smith, *America's Mission: The United States and the Worldwide Struggle for Democracy in the Twentieth Century* (Princeton: Princeton University Press, 1994), 146–76.

16. Which is what the newly elected British Labour government did in fact decide to do with respect to India and Palestine that same year.

17. The best introduction is James Gleick, *Chaos: Making a New Science* (New York: Viking, 1987). Stoppard makes chaos theory a major character in his play *Arcadia* (London: Faber and Faber, 1993).

18. John Lewis Gaddis, *The United States and the End of the Cold War: Implications, Reconsiderations, Provocations* (New York: Oxford University Press, 1992), 59–63.

19. See John Lewis Gaddis, *We Now Know: Rethinking Cold War History* (New York: Oxford University Press, 1997), 189–220.

20. For the arguments for and against this proposition, see Niall Ferguson, *The Cash Nexus: Money and Power in the Modern World, 1700–2000* (London: Allen Lane, 2001), 309–12.

21. An early attempt to assess the implications is Strobe Talbott and Nayan Chanda, eds., *The Age of Terror: America and the World after September 11* (New York: Basic, 2001).

22. "The Pursuit of the Ideal," in Isaiah Berlin, *The Proper Study of Mankind: An Anthology of Essays*, ed. Henry Hardy and Roger Hausheer (New York: Farrar, Straus and Giroux, 1998), 15.

Dinner with Democracy

CYNTHIA FARRAR

On a Thursday evening in January, twenty-one people stood in line in an undergraduate cafeteria, collected their food on trays, and slowly gathered in an adjacent room. A few were affiliated with the university; most were not. Lawyers, political activists, a judge; neighborhood leaders, community organizers, a former mayor; business and religious leaders, a journalist, Yale undergraduates; men and women, of various ages, races, ethnicities, and backgrounds—all stood uncertainly around the room. They had been invited to participate in an extended discussion of democracy. Each week, they would join Yale students and other members of the public at lectures in a special course called Democratic Vistas, taught by fifteen Yale professors from different disciplines. Each week, they would read assigned texts. And each week, they would meet for dinner, with me, and talk.

The first conversation was stilted. I talked too much. Their eyes flicked around the room. They wondered what they had gotten themselves into. To get the discussion going, I asked the group to analyze itself in democratic terms. If this group were to make decisions on behalf of the larger community, how would we assess whether they could legitimately do so? By way of answer, individuals offered guesses as to why they had been invited, why someone (me) had thought they had something to contribute to the discussion: certain kinds of experience or understanding? representing or resembling a particular group in society? commitment to the process itself or to the common good? ability to enlarge the perspectives of others? I posed a further question: if we were to consider ourselves a democratic entity, what would that mean? Would we have to operate in a particular way, such as take turns running the class? What would each person be entitled to expect and be required to contribute? What if some people talked all the time, others not at all? In response, some said that each person brought his or her own agenda. Others questioned the premise that we could act like a democracy: there wasn't enough time; not everyone who needed to be present was there; we weren't trying to produce anything, not even decisions. At the end of the hour and a half, amid the clattering of trays and scraping of chairs, I wondered if anyone would return the following week.

I also wondered what I had gotten them into. I had started from an intuition: that this discussion group would not just talk about democracy, but enrich it. What this might mean became clearer to me over the course of the term. Certainly the initial session was a blind alley. Whatever I may have thought they might accomplish as a group, it would definitely not be defined by adherence to standard democratic procedures and the traditional framework of democratic legitimacy: for example, being chosen by a larger constituency through a fair and open process, making decisions on behalf of that constituency through mechanisms such as majority rule, being accountable for the consequences of those decisions, and the like. Indeed, their contribution might well reside, I thought, in a region not often explored by democratic theorists or reflected in attempts to reform democratic practice. This region was charted by the ancient Athenians and has begun to be mapped more systematically in recent years. Call it participatory democracy, or deliberative democracy. Its defining features are, roughly, these: active participation by a broad range of citizens, a deliberative and at times contentious process of problem solving and decision making, a process that is seen as transforming the individual citizens' civic capacity but preserving their individuality. My own study of the origins of democratic theory in Athens, and my attempts to expand the scope of public participation in local governance, had led me into this territory.

Thirteen weeks after our initial meeting, eighteen people reflected on what we had been through. Their remarks suggest that they too had glimpsed hitherto unfamiliar but appealing democratic terrain:

- "I think it's rare to find one's self in a setting with people who live their lives in a different place in this culture. I don't normally find myself in settings where people have views and experiences that are so totally different from my own. And people who are in the world of business or academia or the judiciary. I think that one of the things that is peculiar, in a way, about this democracy is the extent to which we all do tend to hang out with people who are like ourselves."

- "There's a certain awe and wonder you get when you sit in a large group of people and discuss in an academic context intensely personal ideas and approaches. Because it really forces you to bring more out than you might otherwise."

- "Before the class started, if you had asked me my thoughts about democracy, I probably would have answered in exclusively political terms. And because of the nature of the class, I would hardly exclude the political, but I now think of it as a much more complex mosaic and I can appreciate the fact that democracy has a lot to do with the way that we think and the way that we live, apart from the way that we vote."

- "A lot of my experience with people who disagreed with me politically, or with whom I disagreed politically, was of a nasty contention. And to see that you could do this and if you did it right, you would still be civil to each other and reach some sort of mutual understanding while perhaps not agreeing, but nonetheless, some sort of civility. It was encouraging. And it has made me think very seriously about running for office."

- "I, who am thirteenth generation in the U.S., have always considered myself a persecuted underdog as a woman. And it seems really odd to other people. But I now see people who feel like underdogs in different kinds of ways, and I think that's what I will take forward."

- "The effect of severing these ties that we have with constituencies we normally represent is that we were able to create a little political community in which we were all created equal. While outside of this room, we are really unequal in social status and wealth and ability, age, other variables. So this was sort of an ideal of citizenship, in which people come together and leave aside their constituencies or the social position they represent and are able to interact with each other as equals."

- "I think one of the other things that made this group successful is that it's not only that there's a defined amount of time and structure and an ending point and sort of an abstractness, but also that we all made a commitment to be here. Even when we disagreed, we got to know who the personalities were and how the discussion went and how people interact with each other and how to talk and not talk and listen, and feel part of this group. And knowing that the same faces would be there each time."

The democratic meaning of what we came to think of as Dinner with Democracy rests not primarily in what people said about each week's topic—

though what they said was shrewd, thoughtful, and enlightening—but in what they did together and what the experience did to them. This structured, extended, and challenging discourse among a diverse group of individuals offers a glimpse of an aspect of democratic citizenship not comprehended—indeed, sidelined—by most theories, and many practices, of democracy. Some forms of political theory are concerned with abstract questions of legitimacy (and some political theorists of this kind do invoke ideals of collective civic deliberation to make their case).[1] Another kind of political theory considers the actual activity of political communities—which is my concern here—but tends to ignore the as-yet-unrealized potential for different forms of political engagement.[2]

Interpreters of democracy often frame their analysis in terms of contrasting extremes. Discussions of democratic governance offer two alternatives: (1) reliance on the modern structures of the bureaucratic state, overseen to some degree by a system of representative government said to reflect the will of the people; (2) partly in response to the detachment of the administrative model from popular influence, direct involvement by the people in decision making, through a system of initiatives and referendums. Left off the spectrum is the possibility of regular, ongoing, and direct participation of the people in a governance system that requires collective deliberation and a process of mutual political education, not just the casting of individual votes for either a candidate or a proposal.

Discussions of the relationship between individual and society in a democratic context also offer two alternatives: (1) extreme individualism (libertarianism or assimilation of political processes to the workings of the market); (2) partly in response to the perceived excesses of democratic capitalism, an appeal to community solidarity, to the shaping of individual preferences and values through identification with a group. The invocation of community carries the risk of repressing individuality.[3] Left off the spectrum in this second contrast is the possibility of substantive political engagement with others who are not part of a "natural" group, but who are fellow citizens different in other respects from oneself. From this perspective, citizens are neither members of a tribe nor consumers; what they have in common is citizenship, and they engage in constant renegotiation of the inevitable tensions between public goods and private interests, community and individual.

In both cases, what is missing is recognition of the power of structured engagement among political equals, which not only permits them to express and aggregate existing preferences, but also transforms their understanding of and capacity to contribute to civic decision making. The participants in Dinner with Democracy did not in any meaningful sense "choose" what occurred.

They agreed to join a process and to be open to the possibility of being transformed by it. The structure of the discussions worked on them. They attended,
perhaps, because each in his or her own way had an intuition that however
rich their lives, however active their involvement in civic affairs (and they were
unusual in their civic commitments, from coaching youth baseball to running
a program for ex-cons to serving on every significant nonprofit board in New
Haven), some important elements were missing: exposure to people different
from themselves, the opportunity to argue and articulate their views under
challenge, a chance to reflect on the truths they held to be self-evident. They
entered, and sustained, a genuinely "political" space of a kind that modern
democracy tends to spurn or, at the very least, to corrode.

This antique notion of the "political," and its incongruity with modern
practice, surfaced in the very first lecture that the diners-with-democracy attended. In that lecture, Anthony Kronman characterized the soul of democratic man by invoking Plato's appalled account, in the *Republic*: the democratic city, Plato said, is "full of freedom and free speech." The citizen of a
democracy "lives along day by day, gratifying the desires that occur to him, at
one time drinking and listening to the flute, at another downing water and
reducing; now practicing gymnastic, and again idling and neglecting everything; and sometimes spending his time as though he were occupied with
philosophy. Often he engages in politics and, jumping up, says and does whatever chances to come to him; and if he ever admires any soldiers, he turns in
that direction; and if it's money-makers, in that one." In response, Plato develops the idea of a formal human good, or end, attainable only by a few, and
describes in detail the ordered state that alone can enable all men, whatever
their capacities (indeed, including slaves and women, excluded from participation in the Athenian polis) to realize their full potential and for some to achieve
the highest good for man. Kronman argues that the Christian worldview permits, even encourages, the chaos of soul and society characteristic of democracy as portrayed by Plato. Christian man believes in creation (by God) of
something from nothing and, relatedly, in the idea that the only form the
world has is accomplished through the interaction of free individuals. Every
desire is on the same footing as every other. Society seeks to prevent deadly
clashes between desires, but otherwise exists only to enable individuals more
effectively to achieve their individual objectives. Democratic man is a consumer. The democratic city is as Plato depicts it: "a general store."

Plato's proposed alternative is a state in which souls and polity match and
sustain each other precisely, and the polis demands and cultivates each soul's
contribution to civic order. If this is the only alternative, then moderns are
bound to choose virtually untrammeled individual freedom. But again, these

are extreme choices. What is missing here is the possibility instantiated by the actual workings of democratic Athens, which Plato caricatures and Kronman ignores. The Athenians created a genuinely political realm—a realm in which individual citizens, whatever their social status or breeding or talents, were expected to abstract to some degree from their personal interests and to engage with other perspectives. Order emerges from the interaction of free individuals, but only because they genuinely interact. The polity treats citizens as if they are capable of identifying and contributing to a common good, and helps them to fulfill this expectation. Like Plato's Republic, the Athenian democracy shaped its citizens; but for the Athenian democrats, the political structure was itself shaped by the citizens themselves. Plato rejects this vision as likely to lead to radical disorder: he argues that each soul, and the polity as a whole, must hew to the eternal and unchanging order laid up in the heavens.

Modern democrats often reject not just the Platonic but also (to the extent they consider it at all) the Athenian vision as likely to violate the individual's freedom. We tend to share Plato's view that democracy of the Athenian kind—where power is actually exercised by ordinary citizens—could lead to factional disputes, enable the hoi polloi to trump the judgment of the best-educated and best-informed citizens, and undermine the professionalism required of modern leaders. (Note that the founders did not reject direct democracy as impractical in a large society; they preferred the system of electing representatives because it would produce an elite capable of leading the republic.) Modern democracy treats individual beliefs and preferences as givens. The task of reconciling the claims of individuals and society is therefore largely procedural: voting, majority rule, and (often) the workings of the "market" in ideas and preferences. The actual experience of Athenian democracy—as opposed to Plato's caricature—is evidence that there may be a middle way.[4] Dinner with Democracy is also suggestive.

In recent years, philosophers and political theorists have been arguing that interaction among citizens is important to the legitimacy and the functioning of democracy. Those who are primarily concerned with questions of legitimacy use deliberative democracy to establish the foundations for democratic practices.[5] The idea is that our assessment of the legitimacy of particular practices should be based on whether the individual members of the society, if they were to engage in free and reasoned deliberation under conditions in which they are treated as moral and political equals, could be expected to sanction those practices. What does this kind of reasoning mean for democratic societies in practice? Inferences about what this idealized kind of deliberation would yield have been used to criticize the outcomes actually generated by the existing political system.

Those more concerned with the functioning of democratic institutions than with establishing their fundamental legitimacy have suggested that we need to give greater attention to the ways in which individuals actually engage with each other in a variety of settings, political and otherwise. Experiences of earlier, and arguably more civic, eras are often invoked: bowling in leagues on a regular basis rather than occasionally, with a few close friends and family; participating in the Elks as a local social club; and functioning nationally as a broad-based political pressure group.[6] Or, harking back to ancient practices, they suggest introducing elements of direct, participatory, inclusive democracy into our systems of representation and administration.[7] Dinner with Democracy points to the need for and the potential of contexts that are political in the ancient sense, capable of fostering genuinely civic interaction and cultivating the capacity for engaged citizenship. It also suggests the difficulty of creating such settings and of making them relevant to the realities of modern democratic politics.

Dinner with Democracy did feature characteristics that, for the deliberative democrat, define a legitimate political space: it encompassed difference; participants were expected to give reasons for their views; there was no real possibility of escape from being implicated in what was discussed; and each member — whatever his or her economic or social status or education or cognitive abilities — functioned as an equal for purposes of the discourse and was expected to observe and sustain operating principles that foster respect and clarity. The meaning of this experience lies not in the ability to generate inferences from a hypothetical — "if people had a chance to reflect on their interests and their understanding of the good under circumstances like these, they would reject x" — or even primarily in what a group of real individuals came to think about particular issues under circumstances of free and equal discourse, but rather in what happened to these individuals in the process. Participants were transformed by this political structure in ways that could not have been predicted.

Through its transformative power, the table setting itself offered a cogent response to claims that politics is simply the art of balancing different interests. The apparent "givens" of human society need not be treated as fixed, even in a system that respects individual differences. Thus, for example, unconscious prejudice can plausibly be treated as irrelevant in a mixed group in which reasons are given and scrutinized and individuals learn to read each other's inflections of figure and voice. This is a reminder that nature, nurture, and culture are not the only forces capable of shaping human interaction: explicitly political exchange can literally put the unconscious self (prejudices and all) in its place. Similarly, psychological adaptation to, even rationalization of, structural inequalities by those most harmed by them, and the entrenched racial and economic segregation characteristic of the United States, may seem to be the inevitable consequence of the exercise of human preferences. But these blinders cannot long survive the sustained scrutiny of a group of people from markedly different backgrounds and affiliations. And the pointed debate characteristic of the group ensures that no aspect of society is considered off-limits, so long as views are expressed respectfully. There is no restricted menu of "political" topics, and no "veil of ignorance," to use political philosopher John Rawls's phrase, about where one's own interests lie.

Because Dinner with Democracy encouraged participants to bring their full personalities into the conversation, and to consider all aspects of the life of the individual in a democratic society, concerns grounded in the "private" spheres of life — religion, family — also surfaced. The most impassioned and contentious debate the group had was about the relationship between faith and citizenship. The disagreement was in part about whether a "wall" should exist between church and state, and if so where and why and of what kind. This was not just a dispute about the boundaries of the political (which is itself a political issue), but an expression of different kinds of faith and a demand that others not simply tolerate such views, but also take them seriously. The group achieved something of the intimacy of a family, and views were expressed that appealed to the kind of sympathies and shared intuitions and eliding of questions of power that often characterize the private realm, and indeed make this realm problematic for democracy. Yet because the group was, in the end — and like polities in this respect — a contrivance, not in any sense a "natural" society like the family, issues of power were never far from the surface.

Indeed, the conversation continually returned to fundamental questions of power: Is choice freedom? Is equality of opportunity really equality? Or are appeals to "choice" and "equality of opportunity" — at least at times — masks for the exercise of power and freedom by those with resources, and the disempowerment of those without? They wished not to challenge the basic commitment of American democracy to freedom and to equal opportunity, but rather to ask what those commitments yield in practice. The participants recognized that the market simultaneously promotes the general welfare and greater inequality, and that other practices considered essential to our democratic society have a comparable effect. Public education, they acknowledged, both diffuses knowledge among the general population and accelerates the advancement of the talented. What seemed important to many of the diners-with-democracy was the resulting increase in fragmentation and polarization. With respect to both wealth and knowledge, they argued that the greatest risk of investing in freedom of choice at the expense of commonness was isolating those left behind both economically, by technological advances, and physically, in concentrated pockets of rooted poverty and despair created by the choices made by others.

As one participant said, "The great contribution of a common school to a democracy is when we can go to school with people different from ourselves because, in a stratified society, we're likely to spend much of our lives apart from people who we don't choose to be with." Yet he admitted that he and his wife had themselves ignored this principle when they chose schools according to how well they suited the temperaments and talents of their individual children. "But," he added, "there is a very big price to be paid for that and part of that price is our whole sense of community and the innate sense of democracy that a true common school would give us." Another emphasized the importance of choice: "It cannot be the community above freedom. That's not democracy." The common ground discovered by the group was the conviction that beyond a certain (indeterminate) extent, relative inequality (or, indeed, absolute poverty) and fragmentation would prevent some people from participating in the community of choosers or making their voices heard, and that this outcome would violate the premises of democracy as they understood them.

The diners-with-democracy identified two characteristics of their own dinner discussions as the key to dealing with the tensions between liberty and equality inherent in democracy: exposure to difference; and a sense of commonness, initially contrived, and then forged. Their experience offers a distinctively political perspective on citizenship. That is, what the citizen-diners said and what they did suggested that it is essential to create a space within which the claims of the individual and society, of money and power and justice, can be explicitly addressed by those affected, treated as equal members. They intimated that a threshold level of resources and education is required for this. Yet they were skeptical that the operation of the existing political system could accomplish any of these ends. These citizens of New Haven and surrounding towns talked in detail about the ways in which politics, perhaps especially at the local level, had been corrupted:

- "[If you're running for office], you focus only on those people who are for you or leaning for you. Some of those people, after the first phone call, never hear again from a political person. And that's the way the system works today. And it's become more and more sanitized to the point where there isn't really an election anymore. It's who's got the most friends to come out to the polls."

- "How do decisions get made and who makes them? . . . It seems to me that the aspirations associated with the founding of this country had to do with the idea of no taxation without representation. And the idea that people should be able to have some degree of power over things that they care about, things connected to their own self-realizing activities. How many of us think that we have any power to affect things that matter to us?"

- "In my neighborhood, it was a policy of people to state that they had no intention of running for office. And they say that in order to develop a trust to get things done."

- "Periodically, in my twelve years in New Haven, people have asked me about whether or not I would run for mayor. And my response is, 'I am queen of my own bedroom, I am captain of my own tub, I am head of my own organization.' And the reason why I say that is because it's very, very hard not to be corrupted in the current political process. And you have to know that the pressure's going to be there and that's going to work against the very reason why you decided to run for political office or the very reason why you decided to participate in community activities anyway."

- "Last night I had to go in front of the Board of Aldermen to ask the mayor to put us in for $35,000 in the Community Development Block Grant allocation. . . . One of them says, 'Well, why should we give you this money?' By the end of five minutes, it dawned on me, they were talking about our money as if it was their money. It's not your money. I'm a representative of a community coming to the representatives of the people for a piece of the people's money to do people's work. Can you stop it? But this is the kind of thing that turns people off."

For a few, renewing or reforming the traditional political realm (getting people to vote, reminding people of the rights they enjoy and the need to defend them) seemed the most desirable route. But most believed that a genuinely political form of engagement might well have to occur outside politics as presently understood.

If this conclusion is valid, then why treat Dinner with Democracy as in any significant sense political? This group of citizens did not have to face the challenges of ordinary political life — making decisions, allocating resources and authority — nor indeed did it fully achieve the deliberative ideal. Although the group was a more diverse one than most participants had ever engaged with on a regular basis, it was not fully so. Everyone who participated was above average in educational attainment, and no one would have qualified as impoverished or marginal. In this respect, Dinner with Democracy speaks directly to debates among thinkers who, in one way or another, value more extensive, structured, and reflective interaction among individual citizens.[8]

Advocates of the value of social capital tend to characterize the public sphere as consisting of all associations and organizations that bring people together, however little they may succeed in attaining deliberative norms. And yet, when decisions affecting a group of citizens are at stake, or when the aim is to establish normative criteria of legitimacy, then theorists stress stringent standards of impartiality and transparency and inclusiveness, and the giving of reasons that could in principle be acceptable to everyone. In the discussion about the meaning of citizenship, one citizen-diner observed, "I agree that there's something more to being a citizen in this country than having a passport. On the other hand, I think that it's probably different than just any type of general participation within our community. Do we really think that bowling societies are a form of citizenship? And when I go home and see my friends, is that citizenship? If I go out with people to see a performance in public, is that citizenship? I think that we maybe can consider that participation in general is a good thing. We want to . . . generate social capital, to be a group. But I think citizenship is probably a little different than that . . . I suspect it would have something to do with participating with a broad continuum of what the society is."

What kinds of contexts meet the standard of enabling members to function as political equals who see themselves as sharing a political identity and belonging to a single political entity? And can they be expanded to include all citizens? And to make a difference to political decision making? Or are they limited to having an effect on select participants, who may themselves then contribute to a more deliberative and inclusive form of political life? Participants in Dinner with Democracy recognized that they were able to engage with each other as equals in part because they left their constituencies and pet projects at the door to the dining hall—and perhaps also precisely *because* they were not being asked to make decisions that would affect others. Members of the group dealt with each other openly and flexibly, as individuals rather than as "representatives" of any particular group or initiative. In a comment quoted earlier, another participant noted that "the effect of severing these ties that we have with constituencies we normally represent is that we were able to create a little political community in which we were all created equal." If they were to make decisions, they would have to take particular groups into account—to act as if they had been selected to represent some group or other, and to be accountable to them for the outcome. This would increase partisanship, inflexibility, a focus on particularist interests, perhaps. As one remarked, "It's a real luxury not to come to any conclusion." But he went on to draw an inference about reforming the way in which existing political structures function: "It's an argument for the point that there ought to be more times when we're not sitting down in a crisis, trying to come out with a conclusion because, then, maybe we'd be more prepared to listen to each other when it was important."

More than one participant was uneasy with the idea that Dinner with Democracy had been an escape hatch, valuable for their own personal development but removed from practical politics. They sought ways of translating what they had experienced into larger and more consequential spheres, or to bring the problems of civic life more concretely into the group's discussion. And all the participants felt that the experience would somehow make a difference. One of the undergraduates (quoted earlier), inspired by the revived belief that civility was possible in political discourse, was considering the possibility of running for elected office one day. Mechanisms of various kinds are now being proposed that seek to reintroduce something of this spirit into the practice of democratic decision making.[9] Assembling groups of ordinary individuals to deliberate and make decisions need not necessarily run counter to the premises of modern representative democracy so long as the selection and decision principles are clear and fair, and rotation occurs among individuals, so that continuity with the rest of the population and some measure of ongoing accountability are engendered. In the Athenian democracy, sovereignty rested with the people's assembly; the agenda-setting council and administrative offices and juries were chosen by lot, and those who played these roles were paid, so that poverty was no bar to participation. Attendance at the assembly was voluntary, and the magistracies rotated, so over time many different individuals helped to rule the city. This system provided incentives for each citizen, when he was functioning as a decision maker, to see himself as continuous with other citizens, who would soon take his place. Because ordinary Athenians ruled and were ruled in turn, each council member or official made decisions with his fellow citizens in mind, and not with an eye to a particular "constituency."[10]

But it is not my purpose here to explore these possibilities in detail. Rather, I would suggest that even more modest spaces, like Dinner with Democracy, consisting of a conversation among a relatively diverse group of individuals, sustained over a period of months, activated by systematic explorations of basic principles (in this case, a set of academic lectures), structured to promote respectful debate and disagreement as well as identification of common ground, can help to keep democracy alive. Dinner with Democracy is an improvement in this respect over bowling leagues and Elks clubs or their modern-day equivalents, which may build social capital but do not necessarily build more informed, broad-minded, and reflective citizens. Democracy — alone among political systems — relies on the virtue but also the stubborn individuality of all of its citizens. Disorder is a risk; so is conformity. The challenge is to keep alive both quirkiness and solidarity, both equality and realization of man's individual potential. No system can deliver this result — though some make it easier, while others prevent it entirely. What is required, as both Whitman and Lincoln perceived, is continual engagement, imagination, persuasion, openness. This can be accomplished only through the process of interaction between self and other, which is often too ragged and contingent, too much influenced by status and power, and too narrowly bounded, to serve democratic purposes. A more varied and rich and demanding fare — dinner with democracy as the table setting, perhaps — may be needed to sustain the democratic experiment.

Notes

1. The most prominent modern expositors of theories of this kind are Jürgen Habermas, in *Theory of Communicative Action*, trans. Thomas McCarthy (Boston: Beacon, 1984), and John Rawls, in *A Theory of Justice* (Cambridge: Harvard University Press, 1971) and *Political Liberalism* (New York: Columbia University Press, 1993).

2. I have in mind the tradition that views interests as givens and politics as a process of aggregation, bargaining, and/or balancing. Modern theorists in this tradition include Joseph Schumpeter, in *Capitalism, Socialism, and Democracy* (New York: Harper and Bros., 1942), and Robert Dahl, in *A Preface to Democratic Theory* (Chicago: University of Chicago Press, 1956), *Dilemmas of Pluralist Democracy* (New Haven: Yale University Press, 1982), and *Democracy and Its Critics* (New Haven: Yale University Press, 1989).

3. For the libertarian option, see especially Milton Friedman, *Capitalism and Freedom* (Chicago: University of Chicago Press, 1962), and Robert Nozick, *Anarchy, State, and Utopia* (New York: Basic, 1974); and for the communitarian, see, for example, Amitai Etzioni, *The Spirit of Community* (New York: Crown, 1993).

4. For further elaboration of this point, see Cynthia Farrar, "Greek Political Theory as a Response to Democracy," in *Democracy*, ed. John Dunn (Oxford: Oxford University Press, 1992), 17–39; and Jon Elster, "The Market and the Forum: Three Varieties of Political Theory," in *Deliberative Democracy*, ed. James Bohman and William Rehg (Cambridge: MIT Press 1997), 3–34.

5. For example, Habermas and Rawls; see note 1.

6. See Robert Putnam, *Bowling Alone* (New York: Simon and Schuster, 2000), and Theda Skocpol, "How Americans Became Civic," in *Civic Engagement in American Democracy*, ed. Theda Skocpol and Morris P. Fiorina (Washington, D.C.: Brookings Institution, 1999), 27–89.

7. See James Fishkin, *Democracy and Deliberation* (New Haven: Yale University Press, 1991) and *The Voice of the People* (New Haven: Yale University Press, 1995); John Gastil, *By Popular Demand* (Berkeley: University of California Press, 2000); and Ethan Leib, "Towards a Practice of Deliberative Democracy: A Proposal for a Popular Branch," *Rutgers Law Journal* 33 (2002): 359–455.

8. The character of the burgeoning literature about "deliberative democracy" is well captured in several collections: Stephen Macedo, ed., *Deliberative Politics: Essays on Democracy and Disagreement* (Oxford: Oxford University Press, 1999); James Bohman and William Rehg, eds., *Deliberative Democracy* (Cambridge: MIT Press, 1997); and Jon Elster, ed. *Deliberative Democracy* (Cambridge: Cambridge University Press, 1998).

9. See works cited in note 7.

10. See Bernard Manin, *Principles of Representative Government* (Cambridge: Cambridge University Press, 1997).

American Democracy and the Origins of the
Biomedical Revolution

JOAN A. STEITZ

In June 2000 headlines blazed with the announcement that scientists had finished assembling the sequence of the human genome. Craig Venter, head of Celera Genomics — a private company — and Francis Collins, head of the National Human Genome Research Institute, shook hands with President Bill Clinton and declared the book of life decoded. Despite some ugly aspects to their competition, their work had produced a rough draft of the sequence of close to 40,000 genes. Those of us in the know recognized that the job was far from done. With only 85 percent of the sequence of the 3 billion base pairs of the DNA in human chromosomes assembled, much of the work still remained. Often piecing together the last 5 percent of a sequence takes as long as determining the first 95 percent. Nonetheless, this international achievement — resting as it did on the shoulders of thousands of participating scientists from academia, industry, and government — was a triumph of modern biomedical research.

A third person who, in my opinion, should have joined in the handshaking was Eric Lander, a professor at MIT, the director of the Whitehead Institute Center for Genome Research (which contributed roughly one-third of the assembled sequence), and the ingenious architect of much of the critical technology that brought the genome project to fruition. Lander summed up the promise of this momentous accomplishment: "With the availability of the complete genome sequence, biologists in the twenty-first century will finally be able to see the big picture — health and disease described in terms of the complete symphony of DNA, RNA, and protein variation, both within an organism and across the evolutionary tree. The years ahead will see far-reaching reclassification of disease based on underlying molecular mechanisms and powerful, new therapeutics based on a sophisticated understanding of cellular circuitry."[1]

Even before the human genome, the products of the Biomedical Revolution have been increasingly evident by their impact on our lives. Blood-supply monitoring, DNA forensics, prenatal screening, new vaccines, cures for various cancers, treatments slowing the progression of AIDS, and genetically modified foods are but a few of the changes brought about by biomedical research. With these stunning advances have come legal and ethical concerns: How do we protect against the abuse of genetic information? What is the best design for clinical trials of new drugs and therapies? How do we balance reproductive rights against the future of our genetic lineage? These are questions we all must join in answering — biologists, ethicists, lawyers, and citizens. But they are not the subject of my essay. Rather, I wish to consider a historical question.

What is striking about the Biomedical Revolution is that it occurred largely in the United States, rather than in other countries with comparable intellectual capital. How did the unique form of democracy being examined in this book — American democracy — contribute to this development?

Origins

The Biomedical Revolution dates its beginnings to 1953, when a young American postdoctoral fellow, James Dewey Watson, and an older English graduate student, Francis H. C. Crick, proposed a model for the double-stranded structure of DNA. At the time controversy still centered on whether DNA was in fact the genetic material. Watson and Crick's famous letter that year to the British journal *Nature* contained no data; the model relied entirely on the results of others — in particular, the X-ray pictures of Rosalind Franklin, who died too young to share in Watson and Crick's 1962 Nobel Prize. Watson had graduated from the University of Chicago at the age of nineteen. There he had forsaken his first love, bird watching, and developed an interest in the gene, subsequently earning a Ph.D. at Indiana University studying bacterial viruses. During his postdoctoral stint in Europe, Watson's obsession with the nature of the gene and the structure of DNA grew. Crick, on the other hand, had worked for the British admiralty developing noncontact mines during

World War II and in 1953 was still completing his Ph.D. on the X-ray structure of proteins. The two met at Cambridge and became partners in the race to decipher the structure of DNA.

Their primary adversary was the famous chemist Linus Pauling of Caltech, who had correctly predicted helical structures in proteins and now had turned his interest to DNA. The structure proposed by Watson and Crick was compelling because of its predictive quality. Their *Nature* paper ended, prophetically, "It has not escaped our notice that the specific pairing we have postulated immediately suggests a possible copying mechanism for the genetic material."[2] Indeed, if the two strands of DNA simply separated, and each paired up with a newly made strand, the result would be two copies of the original molecule. The model had to be right. And everything we have learned since has only served to confirm Watson and Crick's double helix.

The seeds for a new academic discipline had been sown. But beginnings are slow. When I began graduate school at Harvard ten years after Watson and Crick's breakthrough, there were still no departments of molecular biology. Nor were there textbooks in the field. I enrolled in a graduate program run by the Committee on Biochemistry and Molecular Biology, consisting of a subset of faculty from the chemistry and biology departments. Like a handful of similar programs at other U.S. universities, the faculty all came from other fields. These professors had become fascinated by the question of how life works at the molecular level and had shifted their research focus away from the standard fare of their departments — usually biology, chemistry, or physics. And this is where American individualism becomes relevant: these academics had the courage to stray from the relative security of the disciplines in which they had been trained and hired as faculty. Moreover, the university system in which they worked was flexible enough to tolerate their shift in focus.

At first molecular biologists studied only bacteria and their viruses. The accepted notion was that one needed to examine something simple in order to learn anything. Biologists who studied more complex higher cells were derided for wasting their energies on systems that were too complex to understand. This notion was the legacy of the Phage Group, a small cadre of American scientists from various disciplines, including physics, who met in the summers at the Cold Spring Harbor Laboratory on Long Island. As their object of study, they had chosen what they believed were the simplest living entities, viruses that infect bacteria (phages). The experimental approaches they developed were based on the belief that genes could be explained by a combination of genetics, physics, and biochemistry. Theirs was a reductionist approach. As explained by Leo Szilard, a leading physicist who was among the converts, what physicists brought to biology was "not any skills acquired in physics, but rather an attitude: the conviction which few biologists had at that time, that mysteries can be solved."[3]

And the results came pouring in. After the structure of DNA came the discovery of messenger RNA, the middle molecule in the "central dogma," which was first enunciated by Crick and can now be quoted by schoolchildren: "DNA makes RNA and RNA makes protein."[4] Next came the elucidation of the genetic code. One of the highlights of my graduate school career was crowding into the back of the ballroom of the Hotel Americana in New York City for a plenary lecture of the International Congress of Biochemistry. Excitement was palpable in the hall as we heard about the breakthrough experiment that had at last cracked the genetic code. A year or so later, one of my fellow graduate students in Watson's lab earned his Ph.D. by determining the identity of just *one* base at the end of a bacteriophage RNA genome. And by 2000 we had a working draft of the 3 billion bases of the human genome!

In the early years of molecular biology (the 1960s and 1970s), the science was wonderfully fascinating, but only the best minds could even conceive of the magnitude of its practical implications. Recombinant DNA, developed by molecular biologists in the mid-1970s, was the keystone that provided the ability to isolate genes and determine their structures. With the subsequent exponential growth of the field, it became acceptable for molecular biologists to study more complex organisms, and the techniques of molecular biology were embraced by all the related biomedical disciplines. Today, just a few decades later, we have a biotechnology industry worth more than $200 billion that has already contributed dozens of new drugs to treat a host of human illnesses. How and why was this fledgling, esoteric scientific enterprise supported financially during those early decades? Why did molecular biology flourish primarily in the United States rather than in other nations?

Funding for Basic Research

Money is key to all scientific research. But money in itself is not enough. The sources and the recipients of funds for basic research, as well as the nonhierarchical structure of our institutions of higher learning, have nurtured the growth of molecular biology in the United States. The significant differences between how and to whom research money is distributed in the United States and how it is apportioned in other developed nations are the product of our democratic system, which encourages pluralism and rewards individualism.

Let us consider sources of funding. First, it is important to understand that U.S. universities do not fund research in the natural sciences, even though it is carried out by their faculty on their premises. Research funding is competitive and comes from outside sources — agencies of the federal government and private foundations. The university provides an environment where enough scientists are gathered together to form a critical mass. This concentration fosters creative interaction, and students — both undergraduate and graduate — have the opportunity to participate in cutting-edge research in the course of their training. To give you an idea of how this funding works, let's look at some typical numbers.

The current running costs for my department at Yale, Molecular Biophysics and Biochemistry (MBB), are slightly over $20 million per year, of which less than $4 million is provided by the university. Altogether there are about three hundred people (not counting undergraduate majors) engaged in the research, teaching, and administrative functions of the department. The university funds cover many (but not all) faculty and support-staff salaries, set-up costs for new faculty, undergraduate lab courses, and partial maintenance of the graduate program. A substantial portion of the funds acquired from outside sources is turned over to the university in the form of overhead, which is determined by negotiation between the university and the government, to reimburse the university for space and the administrative costs of research. Graduate student tuitions are also paid to the university. But the salaries of the technicians and the graduate and postdoctoral students who execute the experiments, as well as the costs of equipment and supplies, come from non-university sources.

The federal government has been the major source of funding for basic research for the past half-century. Before World War II, most basic research in the United States was supported by private foundations; federal expenditures for research and development were only about 1 percent of what they are today, even when adjusted for inflation. Nonetheless, the tradition of the federal government providing funds for scientific research has a long and noble history. Our Constitution itself promotes what the founding fathers called "science and the useful arts." In 1803, President Thomas Jefferson persuaded Congress to appropriate $2,500 to fund an expedition led by Meriwether Lewis to explore the American West. Although Jefferson cloaked the enterprise in economic terms — saying it was "for the purpose of extending the external commerce of the United States" — his real interests were scientific. He saw the expedition as an opportunity "to advance the geographical knowledge of our own continent" and made certain that Lewis (who had been his personal secretary for two years before the expedition) was trained in botany, mineralogy, astronomy, and ethnology. Jefferson even showed Lewis how to use a sextant. Indeed, the Lewis and Clark journals are a veritable treasure trove, the first systematic survey of the flora and fauna, climate and fertility, and peoples, wars, and economics, of the American West.[5]

The current era in federal funding for science dawned in 1945 with the report by Vannevar Bush entitled *Science, the Endless Frontier*. Bush had headed the war research and development effort, and President Franklin Roosevelt had challenged him to find ways to sustain in peacetime the wartime partnership in research forged between the universities and the government. Bush's report provided both the intellectual rationale and a blueprint for government support of basic research in areas related to medicine, the natural sciences, and defense. As President Bill Clinton noted at the 1999 ceremony awarding the National Medals for Science and Technology:

> Vannevar Bush helped to convince the American people that government must support science, that the best way to do it would be to fund the work of independent university researchers. This ensured that, in our nation, scientists would be in charge of science. And where before university science relied largely on philanthropic organizations for support, now the national government would be a strong and steady partner. This commitment has helped transform our system of higher education into the world's best. It has kindled a half-century of creativity and productivity in our university life. Well beyond the walls of academia, it has helped to shape the world in which we live and the world in which we work.[6]

Specifically, Bush's report led to the creation of the National Science Foundation (NSF) in 1950 and to a system for allocating federal money based on scientific merit. Other federal agencies, such as the National Institutes of Health (NIH) and the Department of Energy (DOE), have adopted comparable competitive procedures for allocating their funds in support of basic research. Another boost for federal research and development funding was provided by the Soviet Union's launch of *Sputnik* in 1957. The launch raised anxiety in the United States that perhaps the country had slipped in scientific and technical superiority. As a consequence, funding for science and math education made double-digit increases annually over the next decade.

For example, by 1998 government funding of basic research exceeded that of private industry by $10 billion ($18 billion to $8 billion). Such publicly funded research has been critical to private sector innovation. Economic returns on investments in basic research are high, being widely dispersed and delivered over a lengthy period. A recent study found that 73 percent of research publications cited by industrial patents were derived from government-funded research.[7] Although occasionally a scientific breakthrough finds immediate application, usually the yields on basic research are realized far into the future. Often the greatest benefits are the least anticipated. For instance, the war on cancer of the 1970s delivered its most significant benefits in the treatment of AIDS in the 1990s. A host of other examples can be found in an article by S. C. Silverstein and colleagues, "A Few Basic Economic Facts About Research in the Medical and Related Life Sciences."[8]

The most important U.S. institutions that receive federal funds to conduct basic research are the country's two hundred major research universities. Federal laboratories (such as the NIH) do exist and do contribute significantly to research in defense, health, and energy, but because they are mission oriented their impact in basic research has never been comparable to that of universities, and in most cases it has decreased in recent years. The few high-profile biomedical research institutes in the United States (the Cold Spring Harbor Laboratory, the Salk Institute, the Whitehead Institute, the Fred Hutchinson Cancer Research Center) are private, nonprofit organizations with close ties to individual universities. The migration of U.S. students and young researchers from university to university spreads ideas and brings fresh insights to the scientific enterprise. It is often said that the best science comes from the bottom up, not from the top down.

A contrasting situation exists in the nations of Europe and the Pacific, where most basic research is conducted in government-supported institutes. These are staffed by well-trained scientists but lack significant input from creative, highly motivated undergraduate and graduate students. Moreover, like most professionals in their countries, foreign scientists tend to stay put, usually working in the same institute for their entire careers. Their science suffers from too much stability and from top-down control.

Equally important for understanding differences between the United States and other countries is the fact that federal funding for basic research in the United States is given to individual scientists, as President Clinton emphasized, not to their institutions. These individual investigators compete directly for government grants, and the majority of grant recipients in the United States are faculty at the research universities.

In addition, our universities are structured differently from those in Europe and other developed countries. In foreign universities, a department is usually headed by a single professor, who wields absolute power. The system allows (and encourages) the appointment of a cadre of younger academics as assistants (and dependents). They have no choice but to work toward the professor's goals. Often independent sources of funding for their own ideas are unavailable to these younger scientists. And this hierarchical system stretches even farther in some countries. For instance, in 2001 the Japanese government had only recently considered turning the national universities into independent administrative units, freeing them from total regulation by a central authority.[9]

In contrast, in U.S. universities each department has many professors. Independence in research from other faculty within the department is regarded as a virtue, regardless of whether the member is an assistant, associate, or full professor. Even the most recently appointed assistant professor can (and must) apply for competitive outside grants in order to fund the experiments that will attract students to the lab and produce the publications that eventually lead to tenure.

Peer Review

Earlier I referred to Vannevar Bush's blueprint for allocating funds for research based on competitive merit review. This system was developed principally by the NSF and NIH, but it is used by many other federal and nongovernmental agencies. It ensures open competition for available resources with evaluation of merit by peers. In open competition, within the framework of an agency's mission researchers propose their best ideas, and anyone can apply for funding, regardless of his or her institution or geographic location. The evaluation of applications and awarding of funds by peer review is regarded as the primary reason for the remarkable quality, originality, and success of basic research in the United States. But peer review is largely an American success story. Why?

First because of the way it works. The agency that has issued a request for applications also assembles a "study section," a group of about a dozen active scientists who are specialists in the particular discipline and are willing to serve as reviewers of the grant applications. These are primarily faculty from research universities, but no more than one member comes from any institution. Study section members will normally serve terms of several years with two or three meetings per year to discuss and rank applications. They receive all the applications to be considered at least a month in advance of the study section meeting. A primary and one or two secondary reviewers are assigned to read and write a critique of each application. At the meeting these scientists lead the discussion of the application, mostly focusing on the science proposed and the track record of the applicant but also including consideration of the appropriateness of the budget request. Then all the members vote. Applications whose priorities fall above the funding line receive support, usually after a relatively perfunctory review by a higher panel within the organization.

Membership on a study section is voluntary; it involves a lot of work and is basically unremunerated. (The expenses of traveling to and attending the study section meetings are reimbursed, with perhaps a token $200 per day stipend offered for time spent at the meeting. The much longer preparation time required beforehand is uncompensated.) Scientists participate because they realize that the system is the best way of allocating funds for research. One of the important ground rules is that scientists do not participate in the review of an application from anyone at their own institution or from anyone with whom they have had a close scientific association in the past five years, as student, mentor, or collaborator.

The United States is fortunate that it is so large. Thus, appropriate experts can be found for applications, people with whom the applicant is not closely connected. A relatively impartial decision can be made — essential to the success of the peer review system.

Consider now the problem of mounting effective peer review in a small country, for instance a Scandinavian nation with a population of 5 million as compared to our 280 million. A 1997 study entitled "Nepotism and Sexism in Peer Review" (1997) examined the reasons why men were twice as successful as women in their application to the Swedish Medical Research Council for postdoctoral positions in 1995. The "scientific competence" of the applicants was judged on a scale of 0 to 4 by the evaluators who made up the study section. In the published study, using multivariate analysis the competence scores assigned were related to characteristics of the applicants, including their scientific productivity (number and impact of papers, citations in other scientific papers, and so on), gender, and research field. Three factors were discovered to be independent determinants of high scores for "scientific competence": the applicant's scientific productivity, gender (men received higher scores than women with comparable productivity), and affiliation with one of the review committee members. For example, applicants who had been supervised by one of the evaluators obtained significantly higher scores for scientific competence than other applicants with comparable productivity. But in a small country, it is almost impossible to assemble a review group where a reviewer does not have close ties to any of the applicants. Thus, peer review has not been an effective mechanism for distributing funds in most European nations.[10]

Because peer review has worked so well for the U.S. agencies that have used it, a 1995 report from the National Research Council called *Allocating Federal Funds for Science and Technology* advocated extending competitive merit review as the method of choice for future decisions about federal science and technology funding. It advises that merit review should be used not only in "extramural funding" (what I have been discussing: grants that go to faculty at universities) but also in allocating internal funds for running government laboratories.[11] In recent years, there has also been an active reevaluation of the criteria study sections use in ranking investigator-initiated proposals. Input from both applicants and study section members has resulted in a new statement of what reviewers should look for in applications for NIH funding.

Reviewers are asked "to judge the likelihood that the proposed research will have a substantial impact on advancing our understanding of biological systems, improving the control of disease or enhancing health." Five criteria are to be assessed: significance (how will scientific knowledge be advanced?), approach (is the conceptual framework adequately developed?), innovation (does the project challenge existing paradigms or develop new methodologies?), investigator (appropriate training and past record), and environment (can it contribute to the success of the proposed investigation?).[12]

The development and extensive use of the peer review system in allocating funds for science has been uniquely successful in the United States. Even though it is far from perfect, it is a system that embraces equal access, strives for impartiality, and rewards individualism. These are principles that reflect the best of the American democratic tradition.

Funding for Molecular Biology

I would like now to focus on how the availability of funding opportunities from multiple sources has enhanced progress specifically in molecular biology and the other biomedical disciplines.

Today the federal government provides about 80 percent of the dollars spent annually for basic biomedical research at universities, medical schools, and nonprofit research institutes. But what happens when a researcher sends a grant application to a federal agency, and the study section does not consider it important enough to be funded? Luckily, in the biomedical sciences there are multiple federal agencies whose mission might benefit from the applicant's research, including the NIH, the NSF, and the Department of Energy. In addition, the private foundations that contribute the remaining 20 percent of research funding also employ peer review. Since study sections are made up of active scientists, all with their own personal views of what is important, a project that does not appeal to one study section might be viewed enthusiastically by another. This is particularly true of proposals that are highly innovative or out of the mainstream of current endeavor. In most cases a worthy project that is not funded by one agency has a good chance of being funded by another.

Thus, the diversity of funding sources available to a faculty member at an American research university has made the pursuit of truly creative ideas a reality in the United States. In contrast, the typical European or Japanese scientist working in a government-funded research institute is likely to be dependent on a single source for support. The administrators in charge of the money may not view an innovative project positively.

I would like to examine in more detail three representative organizations, each of which has peculiarly American features and reflects certain values of our democratic culture. These are the National Institutes of Health, a federal agency; the American Cancer Society, a mission-oriented voluntary health agency; and the Howard Hughes Medical Institute, a private foundation.

THE NATIONAL INSTITUTES OF HEALTH

Almost 90 percent of all federal support for biomedical research comes from funds allocated by Congress to the National Institutes of Health (NIH). Significantly, about half of NIH monies take the form of investigator-initiated grants to faculty at American research universities, medical schools, or non-profit research institutes. These funds support the most innovative ideas of the most creative American scientists. A much smaller fraction of the NIH allocation (about one-tenth) pays for its own research laboratories (the "intramural program"), located primarily on the NIH campus in Bethesda, Maryland. Why is such a large percentage of NIH funding dispersed off-campus (extramurally)? And why has a wide range of basic research, rather than just disease-oriented projects, been supported?

The NIH traces its origins to the 1880s, when a one-room laboratory was created in the Marine Hospital on Staten Island, New York, for a young physician, Dr. Joseph Kinyoun, who had identified cholera bacilli in merchant seamen. The Hygienic Laboratory, as it came to be called, moved to Washington, D.C., in 1891. In 1901, Congress authorized the building of a new laboratory to investigate infectious and contagious diseases related to public health. Two congressional acts in 1902 allowed the laboratory staff to expand to include Ph.D. specialists, as well as M.D.s, and charged the laboratory with regulating the production of vaccines and antitoxins. (This occurred four years before the landmark Pure Food and Drug Act.) Between 1912 and 1930, the laboratory was called the Public Health Service, and its officers dealt with such problems as the cause and cure for the dietary deficiency pellagra, the effects of pollution on lakes and rivers, and the basis of anthrax outbreaks at military bases.

In 1930 the laboratory's name was changed to the National Institute (singular) of Health, and further legislation authorized the establishment of fellowships for research into both basic biological and medical problems. Seven years later, the National Cancer Institute (NCI) was created, again with visionary authorization—to award grants to nonfederal scientists for research on cancer and to fund fellowships. (In 1944 the NCI was designated a component of the NIH.) Thus the NIH established early three important traditions in its strategy for advancing the health of the nation: funding for basic (rather than exclusively medical) research, support for training (in the form of fellowships), and grants to non-NIH scientists.

The Public Health Service Act of 1944 redefined the NIH in its current form and determined the shape of biomedical research in the modern era. In 1946 the successful grants program of the NCI was expanded to the entire NIH, and the NIH budget grew from $8 million in 1947 to $1 billion in 1966. Also in the late 1940s, the NIH was authorized to conduct clinical research, and new, mission-oriented subinstitutes, such as the National Heart Institute and the National Institute of Dental Research, were created. Today there are two dozen institutes and centers under the NIH umbrella. The scope of NIH activities varies widely, and includes issuing guidelines for animal care, for the use of recombinant DNA, and for the ethical conduct of research, as well as launching special programs like the Human Genome Project (jointly with the DOE). In 2001 the NIH appropriation was $20 billion.

The NIH's policy of dispersing almost half its funds extramurally has paid off handsomely. As one measure of success, more than eighty Nobel Prizes have been awarded for NIH-supported research. Of these, only five went to investigators in NIH intramural programs.[13]

THE AMERICAN CANCER SOCIETY

The American Cancer Society (ACS) is the largest supporter of basic research among voluntary health organizations, spending about 2 percent as much as the NIH. The ACS was founded by fifteen New York physicians and business leaders in 1913, at a time when the word *cancer* was taboo in public. These leaders set about trying to bring cancer out into the open by writing for popular magazines and recruiting physicians to educate the public. In 1936 a legion of volunteers called the Women's Field Army was created to wage war on cancer; by 1938 the group had expanded to 150,000 members, ten times its original size. After World War II, the philanthropist and advocate for medical research Mary Lasker helped raise $4 million for the ACS to fight what was termed "the enemy at home." A full $1 million of this was earmarked for the ACS's research program.

In subsequent years, the ACS—a disease-related organization—has spent more than $2 billion on research. It solicits investigator-initiated applications and relies, like the NIH, on peer review carried out by study sections. Much of the funded research has been basic, with only tenuous ties to cancer evident at the time of funding. Thirty Nobel Prize winners have been recipients of ACS funding, often early in their careers, before they received support from other sources.[14]

THE HOWARD HUGHES MEDICAL INSTITUTE

The Howard Hughes Medical Institute (HHMI) is a relative newcomer, but it has recently expanded and is now the single largest nongovernmental supporter of basic biomedical research. The institute currently distributes more than $500 million annually, about 5 percent as much as the NIH extramural program. Support to U.S. researchers is not provided in the form of investigator-initiated grants, but recipients are chosen by a mechanism similar to the study section.

The HHMI was founded in 1953 by the eccentric billionaire businessman Howard Hughes. Although Hughes had long been interested in supporting medical research, the institute's mission was framed in impressively broad terms. Its charter states: "The primary purpose and objective . . . shall be the promotion of human knowledge within the field of the basic sciences (principally the field of medical research and medical education) and the effective application thereof for the benefit of mankind."[15] Hughes's Medical Advisory Board was made up of prominent medical scientists from the country's most prestigious medical schools. By 1957, forty-seven investigators, all at major medical schools, were being supported by the HHMI.

A new era at HHMI began in 1985, when the trustees sold the Hughes Aircraft Corporation and agreed to disperse 3.5 percent of its assets (held primarily in the stock market) annually. Since then, the number of investigators has grown to 350 at more than 70 locations; they are faculty not only at medical schools and institutes but also at basic science departments at the nation's research universities. The HHMI differs from the NIH and the ACS in funding people, rather than projects. Thus, HHMI investigators cease to be employees of their universities, although they remain on the faculty and are expected to participate fully in the teaching and training missions of their departments.

New HHMI investigators are appointed every several years in a nationwide competition in which the leading U.S. universities and medical schools are asked to propose candidates. Investigators are selected and then reviewed every five years by a board of peers. They are expected to perform innovative, creative research but are not tied to a particular project or field. Thus, the HHMI has been instrumental in the development of certain fields, such as structural biology (which was struggling because of minimal NIH support in the late 1980s but is now flourishing). Today, the HHMI funds do not go exclusively to support the laboratories of the investigators. There are also substantial grants to international researchers (in the former Soviet Union,

Eastern Europe, and South America, for example) and for creative ventures enhancing science education in high schools and at liberal arts colleges.

FUNDING OPPORTUNITIES FOR TRAINING

There are dozens of other U.S. organizations that fund basic biomedical research. Private foundations are particularly prominent on the American landscape, providing a diversity of opportunities for investigators to obtain support for creative research. These are particularly important in supporting training in the various biomedical sciences. Here the NIH bears the bulk of the burden, providing both stipends and tuition for Ph.D. and M.D.-Ph.D. students at leading universities and medical schools. Training grants from the NIH are awarded by the same procedures as research grants, based on competitive merit review conducted by study sections. But increasingly other sources are funding training and thus helping to shape the future of biomedicine. In February 2000 an important conference entitled "The Role of the Private Sector in Training the Next Generation of Biomedical Scientists" was organized by the ACS, the HHMI, and the Burroughs Wellcome Fund. The latter is an independent private foundation that funds outstanding scientists early in their careers to help them develop as independent investigators. The conference attendees considered how private foundations, even with limited funds, can have important impact on training at both the undergraduate and the graduate levels. Specific attention was given to building bridges between clinical and basic sciences, as well as to the many new interdisciplinary areas that represent emerging frontiers of research in the postgenomic era.

Once a young biomedical scientist has obtained a Ph.D. or M.D. degree, there typically remains a minimum of at least three years of training before he or she can secure an independent position. Funding can come either from the grants supporting the postdoctoral laboratory or from an independent postdoctoral fellowship. In addition to federal agencies and voluntary health organizations, there are numerous private foundations that award postdoctoral fellowships, again based on competitive merit review. They provide a living stipend and often additional funds for travel or research supplies. Receiving such a special fellowship is a distinction for a young investigator since it ensures a degree of independence while in the host lab and a leg up in acquiring a later position.

In addition, within the past several decades a number of private foundations such as the Burroughs Wellcome Fund have developed programs to sponsor the best new assistant professors, providing both salary and partial research funds. Applications for these prestigious awards, which are limited to a certain number per institution, often require a letter of assurance from the department chair that the faculty position is truly independent. The principle that independence is essential for innovative research imbues the American funding system at all levels.

People

Science is done by people. And U.S. scientists stand out for the active role they have taken in shaping environments for doing science and ensuring its funding. The notes cite writings by three contemporary American scientists I particularly admire — Tom Cech, president of the HHMI; Harold Varmus, director of the NIH from 1993 to 1999; and Jim Watson, president of one of the premier U.S. research institutes, the Cold Spring Harbor Laboratory. All three won Nobel Prizes before they took on their roles as administrators of science. Their words reveal aspects of the democratic soul described by Anthony Kronman as being peculiarly American. What is it about American scientists that has led to the American Biomedical Revolution?

THE ROLE OF LIBERAL ARTS COLLEGES

It may come as a surprise that graduates of liberal arts colleges are overrepresented among American scientists. Although only 8 percent of students attending four-year colleges or universities are enrolled at liberal arts colleges, they account for 17 percent of those receiving Ph.D.s in science. Even more impressive, as judged by election to the prestigious National Academy of Sciences, these graduates are disproportionately represented among the most successful American scientists. In a recent two-year period, 19 percent of newly elected members who were educated in the United States obtained their bachelors degree from a liberal arts college.

Do undergraduates experience something special at liberal arts colleges that better outfits them for a scientific career than their peers at large universities? Or do liberal arts colleges preselect those students who have an aptitude and a predilection for science? Of course the nature-versus-nurture argument is always problematic. However, it is noteworthy that of the 20 percent or so of students who profess an interest in science upon entering college, those attending a liberal arts college are more likely to maintain that interest. Liberal arts colleges graduate a percentage of students with majors in science comparable to those who declare an interest initially, whereas the defection rate is much greater at large universities. Whether it is the more intimate contact with faculty or the critical thinking encouraged by a curriculum that emphasizes the arts and humanities, the "intellectual cross-training" (as Tom Cech dubs it)[16] obtained at a liberal arts college clearly provides an extra edge for success in science.

By contrast, there is essentially no such thing as a liberal arts college elsewhere in the world. Post–high school education is almost exclusively government funded and occurs at large universities. These have their advantages as well as their disadvantages. But the lack of influence from the uniquely American breed of higher education — the liberal arts college — surely contributes importantly to differences between how scientists in the United States and those elsewhere conduct their affairs.

REPRESENTATION OF WOMEN

Women are underrepresented in academia the world over. Science is no exception, and the record is worst in the physical sciences. The exclusion of women means that science is not exploiting its intellectual potential to the maximum. The problem in the United States as elsewhere is a leaky pipeline. Whereas approximately half of undergraduate degrees in the biological sciences are awarded to women, the number drops for Ph.D. recipients and further for those in postdoctoral training. Women account for about a fifth of the faculty in science and engineering at U.S. universities and four-year colleges. At the top of the academic ladder the numbers become smaller: at the assistant professor level (in all fields) there are about 40 percent women, dropping to under 30 percent at the associate professor level, and just over 10 percent at the full professor level. Even in medicine, where about half the M.D. degrees now go to women, the statistics on female faculty in medical schools are no better (and perhaps worse). The causes are complex and a topic of much discussion.[17] Some funding agencies have adopted forthright measures to attempt to rectify the inequities. For instance, the NSF currently refuses to provide support for a conference if no women are included as speakers in fields where substantial numbers of women are trained (such as subdisciplines of biology, where 34 percent of the Ph.D.s are women).

But the record of promoting women to academic positions in science is about twice as good in the United States as in Europe, Japan, and elsewhere.[18] And the record in molecular biology is better than that in other, more established disciplines, such as medicine, chemistry, and physics. Why? I mentioned above that molecular biology, at least at its inception, was peopled by scientists who had been trained in other disciplines. These scientists possessed the courage to abandon established research paths and embark on investigations that were viewed as esoteric even when successful. Such adventuresome people are also more willing to acknowledge others based on their contributions rather than on pedigree or status. Thus, women, minorities, and eccentrics of various kinds have thrived in molecular biology. And the inclusive tradition has benefited molecular biology in return.

Scientific Activism

Harold Varmus's "Basic Science and the NIH" contains some surprising revelations.[19] When Varmus assumed the directorship of the NIH in 1993, he had had no previous administrative experience beyond running his own laboratory (with a budget one ten-thousandth of the NIH's). However, a year previously (in January 1993), before it was known that the NIH directorship would become vacant, Varmus and two of his colleagues at the University of California, San Francisco, had composed a bold letter of advice, published in *Science* magazine, exhorting the Clinton-Gore administration to act on eleven concrete recommendations in support of basic biomedical research.[20] And in his first public policy talk as director of the NIH, Varmus charmingly confessed to considerable political naïveté regarding the specifics of some of those recommendations. He quipped, "You don't have to live in Washington very long to learn that our proposal to double the budget [of the NIH] by FY '98 is simply not realistic."[21]

Indeed, in the early years of Varmus's leadership at the NIH, with five-year caps on discretionary spending and a monstrous national debt, the struggle was to avoid cuts, rather than obtain even inflationary increases for the NIH budget. Varmus's 1995 lecture to the Annual Meeting of the Massachusetts Medical Society was grimly entitled "Biomedical Research Enters the Steady State." But he did not hesitate to recite the enviable record of scientific accomplishments and improvements in the nation's health that could be traced to forty-five years of steadily increasing support for the NIH. He ended his address by asking, "Why should the NIH — with its popular goals, productive record, economic benefits, central role in sustaining our universities and training new scientists, and prospects for improving health — be valued any less by the federal government than Social Security and other mandatory entitlement programs?"[22]

Varmus did not give up, and by 1998 his unrealistic dream of increasing the NIH budget twofold within five years had almost been fulfilled. The drive to double spending by the NIH did occur and reached its halfway point with congressional approval in December 2000 of a 14 percent hike for the third year in a row.

What is incredible about America is that individuals with vision have the opportunity for leadership positions that will enable them to implement that vision on a large scale. Harold Varmus, the son of a physician, was an English major at Amherst College. He had trouble deciding what to do with his life, and "prolonged his adolescence as a graduate student, reading Beowulf and Shakespeare." Finally he went to medical school, as he says, "in part because someone once told Gertrude Stein that it 'opened all doors,' in part because medical students seemed more eager than I was to get out of bed in the morning." Later, while working at the NIH as an alternative to service in Vietnam, he experienced "the intoxicating power" of scientific discovery. More than twenty years later, with his UCSF colleague Mike Bishop, Varmus showed that cancer genes in viruses are derived from normal cellular genes, which undergo mutations that are the defining events in cancer. The two shared the Nobel Prize for the discovery of oncogenes in 1989. Four years later, when offered the directorship of the NIH, Varmus could not say no. His record in the six years he spent at the NIH is enviable.[23]

Jim Watson is another scientist who has never failed to let his opinions be known. His views of the war on cancer, which he helped initiate in 1971, are both amusing and poignant. Of massive cancer centers, he commented, "No matter how hard you try, you can't pull qualified specialists out of a hat." He was not bashful in stating his concern that by granting new cancer money to large-scale programs, "we may be witnessing a transference of power (money) from the research-oriented universities (departments) that have made American biology as it now exists, to a new power base whose past existence was derived from its willingness to work on cancer at a time when most scientists thought it to be an intellectual graveyard."[24] In "The Necessity for Some Academic Aloofness," Watson acknowledges the "quiet unease" of the academic environment and cites "a major factor determining the quality of a given institution" as being "the ability of its faculty to reward intellectual success even when it leads to the effective academic redundancy of many of its older members." He goes on to detail how the immensely important commercial exploitations of recombinant DNA and of monoclonal antibodies can be traced directly back to seemingly esoteric discoveries of pure science. He concludes, "We must never forget that ideas are not only beautiful, but necessary."[25]

Yet Watson's impressive leadership both of the Cold Spring Harbor Laboratory and on the national science scene has been anything but aloof. Subsequent to deducing the DNA structure in 1953, Watson joined Harvard, where his laboratory made many contributions to uncovering the molecular mechanisms and regulation of gene expression. (He always allowed his students to publish their papers solely under their own names.) He wrote the first textbook on molecular biology and a startlingly frank account of the discovery of the structure of DNA, the best-selling *The Double Helix*. In 1968 he became director of the Cold Spring Harbor Laboratory, then a sleepy collection of a few small labs and a summer meeting place (with miserable beds) for molecular biologists. Using his distinctive combination of eccentricity and charm, Watson wooed the affluent Long Island community, urging his neighbors to get involved in (and provide support for) the affairs of the laboratory. Today the Cold Spring Harbor Lab is known for its innovative research, its short courses that draw scientists from around the world to learn new technologies, and its premier meetings on both scientific and ethical topics. The Cold Spring Harbor Press publishes books and journals, the DNA Learning Center provides an introduction to the molecules of life for Long Island schoolchildren, and the local environment boasts a thriving biotechnology industry spawned by discoveries in the lab. Meanwhile, Watson's vision has spurred the application of molecular biology to the study of the brain and neurological disease. He became the first director of the National Center for Human Genome Research of the NIH, serving from 1989 to 1992, for he believed—at a time when few others did—that the sequence of the human genome was achievable. As always, his intuition was correct.

In contrast to scientific activists like Varmus and Watson are European scientists. A short article by A. Moore bemoaning the current crisis in European science ascribes the success of U.S. science policy partly to political lobbying by scientists—"accepted as a rightful activity; almost a professional duty." It exhorts European scientists to follow the example of their American peers to fight the tendency of the European Commission to fund demand-led, short-term science and ignore basic research, which is necessary to lay the foundation for future development and application.[26] My own experience in sitting on scientific advisory boards in Europe is that criticism is invariably delivered with such politeness that it is sometimes difficult to grasp the true message. In contrast, our forthright and often blatant ways of communicating with one another allow no possibility of misunderstanding.

These contrasts in the European and American scientific scenes seem remarkable in the context of the nineteenth-century observations of Alexis de Tocqueville. In *Democracy in America*, Tocqueville concluded that Americans were "more concerned with the applications than with the theory of science," and that "hardly anyone in the United States devotes himself to the essentially theoretical and abstract side of human knowledge." If I have succeeded in conveying no other message, I hope that I have communicated that it is basic research—performed because scientists have been in charge of science in the United States—that has fueled the Biomedical Revolution. Either Tocqueville was wrong or we have changed.

Molecular Biology and the Democratic Soul

I have tried to paint a picture of the distinctly American institutions, traditions, and scientists that together have contributed to the flowering of biology and thus to the Biomedical Revolution in the past fifty years. I have not touched on other, probably relevant contributing factors. For instance, what was the impact of the migration of many European scientists to the United States during the World War II era? How important was the devastation of European economies relative to the comparative prosperity that the United States enjoyed after the war? How has the transformation of southern universities as a result of the civil rights movement contributed to scientific development? What spurred the origin and explosive growth of biotechnology, which has revitalized the pharmaceutical industry, primarily in the United States? The influence of the American entrepreneurial spirit and of the American version of the democratic soul, with its striving for individuality, is everywhere in evidence.

I would like to end by sharing with you Jim Watson's advice to young scientists. His after-dinner remarks, found in "Succeeding in Science: Some Rules of Thumb," capture the quintessential Watson.[27] He begins by noting that "you need some luck." For instance, he was turned down for graduate school by Caltech (why would they want someone whose undergraduate interest was in birds?) and went instead to Indiana, where his mentor encouraged his study of the gene. But luck is not enough. Nor does intelligence suffice. Watson offers five sound rules for success in science.

Rule 1. "To succeed in science, you have to avoid dumb people." Watson explains that the goal isn't simply to win but to win at something difficult. Hence it is necessary to surround yourself with the brightest people.

Rule 2. "To make a huge success, a scientist has to be prepared to get into deep trouble." This means that when your superiors tell you that you are not adequately prepared or qualified to do something, you need to ignore them, regardless of how traumatic that might be.

Rule 3. "Be sure you always have someone up your sleeve who will save you when you find yourself in deep s——." Watson contrasts the situation of himself and Crick, who always found someone to help them out of trouble, to that of Rosalind Franklin, who had no one to support her and was excluded from the DNA race.

Rule 4. "Never do anything that bores you." If you dislike something, you can't possibly do it well. Moreover, you need to constantly expose your ideas to informed criticism. You must chat with your competitors, even if you find them objectionable.

Which leads to Watson's final rule: "If you can't stand to be with your real peers, get out of science."

Notes

1. Lander, E. S. (2000), "The View from Half-Time," *Discovery* (July): 2.

2. Watson, J. D., and Crick, F. H. C. (1953), "Genetical Implications of the Structure of Deoxyribonucleic Acid," *Nature* 171:737–38.

3. Grandy, D. A. (1996), *Leo Szilard: Science as a Mode of Being*. Lanham: University Press of America.

4. Crick, F. H. C. (1958), "On Protein Synthesis," *Symposium of the Society for Experimental Biology 12*, 548–55. New York: Academic.

5. Ambrose, S. E. (1996), *Undaunted Courage: Meriwether Lewis, Thomas Jefferson, and the Opening of the American West*. New York: Simon and Schuster.

6. Clinton, W. J. (1999). "Remarks by the President During the National Medal of Science and Technology Awards Ceremony." www.whitehouse.gov/WH/New/html/199990427–4646.html.

7. Committee for Economic Development (1998), *America's Basic Research: Prosperity Through Discovery*. New York: Committee for Economic Development.

8. Silverstein, S. C., Garrison, H. H., and Heinig, S. J. (1995), "A Few Basic Economic Facts About Research in the Medical and Related Life Sciences," *FASEB Journal* 9:833–40.

9. Normile, D. (2001), "Women Faculty Battle Japan's Koza System," *Science* 291: 817–18.

10. Wenneras, C., and Wold, A. (1997), "Nepotism and Sexism in Peer Review," *Nature* 387:341–43.

11. Committee on Criteria for Federal Support of Research and Development (National Research Council) (1995), *Allocating Federal Funds for Science and Technology*. Washington, D.C.: National Academy Press.

12. "Recommendations for Change at NIH's Center for Scientific Review" (2000), Phase 1 Report, Panel on Scientific Boundaries for Review. Draft, Executive Summary, www.csr.nih.gov/.

13. Harden, V. A. (2000), "A Short History of the National Institutes of Health," www.nih.gov/od/exhibits/history/index.html.

14. American Cancer Society (2000), www.cancer.org.

15. Howard Hughes Medical Institute (1999), *A Twentieth-Century History*. Chevy Chase, Md.: Howard Hughes Medical Institute. See also Russo, E. (2000), "Making an Impact," *Scientist* 14:1, 14–15.

16. Cech, T. R. (1999), "Science at Liberal Arts Colleges: A Better Education?" *Daedalus* 128:195–216.

17. Valian, V. (1998), *Why So Slow? The Advancement of Women*. Cambridge: MIT Press.

18. European Technology Assessment Network on Women and Science (2000), *Science*

Policies in the European Union: Promoting Excellence Through Mainstreaming Gender Equality. Luxembourg: Office for Official Publications of the European Communities.

19. Varmus, H. (1994), "Basic Science and the NIH," *Molecular Biology of the Cell* 5:267–272.

20. Bishop, J. M., Kirschner, M., and Varmus, H. (1993), "Science and the New Administration," *Science* 259:444–45.

21. Varmus (1994), "Basic Science and the NIH."

22. Varmus, H. (1995), "Biomedical Research Enters the Steady State," www.nih.gov/about/director.

23. Varmus, H. (1993–1998), Speeches, www.nih.gov/about/director.

24. Watson, J. D. (2000), "The Academic Community and Cancer Research," in *A Passion for DNA,* 129–37. Cold Spring Harbor, N.Y.: Cold Spring Harbor Laboratory Press.

25. Watson, J. D. (2000), "The Necessity for Some Academic Aloofness," in *Passion for DNA,* 109–16.

26. Moore, A. (2000), "Science Funding and Infrastructures in Europe," *Trends in Genetics* 16:329–30.

27. Watson, J. D. (1993), "Succeeding in Science: Some Rules of Thumb," *Science* 261:1812–13.

13

Computers and Democracy

D A V I D   G E L E R N T E R

"Computers and democracy" is a big, vague, hot-air balloon of a topic. I'll try to bring it down to earth; I'm not sure whether I'll succeed. Americans' attitudes toward democracy and computers are curiously similar: we depend on both, believe in both, pride ourselves on both, but we aren't particularly interested in the details of either. The first role of any well-functioning democratic government or desktop computer is to annoy us as little as possible. Traditionally, in this country we have not admired people who are too eager to be part of government; we are not too crazy about computer experts either.

Computers are likely to affect American democracy mainly by influencing American culture—the atmosphere in which democracy lives. Networked computers at their best are like the feeling of spring in the air; among human beings, the feeling doesn't make things happen, but it makes people more eager to make them happen. It puts us in the mood for action. Computers can do that too. They can put us in the mood for change. They can give us an excuse to get good things done.

But good things don't happen automatically. Many of us approach technology deferentially. We are content to sit back, see what happens, let matters take their course. Many are content for software and computers to be left to technical experts. Some of us, for that matter, feel the same way about government: that mere ordinary people aren't equipped to make public policy.

But computers and the Internet have a shaping effect on American culture, American language, and the texture of daily life. Their influence will increase. Their gravitational field will continue to grow.

To design software and help guide technology evolution takes wisdom, experience, and common sense — qualities that are no easier to find among technical experts than anywhere else. Americans ought to take technology in hand, make computers their business the same way they make government their business, not because they are ideally qualified to call the shots but because they are better qualified than anyone else. Computers could be a great thing for American culture, and therefore for American democracy and life in general. They could also bring out the worst in us, leave us richer in money and worse off in spirit than we have ever been before. The outcome will depend on whether we sit back and let the technical experts run the show or assert our right and our duty to shape the evolution of this astonishingly, unsettlingly important technology.

First let's consider the mechanics of democracy: what are the probable consequences of using computers as voting machines, and how would we go about doing so?

For some time people have been considering using computers as voting machines. Proposals come in many formats, but let's focus on a simple, radical concrete plan. Let's say that you could vote by using any Net-connected computer during official voting hours, at home or in any other place. Let's forget about the details: we would have to make sure that only qualified people vote, that no one votes more than once, that voters see only the ballot for their town. We would have to make sure that accumulating vote totals weren't messed with or snooped on. We would have to make sure that Net-connected computers were no less accessible than today's voting machines, ballot boxes, and so forth. We would have to decide what kind of software to use and how the interface should work. (Presumably each state would make its own decisions.)

We would also have to solve other problems that computer voting wouldn't create but would bring to the fore. For example, if we were allowed to vote using computers in our homes, many of us would spend a good part of every election day within a few steps of a voting machine. Inevitably, we would start wondering whether we could change our votes and then change them back. We shall need a policy for computer voting, as well as a way to carry it out.

But let's assume that we have solved all these problems. Some are hard, but we could probably manage them all within a year or two if we worked at it. The real question is: Is computer voting a good idea?

At first it sounds rotten; at least it did to me, for several reasons. The most important thing about the process of an election is not that the final count should be completely accurate (with every last vote recorded and totaled correctly) but that it should be, as far as possible, transparent. Tampering with the results should be difficult and should *seem* difficult. We ought to be able to picture clearly in our minds the procedure that herds millions of scattered, scampering votes into a majestic grand total. If we can picture it, we can believe in it. And today, on the whole, we can picture it; our elections score fairly high in transparency. A paper card or ballot is a concrete thing. So is a voting machine. Personally, I've always liked the solid little crunch that a voting-machine lever makes when you swing it down, and the ringing thrunk when you open the curtain and register your votes. To me these are the sounds of democracy. I suspect other people feel the same way. It's easy to picture the process that connects our tangible voting acts to the final total. Maybe our picture is incomplete, even wrong; and of course computers are already heavily implicated today in vote counting. But at least the voting act itself is easy to understand, and the mental picture exists and is comforting.

Computer voting might be far more accurate but it would be less transparent, and I'm not sure that's a good trade. Every programmer knows not to fix what isn't broken. Every programmer also knows that software is hard to get right and prone to break — and everyone else knows it too. I think we could build voting software that is more reliable overall than the system we use today, even if it were prone to error and fraud. And I think we could sell it to the American public. But our elections would become less transparent; a vote would amount to a handful of bits in a complex series of software structures, and few people can picture software at work. Inevitably, we would pay a price in public confidence: we would have less in the bank when elections were disputed, as they are bound to be occasionally, no matter how we do our voting. The real story of the 2000 Bush-Gore presidential election was the crisis that did not happen. If we change our way of voting, our first responsibility will be to do no worse than we are doing today.

At least one other problem with computer voting comes to mind. Voting shouldn't be difficult, but it shouldn't be too easy either. Making people leave their homes, go to a public place, and maybe even wait on line is hardly an unbearable imposition. But it does quietly underline the importance and dignity of the election. It seems right and fitting that voting be done in a public place — usually with flags on hand, with your neighbors standing around, with the feel of a special occasion. Voting is a little (just a little) like getting married. Other things being equal, the nation has an interest in its citizens marrying and voting. Once people have made up their minds to go through with either process, we don't want to talk them out of it. But we don't want to make it *too* easy either; we want to make it clear that these are not casual acts—deliberation is called for. In theory you could get married in front of a PC, too; you could go to the wedding Web site of your choice and download appropriate music and the necessary forms. But this is a bad idea.

Nonetheless, computer weddings almost certainly will happen, and so will computer voting. When we do make the switch, we ought to stipulate something like this: the company or agency that builds the software must be able to explain how it works to any voter in five minutes, not in comprehensive technical detail but in a fundamentally accurate way. It's a difficult requirement, and admittedly subjective. But it would put pressure in the right direction.

And despite its disadvantages and even dangers, computer voting might even be good for American democracy. It might turn the public's lack of interest in politics into a force to improve politics. By making it easy to get the minimum information you need to vote at the moment you need it and not a moment sooner, computer voting could help make political campaigns as we know them disappear.

Why? Because, first, the social dynamics of computer-based elections would probably allow (and even encourage) voters to spend a few minutes casting their ballots. To take their time. Even when a person is voting via computer in a public place, computer habits are different from voting-machine or ballot-box habits. People expect to sit down and think when they use a computer.

So we might allow each candidate to put a short statement on file, maybe five hundred words; you could read as many of these statements as you felt like before casting your vote. You'd click the "show me the statement" button, or something like that, next to the name you were considering. Our election laws might have to be changed to allow this system, but they might be worth changing.

What's potentially useful here is not the mere existence of these statements—there are plenty such statements floating around today—but the way they would become available at the right moment to be worth reading, in a setting where reading them seemed like a reasonable thing to do. Voters who dump campaign mailings in the trash might nonetheless read these. Voters who ignore the leaflets thrust in their faces by campaign workers hovering hopefully outside the polling-place perimeters might read these statements. There's a big difference between information you ask for and information that is flung at you the way popcorn is thrown at elephants by zoo visitors. When you *ask* for information your attitude is different, and the information itself can be presented differently. Most Americans aren't sufficiently interested in politics to ask for information—but we are a practical people, so we say, and voters who would never ordinarily solicit this kind of information might conceivably ask for it if they were face to face with the ballot and the asking were easy.

This last-minute, point-of-sale message would inevitably carry weight and — more important — give voters an excuse to do what most of them would like to do anyway: ignore the campaign entirely. Block it out, with the thought in mind that candidates' statements will be available when they are needed. The whole plan conflicts with the idea some people have that voters solemnly ponder their election-day choices for months beforehand, but I doubt whether this view of American voters is realistic. In any case, we could gradually increase the amount of information available at voting time — starting with the five hundred–word statement, which would no doubt turn into a video snatch, we could add a two thousand–worder for voters who ask for more, then a five thousand–word statement, and so on. Meanwhile, the rest of the campaign might become increasingly marginal.

The difference between information you ask for and information that is thrown at you affects all of American politics. We turn our politicians into court jesters and professional party crashers, begging for small handouts, mugging and cavorting for attention. And then, naturally, we despise them. Putting a bit of information in the right place, at the right time, in the right way, won't in itself cause our existing campaign system to collapse. But it might give it an *excuse* to collapse.

In fact, computer voting is probably our best shot at giving it an excuse to collapse. I don't think we will ever have publicly financed campaigns in this country, to a greater extent than we have them (at the presidential level) today, and I don't think we should. People don't enjoy paying for things they're used to getting free and didn't want in the first place. Given the state of American election campaigns, forcing the public to pay for them would be like forcing us to pay for junk mail or obscene phone calls. What candidates desperately need from us is not our money but our attention. They want money only to buy attention. Donating a little attention free of charge would be the perfect fix — and if we could do it strictly on our own terms, we probably would. Neither the campaigners nor the campaignees like today's system, and it will fall apart if we give it a chance.

Here is a general point about the probable evolution of technology. The value of a piece of information depends on when you get it. Information that is worthless at the wrong moment can be invaluable at the right one. Using computers to deliver information at the right time in the right way is likely to be a big topic of technology and culture research over the next decade. For example, we've been working for several years on a research software system, now also a commercial project, called "lifestreams," in which users can maintain automatically a comprehensive, time-ordered journal of their electronic lives. Every document, image, email, Web bookmark, news update, or other piece of information they receive or create is dropped at the end of a constantly growing, time-ordered stream. At the head of the stream users see the latest stuff; as new documents arrive, old ones move back. So the stream flows, the way time flows and life flows. The stream has a future too. Users store their plans and appointments in the future. These flow toward the present. When they reach "now," they hop over the "now line" and shuffle off into the past.

But we can also use the stream's future as a staging ground for information that we would like to deliver exactly when it's needed. If you're traveling (for example) and will need information about your plane ticket around three in the afternoon, about ground transportation two hours later, and about your hotel, various phone numbers, and background information for a meeting the next morning, you could lay out all these documents in sequence in the stream's future (like clothes a mythical valet might lay out on a theoretical bed); each piece of information would cruise forward toward "now," and present itself when its big moment arrived.

So changing campaign politics could be one facet of a larger problem of technology and culture. The "information age" is all right as far as it goes (it's been under way for at least a century if it exists at all); but what we really need is an "information at the right time" age.

What does democracy need? Citizens who are well informed and thoughtful, who feel responsible to the community. Computers and democracy intersect as soon as we talk about information: computers and networks supply us with some of our information and, more important, they handle nearly all of it. Almost all the words that are published and nearly all the prepared words that are spoken pass through computer word processors, over networks, and out of printers.

George Orwell wrote in his famous essay on politics and the English language: "If thought corrupts language, language can also corrupt thought." It's no accident that the twentieth century's most notorious tyrannies expressed themselves in opaque, muddy, swollen language. Crisp, clear, clean information — sparkling, if possible — is a necessity of democratic life. A democratic society had better be an articulate society.

Are computers good or bad for prose? In a sense, the word processor and the cheap printer are the best things that ever happened to writing. To write well is to revise obsessively. Word processors are perfect tools for trying out the look, sound, and feel of a sentence before you commit yourself. (Writers don't like to commit themselves to anything as important as a sentence until they are sure of it.) Computer printers let you put your draft on paper, change it, print it again, change it again, and on and on, with the neurotic persistence of a child working a yo-yo, until your editor goes crazy.

Email brought the personal letter back from near death, admittedly in a strange new shape. During the 1970s and 1980s, phone calls grew insidiously less expensive, and then phones themselves became cheaper, smaller, wireless — it was a nightmare out of Hitchcock. It seemed clear that before long we would be crunching cellphones underfoot like cockroaches. Meanwhile, the U.S. mails were nothing to write home about. So by around 1990 the personal letter was gasping for breath. The rise of email has put it back in play.

And yet computers can also be bad for writing. Email resurrected the personal letter. It might also be fostering a culture in which our prose is so feeble we have to load it up with little smiley and frowney faces because otherwise no one can tell whether we're kidding. My sons are often told to write school papers based on research using the Web. The great thing about this form of research is that, for the first time in history, you can write a research paper in less time than it takes to read one. Furthermore there is no quality control on the Web; there are high-quality sites alongside junk sites, where junk information is expressed in junk prose.

Once again the technology is neither good nor bad in itself; what matters is what we make of it. But if I had to guess, I'd predict that the new technology of writing could yield something remarkable for American culture by giving us an opening, a good excuse, to do what we want to do anyway.

Today we have by far the best writing tools that ever existed. We are only a generation or two removed from the greatest outpouring of brilliant writing in American history, an extraordinary eruption that lit up the skies from the 1920s into the 1960s or early 1970s. There are always a few brilliant writers around; you can find them today, guaranteed. But the interesting thing about the great age of twentieth-century American prose is how the formidable parts added up to a remarkable whole, how dozens of sharply defined and distinctive individual voices added up to a national style that caught up the whole country and carried it forward — these authors wrote poems and art stories that were also best-sellers and popular magazine pieces.

Such writers of vivid, crew-cut English as Sherwood Anderson, Gertrude Stein, and Ernest Hemingway led naturally to the great essays and journalism of E. B. White and Joseph Mitchell, A. J. Liebling and Ernie Pyle, and on to a new crop of novelists and essayists who continued in their own voices the same vibrant, funny, often belligerent national narrative: Norman Mailer, Irwin Shaw, Saul Bellow, John Updike, Philip Roth, Eudora Welty, Tom Wolfe, Cynthia Ozick, James Salter. I could go on. This remarkable outpouring ran out of steam in the 1960s or maybe the early 1970s. But that wasn't so long ago—the engine is still warm, and it could easily restart if something were to kick it back to life. Maybe our unprecedented new writing tools will do that, together with email, which makes it easy for writers and editors to work together.

Computers wouldn't cause this big cultural event; all the great writing and editing technology in the world never produced a single decent sentence. But it might give us an opening or occasion or excuse to get back on track and do great things.

Americans have many things on their minds; we are not a monomaniac nation. But it seems to me likely that more or less continuously since the 1930s and occasionally during earlier periods one "big theme" or another has preoccupied us. The big theme is the spare topic in every lagging national conversation. It's the pattern on the national wallpaper. During the 1930s the Depression was the big theme. Then World War II and its immediate aftermath took over, and then for the forty-odd years between the Berlin airlift and the collapse of the Soviet Union it was the Cold War. Today, our big theme has to do with computers and the Internet.

Identifying a single big national theme is a thought experiment, an exercise in deliberate oversimplification. But such exercises serve a purpose. If you are trying to draw a human figure, for example, you will have many complex details to deal with. But you'll also have the problem of finding the one characteristic line of action or tension or flow that makes the drawing come to life. That one line is not the figure or anything close to the figure; it's a radical abstraction. But it's a necessary abstraction. It does not suppress the details; it makes them emerge more clearly.

Granted it seems crazy to propose an analogy between the Cold War and the desktop computer as national big themes—they come from far-apart categories of existence. And I'll admit that such a claim can only be arbitrary and subjective. But I can't shake the strange feeling, and it is strange, that the role the Cold War played in my own childhood is being played in my children's lives by the Internet and computers. When I was a boy President Kennedy, the intrepid Cold Warrior extraordinary, was the official hero of all boys—not because of the Cold War per se but because of *PT-109*, a story of wartime heroism that every child knew. Of course we admired other people too: war heroes, sports heroes, Hollywood heroes, television and pop-music stars, and all presidents of the United States ex officio. Probably we admired presidents most. In around 2000 we were told that Bill Gates was the man children admired most. It seems impossible—but it fits.

Any analogy between the Cold War and computers can only be a half-analogy, similar to a half-rhyme or an unresolved dissonance. The half-analogy is inherently awkward, and it's not an officially sanctioned rhetorical device, but nonetheless it can be useful.

So consider this half-analogy between the Cold War then and computers now. The most important function of a big theme is to answer questions automatically. The big theme is an answering machine with the prerecorded message built in. If it helps our position in the Cold War, it's good. If it has to do with computers or the Internet, it's good. This is a valuable service at times. It keeps us from going over the same ground repeatedly. It allows us to put a national consensus to work and get things done.

But it can also be dangerous. The Vietnam War, for example, was a watershed catastrophe in American life. We fought in Vietnam for many reasons, but ultimately the Cold War made us do it — our global struggle with communism and the Soviet Union. Whether you believe that it was noble or evil for us to have gone into Vietnam, it's hard to doubt that we got involved in the war without thinking carefully about what we were doing. During its early years, as we edged out calmly into those huge rolling breakers step by step — breakers that eventually swept away so much that was good and valuable in American life, above all our endless confidence in ourselves and our future — there was relatively little discussion or argument about Vietnam. Not much discussion of our goals; not much discussion about whether our methods were in line with our goals. The arguments came later. In a sense, they came too late.

Ideology is a sedative. It makes you accept propositions without thinking, gives you the answers without making you solve the problems. It is dangerous to operate a nation when you're under the influence. Today computers are the big theme, and they are a new sort of ideology: an ideology without ideas. Computers are an ideology the way Bill Gates is a hero. American culture is in sad shape.

Today's prerecorded message is: If it has to do with computers or the Internet, it's good. Karl Marx made the famous pronouncement that history repeats itself, the first time as tragedy, the second as farce. (This might be his most important accomplishment.) Probably there is no national tragedy lurking in our fixation on computers. So far there has only been farce: foolish, expensive mistakes.

Take the collapse of the "dot-coms." People poured money into companies that had no logical reason for existing on the theory that commercial reality could be suspended like alternate-side-of-the-street parking rules as long as a business plan centered on the Web. The big theme made people turn off their brains.

Or consider the Clinton administration's aggressive promotion of the Internet in the schools. Most Republicans supported the policy in principle even if they opposed the tax rise that accompanied it. Our schools were evidently failing to teach reading, writing, history, and arithmetic, but few people claimed that our students suffered from information underload, or excessively long attention spans, or too few in-school distractions. I don't claim there was nothing to be said in favor of putting the Internet in schools, but there were definitely things to be said *against* it, on the grounds that at best it was a distraction and at worst an attractive nuisance. But almost no one said them, which should remind us that we have two political parties in this country in order for them to disagree, not congratulate each other on bipartisanship. Especially on domestic policy, political parties are *supposed* to disagree. If they don't, there's probably something wrong with them.

Computers didn't ask to be appointed our national big theme. The situation developed by accident and is nobody's fault. Nonetheless: as big themes go, this is a bad one. It makes us painfully credulous. We need a loyal opposition, and we don't have one. We are setting ourselves up for bigger business failures, and possibly in the long run for an anti-technology backlash. More important, "computers and the Internet" makes an unworthy big theme for a great nation, because it is morally, spiritually, and intellectually vacuous.

Computation is not at all vacuous in itself. Developing the science and art of computation was one of the twentieth century's greatest achievements. But we choose to treat the subject as if it *were* vacuous. More than a generation after most universities established computer science departments, only a handful of people in and out of universities have any idea what computer science *is*. The public generally doesn't care, and computer scientists generally don't care whether the public cares or not.

A nation does not consciously choose its themes, and it would be foolish to suggest what the next theme should be. But we can make predictions if not suggestions. Big national themes are likely to grow out of earlier themes. In a certain limited sense, modern computer technology did indeed grow out of the Cold War. American military research was the driving force behind the original Arpanet of the late 1960s, which became the Internet in the 1980s; military research funding was a factor in the emergence of nearly every aspect of modern computing. Of course, there were many other contributing factors, too — freedom of thought, free teaching and research, free markets, and the nation's tendency to attract many of the world's smartest people to its corporations and universities. Ultimately these are all facets of American democracy.

No one can predict future themes with any confidence, but if we had to guess, we should probably expect the next to grow out of the current one — unless some new, unforeseen national emergency arises (for instance, a resurgent

Russian empire). But we know that the next theme will be something concrete. People have proposed community, civility, and spirituality as important topics for the national agenda, but these wouldn't even make good titles for directed studies courses.

One possible new theme might have to do with the emergence of new Internet-based cultural institutions. During my lifetime, thousands of major new businesses and corporations have been created in this country, but not a single important new university. No important newspapers have been born, although many have died; some first-rate magazines have been created, but only one or two have real cultural weight. Lots of publishing houses have bit the dust. I could go on: it's been an extraordinarily creative era for business institutions and a dead period for cultural institutions.

Creating new cultural institutions is important because successful existing institutions have an obligation to continue succeeding. They are conservative by nature. Yale's most important obligation is to go on being Yale. If technology means that a university could become a radically different kind of institution, Yale is the wrong place for it. Radical experiments make sense at institutions that have little to lose. That's why new institutions are indispensable to American culture; they are the right settings for the risky experiments that can change society.

Of course, technology will change existing successful institutions too — it will change Yale, for example, although the changes had better be in character or they won't have a chance and won't deserve one. Universities like Yale are working hard to deliver courses online. This is an interesting, important project. We might also consider the related but different project of putting the university itself online, building an electronic campus.

The electronic campus would be a meeting ground, like any campus, but it would be laid out in time instead of space. Think of it in terms of the lifestream structure I mentioned before. In this version, the electronic campus would be a stream — the ongoing, emerging narrative history of the university. It would be made up of lots of separate histories shuffled together, like decks of cards shuffled into one stack. The art gallery would have a history: a series of announcements, lectures, acquisitions, new hires, and so forth. Each event in this history would be a separate document posted on a growing, time-ordered stream. The separate documents might be skimpy or detailed; chances are they would start skimpy and *become* detailed. Each course in the college would have a history — a series of assignments, handouts, exams, and so on. The football team would have a history; each college would have a history; the physics department would have a history; the dining halls would have a history (the story of what they served yesterday, last week, last year, last century);

all these documentary stories shuffled together would be the backbone of the electronic campus.

Each member of the community would have a personal history too: your email, notes, and photographs, the drafts of your papers, your address book, your diploma. When you arrived as a freshman you would be set up with your own personal view of the university stream. Your view would have your private documents shuffled in. No one but you would be able to see them; you would see your own documents and as many public documents and conversations as you cared to. Each person would see a different stream, but all these streams would overlap. To put it another way, everyone would see a private foreground — his own story — set against a public backdrop, the university's story. The stream would have a future where the university's plans and your personal plans would be stored. Each document in the future would roll steadily forward toward the present. And the stream would have a past, which in this case goes back to 1701. All the documents, drawings, photos, films, and so forth that document Yale's history would be filed in the stream in proper time order. The future would flow into the present, which would flow into the past. It would all be one stream, constantly moving and growing. You could pick a topic or category and follow it forward or back as far as you wished; or you could sit back and watch the stream move. When you graduated, you would keep your stream account. You could tune into the university whenever you liked. Your history and the history of your class would continue to accumulate on the stream.

There's more to be said, but that's one version of an electronic campus in brief. How does the electronic campus compare to the real one? Its disadvantages are obvious. On the real campus people can talk face to face, play football and Beethoven and look one another in the eye. But the electronic campus has certain advantages too. You can be part of it no matter where you are. Everything takes place in historical context: you can rewind the electronic campus to last term or last decade or last century. Everyone can watch the passing scene from a front-row seat.

Streams like this have been established at a few small institutions, for example at the New Haven technology company that built the commercial version of the software, Mirror Worlds Technologies. One of the stream's big advantages at Mirror Worlds is that when you are tuned in to the stream, you feel that you're right at the center of the action even if you are nowhere near the company's offices. One of the stream's big disadvantages is exactly the same: you *feel* you're right at the center of the action, but you aren't. You've lost face-to-faceness, and that's important. You gain something in return; it can be a reasonable trade so long as you don't kid yourself about the cost.

Before long Yale will probably be in the strong position of having both kinds of campus, the physical one and some kind of electronic one. Similar techniques make it easy to imagine that we could create new universities whose faculty and students are spread throughout the world. These new institutions would exist mainly online. Their members would meet occasionally, but they would be unlikely to have an actual campus. Do the potential gains make up for the big losses? I don't know. But I'm sure we'll have a chance to find out. This experiment will be tried. We're seeing some tentative first steps already.

Everyone knows that it's almost impossible to start a newspaper nowadays. Of course it might be easy to start an electronic one, but on the whole, Web news services have been disappointing. They're good at providing focused, specialized news but not at creating a document that people turn to for the pleasure of browsing and reading. We know one thing about electronic newspapers: when a successful one is created, it won't look anything like an online version of the *Times* or the *Wall Street Journal*. The organization and design of today's newspapers reflect the character of printing on paper. A successful online newspaper will come in a new shape and use new organizing principles that don't exist on paper. It might be a stream, for example, where you could look at the future to find out what's coming up, and the present to find out what's happening now, and as far back into the past as you'd like. Or it might take a completely different shape. In any case, its shape will be new, not a mere translation of paper into a new medium.

Suppose electronic newspapers were structured as streams. You could take the equivalent of the *New York Times* stream and the *Wall Street Journal* stream, mingle them together, and read both newspapers simultaneously. You could follow a story backward step by step to the beginning. You could make everything disappear but the graphs and pictures. You could read a newspaper once a day, once a week, or once a month and it wouldn't make any difference; whenever you tuned in, you could take up exactly where you left off. The stream is an easy structure to navigate — you can go forward or back, look for this or that — and so you could listen to a newspaper while you drove to work; your car computer could read out the newspaper stream. Whether these possibilities are practical remains to be seen. The point is that we can experiment. Newspapers are important to democracy. Nowadays they aren't doing terribly well. Computers will give them a chance to change.

Some of our new institutions won't have any precise analogues in today's cultural universe. Take the following obvious stream-based service, or institution, or whatever you want to call it: New York City is the center of the publishing industry, but it's radically underserved in book reviews. There are only two weekly book reviews for the general public; hundreds of new books are barely mentioned or ignored altogether. In fact, all sorts of New York cultural events receive cursory or no notice. I know an artist who worked for years on a big New York gallery show. When it finally opened not long ago, everyone waited anxiously for the reviews. When a review appeared at last, she and her show were blown away by a single paragraph in the *New York Times*. The art world shouldn't work like that. But in this allegedly information-rich world, the arts are starved for attention.

Before long, someone will found a New York culture stream: it will publish news and reviews but will also be a ticket and shopping and calendar and archive service. When you tuned in this culture stream, you would see late-breaking news and reviews. You could watch everything or focus on books, music, art, Lower Manhattan, whatever you chose. If you read a review for a show you wanted to see, a seating plan for the theater would be on the stream, so you could buy your tickets by clicking the right boxes. The tickets would be delivered to your stream, and a note would be dropped into the stream's future reminding you to go see the play when the date rolled around.

We're already seeing tentative movement in this direction; we'll see a lot more before long. These culture streams and related electronic institutions have no analogues in the pre-Web world, but they could easily become more influential than any newspaper, television, or radio outlet that exists today.

Computer technology in itself accomplishes nothing. If we're going to have an American cultural renaissance, computers won't supply the ideas or the will, let alone the people or the money. Computers won't change our election campaigns or improve the quality of our information supply or create new institutions. But they might give us openings, if we choose to go through them.

Information is no good in itself. It becomes valuable when it shows up at the right place, in the right way, at the right time. The technology world hasn't gotten around to taking this problem seriously yet, but it will. We can make transparency a goal of software design if we want to. We can require that every significant piece of software be able to explain not only how it works but how it's built. Nowadays few people care. As software becomes increasingly central to the workings of society, more people will care; at least I hope they will.

The quality of our language is central to the quality of our democracy. By making it easier to generate written words, computers could be the best or the worst thing that ever happened to our capacity to express ourselves. The outcome depends on whether we believe that good writing is important. To-day, on the whole, we don't. But computers could give us an excuse to change our minds.

We each have a fixed number of hours to dispose of, and we spend some of them dealing with information. Other things being equal, the more bytes of information we look at, the less time we invest in each. It's good to know a lot, have seen a lot, been exposed to a lot. It's also good to study important things in depth. I think we need to recalibrate the balance between depth and breadth in American education and perhaps in society at large. Thanks in part to the Web and to other electronic information sources, our balance is temporarily out of whack. I sometimes think about early American households, where books were rare; you might find a Bible, perhaps Christian or patriotic pamphlets, often the works of Shakespeare. It wasn't an atmosphere that encouraged studiousness, but when a child was studious—when he was Abraham Lincoln, for example—he put all his energy into a relative handful of bytes. But he studied them well and thought about them deeply. His thinking was deep instead of broad. Would his education have turned out better if he'd had the Web to surf? I doubt it. Deep reading, close reading, careful and meticulous reading, is the basis of education. We can't let the Web or anything else make us forget how to do it.

Finally, American society in recent generations has let one big basic theme dominate our national discussion. Today we are focusing on computers and the Net. We can do better. It's time for a new theme. Over the years we've come to accept responsibility for the air we breathe, the water we drink, the schools we operate, the culture at large. We could accept responsibility also for the computers we live with. We could reject bad software, send it back to the factory; we could think carefully about how software ought to behave and what it should do, and about where the field as a whole ought to go. If we do that, if we choose technological democracy, then we can realize the enormous possibilities of computers and the Net.

If we don't, if we sit back and leave computers to technologists and the industry, then society as a whole could easily come to resemble a piece of commercial software. It could grow steadily more complicated, with more and more fancy features that fewer and fewer people understood; with an underlying structure that was opaque and mysterious. The gap between ordinary citizens and expert users would grow larger and more ominous. Gradually the spirit of civil society might come to resemble the spirit of the Microsoft paperclip—an onscreen cartoon character (for those of you who never met it) that Microsoft uses to express its cheerful, charming, easygoing, good-natured contempt for us poor, childlike fools who use its software.

But things don't have to be that way. Computers are one of the most powerful tools we have ever invented. The choices on this ballot proposition are clear. What to do with this amazing tool? (A) We use it. (B) We sit back and let it use us.

I vote for (A).

Contributors

Richard H. Brodhead is Dean of Yale College and A. Bartlett Giamatti Professor of English and American Studies at Yale University.

David Bromwich is Bird White Housum Professor of English at Yale University.

Stephen L. Carter is William Nelson Cromwell Professor of Law at the Yale Law School.

Nancy F. Cott is Jonathan Trumbull Professor of American History and Pforzheimer Foundation Director of the Schlesinger Library at Harvard University.

Michael Denning is Professor of American Studies and English at Yale University.

Cynthia Farrar is Lecturer in Political Science and Ethics, Politics, and Economics, and director of the Urban Academic Initiative at Yale University.

John Lewis Gaddis is Robert A. Lovett Professor of Military and Naval History and Professor of Political Science at Yale University.

David Gelernter is Professor of Computer Science at Yale University.

Anthony T. Kronman is Dean and Edward J. Phelps Professor of Law at the Yale Law School.

Richard C. Levin is President of Yale University and Frederick William Beinecke Professor of Economics at Yale.

Matthew A. Light is a doctoral candidate at Yale University.

Jedediah Purdy is a graduate of the Yale Law School and the author of two books and many essays and articles on law, politics, and culture.

James C. Scott is Sterling Professor of Political Science at Yale University, where he also teaches in the anthropology department and at the Yale School of Forestry and Environmental Studies, and directs the Agrarian Studies program.

Ian Shapiro is William R. Kenan, Jr., Professor of Political Science at Yale University.

Joan A. Steitz is Sterling Professor of Molecular Biophysics and Biochemistry at Yale University, and Investigator at Howard Hughes Medical Institute.

Index